Touch Me Please

Michael Gerwat
&
Patricia Gerwat

Contents

MICK: 1991 - Prologue	3
PAT: 1989 – The Music Stops	5
MICK: The Rock Bands	10
PAT: Coping with the Silence	18
MICK: Sunshine Home	27
The Silent Ordeal I must Face Alone	38
PAT: Rehabilitation	42
MICK: Early Life	50
PAT: The Cochlear Implant	58
Computers: lifeline to the world	66
MICK: North House and Problems at Home	70
PAT: Learning to Have Fun	87
MICK: Linden Lodge	96
PAT: Looking for work	117
MICK: College Life	126
Media Madness	141
MICK: A Bunch of Keys	152
PAT: Plumbing the Depths	163
MICK: New Beginnings	168
PAT: South Pacific	180
MICK: Tuneathon	194
Parting of the Ways	212

Touch Me Please

MICK: Sea of Troubles	220
PAT: Some New Gains	234
MICK: Family Life and Communication	240
PAT: The Final Obstacle	256
MICK: Epilogue	263

MICK: 1991 - Prologue

Just touch me please. Not much to ask is it? I'm imprisoned, I'm bound by circumstances as immovable as the iron bars of a cell. No more venturing out on my own, no longer able to indulge in the social razzamatazz of life: chatting in bars over a pint, meeting strange people in strange places, forming instant relationships, making new friends, entering musical quizzes (and usually winning). I am now denied these everyday aspects of life that people take for granted.

I am condemned to a dark and silent world. The clock has ceased to tick, the rain no longer falls, the stream is hushed. Even the sea has stopped. There are no more singing birds or rustling leaves, or the majestic roll of thunder. The beauty of the spoken word is lost to me forever. Who will communicate with me now? You are all around me, or at least I think you are. I can smell your presence, I can feel the wind of your passing but I cannot hear or see you. Now that I am both blind and deaf, how can I relate to the world outside? Just touch me please. That's all I ask.

Worst of all is the loss of my beloved music. I will never again hear the beauty of Mendelssohn's violin concerto, the drama of a Genesis track, or the awesome power of a classical symphony. For years I was denied a piano. How ironic that now I have one I can no longer use it. No more tuning, repairing or composing on this magical instrument, the mere smell of which intoxicates me.

Can you understand just what I've become? I recall the predictions I was given a few years ago by two palm

Touch Me Please

readers. Jackie told me my life would be like living in a deep cave. I would be shouting out to people and they would be trying to communicate, but would not be able to get through to me. Laura predicted that by the time I was 40 I would have given up my career as a piano tuner, and that if I wanted to get married I should do it now, as I would not want to - or be able to - later. How I scoffed at those prophecies, how we laughed at their stupidity. I wonder what they would think now.

It's a life sentence with no reprieve. Why me? What have I done to deserve the hand of fate to strike in this cruel way? I feel numb, not even able to cry. This last year or so has been a living hell. At least I know I've reached the depths and nothing worse can happen, can it? I can't think beyond the now, I don't want to face any future, not like this, not if I can never hear the beauty of a piano again. What is left to me now? What point is there in any kind of life? Just let me die, just let me go now.

PAT: 1989 – The Music Stops

It is a Monday morning in May. We are sitting side by side in front of a large desk. Various audiological instruments and gadgets are placed about the consulting room. We each have our own thoughts. Mick is terrified of losing his music and losing touch with the world. He understands it only by hearing. I am afraid of losing the person I married less than a year ago. What if he goes deaf and can't play the piano? It was his music that brought us together. Will we find it difficult to communicate? There is an element of fear, but we are optimistic. Mr Fraser is the top consultant in Leeds. We decided to see him privately because we were so worried. We believe we have reached him in time and are confident that he can help. Mr Fraser asks Mick to explain how it all began.

"It started in January" Mick tells him. "I began to feel unwell and experienced some strange symptoms. I was tired, lethargic, and lost all sensation down one side of my body. I was admitted to hospital in February and underwent tests for a week."

I think back to that anxious time. We hardly dared talk of what might be wrong; I feared it was a stroke or a brain tumour. I recall him lying on a couch being prodded with a pin all down one side and not responding to any of the pricks.

"The doctors could find nothing wrong," Mick continues, "so I was discharged and went home. I still felt unwell and had to stay in bed a lot of the time, but went out to a tuning job when necessary."

Although we felt immense relief that there was apparently nothing wrong, clearly he was not well.

Touch Me Please

Sometimes he really wasn't fit to get out of bed. He was anxious to build up his business, but I wonder if complete rest might have cured him. Could he have avoided this situation by taking sensible precautions? After three months things deteriorated.

Mick resumes, "A few weeks ago a buzz began in one side of my head, a constant droning, like a distant aeroplane or a drowsy bee. The buzz moved from one side to the other, gradually increasing. Then I noticed my hearing began to deteriorate in my left ear. I am totally dependent on my hearing, Mr Fraser. I depend on it for my mobility, my work, my social contacts."

"That's why we came to see you," I add. "Mick's hearing is so important we couldn't wait for a hospital appointment."

I have always been amazed at how Mick navigates like a bat. He can always recognise what he is passing as we walk down the street. He can identify a wall, a car or a hedge by the change of sound as we pass, as you do in a vehicle when the window is open and the engine noise changes as it bounces off buildings and spaces along the side of the road. He compensates for lack of vision by interpreting the world through sound. I understand this enough to share his fear. We must prevent him going deaf at all costs.

Mr Fraser nods sympathetically. "Well, let's take a look," he says. He comes round the big desk. Even his secretary looks sympathetic in her corner of the room. I watch as Mr Fraser inserts the otoscope into one ear and then the other, his face inscrutable as he inspects them.

Mick's face is anxious and drawn. How different he has become in the last few months. Apart from his music, it was his ebullient personality that attracted me. I suppose I was the one who proposed. It came to me one day, as a kind of revelation, that I should marry Mick. It just seemed the right thing to do, since he was already living with me and the family. My sister was concerned. "Are you sure you know what you're doing? It's a big commitment being tied to someone who is blind." But we were such good friends; he made me laugh; he introduced me to lots of music I had never heard; I was in love and I knew he felt passionately about me. Now, as I sit and watch the examination, I reflect on how I wanted to make Mick happy to compensate for the difficult life he has had. I know that I can never achieve that if he goes deaf.

When he has finished his examination Mr Fraser sits at his desk and looks at us. I am expecting a diagnosis and perhaps some treatment. I want him to say "Ha, that's the problem; we can soon solve that!" but he looks serious. Instead he says "It is sometimes difficult to understand what causes loss of hearing. Often there is no obvious explanation. In your case, Mr Gerwat, I can't find any cause. The best thing is for you to come to the hospital clinic on Wednesday. We can give you a full hearing test then." His secretary looks at his appointments and gives us a time. Two days to wait. We express our thanks, but leave crestfallen.

It is Wednesday. I am very stressed. Luckily I have managed to find a parking space by the main entrance. Mick can't walk. He is too weak and exhausted and seems totally immobilised. I leave him in the car and set off to find a wheelchair. The buzz and pressure has built up in Mick's head since Monday until he thinks it will burst. I called an emergency doctor last night because the pain was becoming unbearable. When he arrived and heard what the problem was he refused to prescribe any pain killers. Because we had a pending appointment he said we were wasting his time. We found him rude and totally unsympathetic.

I find a chair and collect Mick from the car. He even

Touch Me Please

has difficulty climbing into the wheelchair. We set off to the ENT clinic. As I push Mick along the wide corridors I have only the slightest spark of hope. The worst thing is not knowing what is happening and what the future holds.

Eventually we are seen by Mr Fraser, who is shocked to see how ill Mick is. The hearing in his left ear is gradually fading but it seems the medical profession can't do anything about it. He arranges for Mick to be admitted to hospital at once. As I drive home my heart is heavy. I am thinking that my marriage is going to be very different from how I imagined it. And I am thinking Mick doesn't deserve this.

On Thursday I visit Mick in hospital. It isn't good news. The second ear is now deteriorating as well. In an attempt to prevent any further hearing loss, the doctor has prescribed steroids, but so far they aren't helping. Mick looks depressed. One of the nurses asks him in her Yorkshire accent – as his whole way of life is slipping away from him – "What 'yer sad for?" She is chatting with another nurse about their night out as he lies desperately scared for the future. What a lack of understanding there is of the hidden disability of deafness. People can sympathise with blindness, but do not comprehend the isolation and frustration of being deaf. But coupled with a lack of sight, when your whole world has been built on sound, and the music which is your life, your soul, seems to be slipping away – deafness brings devastation.

The doctors are baffled. They can't diagnose anything and suspect it is psychological. They ask if there are problems in our marriage. I even wonder myself if it could be psychological. Perhaps Mick can't believe that he has found happiness at last, and has subconsciously blocked his hearing. We walk round the hospital grounds, unable to believe what is happening. I am trying not to cry but failing. We have had only a few months of health and happiness together. Mick already knows his hearing is no longer good enough to continue working as a piano tuner. His tells me his career is over. I leave him reluctantly, knowing he will spend a lonely, terrifying night.

Back home I ring my sister. I wonder what she thinks about being tied to someone who is both deaf and blind. I think back to our Quaker wedding a mere nine months ago when we made our promises. "I take this my Friend, Michael Gerwat, to be my husband, promising through divine assistance, to be unto him a loving and faithful wife, so long as we both on earth shall live."

The words were printed on a scroll placed on a small table before us. Naturally, Mick had learnt his speech and spoke it with great feeling, except that he promised to be a 'faithful and loving husband'. Then we signed the scroll beneath the declaration. Unfortunately the table was very small, and as we manoeuvred the scroll the crystal paperweight placed there to stop it from curling up, crashed onto the tiled floor and broke. I remember Mick's words of warning: *"That will bring bad luck"*.

Then I try in vain to sleep, but I cry all night. I cry for Mick, who is alone in a friendless hospital ward. I can only partly imagine what he is suffering. I cry for myself, because it means the end of my world, as well as his. I believe my life is over. Our future dreams are shattered, and I know that it is not only Mick who has lost the music but me as well.

MICK: The Rock Bands

While I was in hospital many thoughts raced through my mind as I lay wondering what the future would have in store. Just when all the dark clouds which had hung heavily over me for most of my life seemed to have cleared away and a bright sun shone from a blue sky, the most shattering thing that could have happened struck within the space of four months. Now the dark shadow of deafness, the one thing I had dreaded, was looming over me. Through a misty, distorted haze the sounds of patients' calls, cries, laughter, mingling with the clatter of wheeling trolleys and rattling teaspoons, filtered through the fog of my senses. No matter which way I turned all the sounds came from only one side. On the right hand side of my body was the outside world, the everyday cacophony of the hustle and bustle of hospital life. The left hand side seemed like a deserted, empty church, quiet and still. The combination of the two diametrically opposed worlds caused me a great deal of confusion.

I was suddenly roused from my musings by Sandra, the cheerful nurse who often raised my spirits with her bubbling personality. Wheeling an ancient, squeaking chair towards the bed she said, "If this will take your weight, sweetheart, it's time for your early morning ride." I returned her banter: "We'll have less of your cheek, young one. Anyone with half an ear can tell this chair needs oiling. I've told you that before." Sandra helped me into the chair and we set off to see Mr Fraser. As I was wheeled through the vast labyrinthine corridors of the hospital a total mishmash and confusion of feelings flooded over me. Rising above the confused background

The Rock Bands

two words began to scream in the centre of my brain: "Why me?"

But worse was to come. Sunday morning dawned, hot and fine. I was listening to the radio when I suddenly found it a little quieter. I asked if it had been turned down. "No it is the same," one of the nurses told me. I froze. Was I just getting anxious? The sound in my right ear almost imperceptibly softened and became more muffled.

The following weekend, when the weather was warm, balmy and like mid-summer, I arrived home from hospital for a short break. I had to return but really saw no point in doing so. The steroids I had been given made absolutely no difference to the final outcome so far as I was concerned. I just couldn't take it all in, I couldn't believe that, in this day and age, nothing could be done to help me. Just how far would this deafness go? Everything sounded muffled, like being in a large bucket. All the brightness of life had gone, all the sharp sounds were missing. I felt like I was hanging over the edge of a bottomless precipice, only managing to keep a slight grip on life.

The first thing I wanted to do when I got home, was to listen to music. Initially I tried the piano. I was shocked, it sounded all out of tune and funny. I rushed to try my stereo but that sounded just as bad. How devastating it was to find out just how much hearing I had already lost. My work was gone straight away, no more tuning for me and that meant forever. I didn't feel anything at this time, simply because the knock I'd received was so hard, the real pain would come later. I just sat around, not knowing what to do with myself.

My work as a piano tuner meant everything to me; it was so closely linked to my love of music. For me it wasn't a job it was a pleasure. I thought over some of the wonderful experiences my work had provided. Certainly,

Touch Me Please

one of the most interesting and fascinating parts of my career was when I worked for the rock bands. I met my first famous person in Leeds at Christmas way back in 1968. It was on the occasion of my engagement party, held at the local club. Before the party, Lin and I went off to see the Bachelors at the Grand Theatre. I didn't particularly like them, but Lin did. I arranged with the theatre manager to meet the stars during their change over. It was a bit congested in the dressing room and I don't think they really wanted us around. It was all very hurried but Lin enjoyed it and that was all that was important.

But this was merely the precursor of what was to come. I did my first famous gig in 1969 for the Moody Blues who were well-known by then. I was able to talk to the band and enjoyed going on stage to see all the equipment. This was the start of a whole chain of meetings with famous bands that was to last twenty years or so. I tuned for Shakin' Stevens, Tears for Fears, Sandy Denny of Fairport Convention and U2, a really nice band with whom I worked a couple of times. When I tuned for the Strawbs they offered me a mellotron for free because they didn't want it anymore. I felt really upset because Lin, my wife, wouldn't allow me to have it. I also remember that one of Mungo Jerry's roadies hurt his thumb badly on a large nail. I couldn't print the language here!

As in all walks of life the bands I met varied. Some were very pleasant to work for, some were not. Lindisfarne did a regular Christmas concert at the university for many years. I would sort out their piano every year and they always remembered me. Hot Chocolate were another really friendly band. I was allowed to play with their synthesisers. The day I tuned for Rick Wakeman the crew were trying out their smoke machines with dry ice. I was surrounded by clouds of smoky dreamy images. They told me it looked as if I were

The Rock Bands

flying.

One occasion stands out. It was early 1973. Elton John was due to appear at the University Union but I knew Barkers had the tuning contract. I had worked for them but lost my job there and was pretty low and depressed. I was married and we were expecting our first child. The phone rang.

"Micky are you busy? What are you doing?" This was Paul Monahan, a student whom I knew from the Union days when I was working there for the bands.

"Nothing particular. Why Paul?"

"Elton John refuses to go on stage because the piano hasn't been done properly." Can you imagine the wave of feelings inside me? I was going to get one over on Barkers at last. Revenge was sweet! "Micky, are you there?" I came out of my reverie. "Can you come now and do the piano?"

"Oh yes, yes!" I replied. I felt butterflies inside me leaping around, this was really something. The van turned up at the door and I boarded it, savouring every moment of the conversation. "Micky, you've saved the day", Paul told me, "Elton was about to pull out of the gig."

I arrived and went on stage. What I didn't know was, the audience was already present while I was tuning the piano. Oh, what a lovely experience it was to tune this Rolls Royce of pianos, this gem, this absolute wonder of the piano world, a nine foot Steinway. I was in heaven. I could see why it hadn't been right. These things need handling with respect and care, they are priceless and should be treated so. I finished the piano and decided to have a play on it. I loved Elton's songs and I struck up with a few of them, singing along quite happily. What I didn't know was that Elton himself had come on stage to see if all was right. I felt a tap on my shoulder.

"Well I'm only the piano player, you can carry on,

Touch Me Please

I've already been paid." You could have knocked me down with a feather. All the audience clapped and stamped. In fact, Elton was there for a couple of nights and I went back at his request, to make sure the piano was tuned properly.

I also remember with fondness Ian Dury, now gone from us. I worked with him on a few occasions. David Essex was a real gentleman. I was allowed to play his vocoda. How interesting that was! It was a keyboard, where you played the notes and if you spoke words into the microphone, you could hold chords down on the vocoda and your words would come out as music. This fascinated me, one could sing words with it and be an entire choir. Oh how I wish I'd been allowed to have a musical instrument back then. And how I wish I'd been allowed to go to all those concerts. I could have had free admission to any of them but Lin said no. I suppose she just didn't understand what it meant to me.

I found that road crews were rough and ready but if you could do a good job and do it efficiently, then it was good enough for them. You had to earn their respect but once you had, they treated you very well. Getting on with the job was the order of the day and my reputation for doing so soon spread far and wide. Over the many years, I got to know the routine of setting up for a concert, from the fitting of the main interface cables to the final sound checks and tweaking of the instruments. At this point I tuned the pianos or other keyboards that were being used. Often though, I had to hang around for hours. I remember Procol Harum leaving their mixers in London. I couldn't do the piano until the mixers arrived.

I saved many a concert as well as Elton's. I clearly remember being called to Judie Tzuke's concert. There were two pianos to be done but the manager didn't think I'd have time to do them. I told him, "Stand back, let the

The Rock Bands

dog see the rabbit" and sorted them both out. He was extremely pleased and I was given a little present to take away with me: a signed LP and some cannabis. You must understand that "spliffing up" was like having a cup of tea, it was tradition in the rock world and I gladly joined in. I was never a hard drug user but I liked a spliff.

My first experience in 1974 was taking cannabis or "hashish". I had very little and it didn't worry me. I had nothing for a few years, then one night I swallowed a large piece of cannabis when I got home. Usually it has to be smoked, but I swallowed it. I imagined bacon men with rubber arms and steel collars, and cheese made out of pottery clay. Hundreds of crazy things went through my mind, but I had to conceal the strange effects of the drug so that Lin would not know. I was cooking tea, and I took the bacon from the frying pan long before it was cooked. Time seemed so slow, every minute seemed so long. Afterwards I knelt down at the sink, laughing at the washing-up. All the while strange things were going through my head – funny pyramids, leather, suede. I found I could recite long, silly poems, pouring them out at great length, dammed up words suddenly being released, but they didn't make any sense. The rhymes were there, and the words were there, but they meant nothing.

During the punk era, I met bands like the Sex Pistols and Elvis Costello. His pianist was a really accomplished musician. Through all the years of meeting folks many managers got to know me and we'd go down to the uni bar for a few beers. This was tradition and it also helped me relax as well. Many's the time I've arrived home a little merry.

The most memorable meeting of all was when I got the chance to meet my favourite band, Genesis. At a really difficult time in my life their music spoke to me, I could empathise with it. I'd waited over four years to see them

Touch Me Please

live. They finally came to Bradford in 1980. Through a friend at the polytechnic, now Leeds Metropolitan University, I got a free ticket to see them. Up till then I had not attended any live band concerts despite all those I could have enjoyed, but this one I was determined not to miss.

We arrived at St. George's Hall in Bradford and I can remember standing in the draughty corridor waiting to be allowed in. I had a pass with 'Ligger' on it, which was the word for someone who got in without paying. I was shaking while I was waiting to meet them. I had always teased hysterical fans outside gigs when I'd been pulled through the massing crowds, parting them like the Red Sea. "Oh please let me carry your bag" women begged or cajoled, sometimes rubbing up against me temptingly, as if I'd fall for that!

"What's so special anyway?" I would say casually, "I meet these folks every day, it's just part of my job and they're no different from you, they are just normal human beings."

"You wait until you find someone you really want to meet, then we'll see how you behave,' they chided me.

Oh, if they'd only been there! I stood, with my wooden stick in my hands, my little memo machine with its micro cassette fitted ready to record what happened. I think I still have that cassette somewhere.

Finally the door was opened and I was pushed hurriedly in. There I stood, trembling. Mike Rutherford was the first to take my hand. His hands were smooth as glass. I thought of that old advert for washing up liquid "Now hands that do dishes...feel as soft as your face." He had a really low voice as well. I stammered out something about how wonderful their latest album was and thanked them for all their music. Phil Collins shook my hand. I asked him about his throat: he'd had problems earlier in the tour and had to cancel a few concerts.

Before I knew it, it was all over. I remember feeling such a fool with my legs as weak as jelly saying to myself, "What's up with you, they are only human beings like you." But I felt as if I were standing before gods!

PAT: Coping with the Silence

While Mick was in hospital I rang Social Services and tried to explain how the loss of his music, his career and his independence represented an overwhelming blow that he just couldn't cope with. I asked if someone could visit him and offer some counselling. Nothing happened.

When Mick was discharged we contacted Centenary House, the Centre for Deaf and Blind People in Leeds. Again, nothing happened. Months later, someone came to fit a loop system in our lounge, but by then Mick's hearing had deteriorated to the point where the loop was not terribly effective and was helpful only for a couple of months.

Eventually Social Services offered some mobility training with the long cane. Mick had always navigated using his ears, carrying a white stick mainly as a signal to other people. The long cane is held diagonally in front, swept in arcs from side to side to indicate any obstructions or craters. Many people who go blind later in life depend on this form of mobility, but without hearing it is rather scary. Once Mick's hearing had gone completely he could never risk going out alone.

By sheer chance I had just given notice from my job, having been summarily and unjustly demoted from a post of responsibility by the tin-pot dictator who owned the business. When they heard about the circumstances, friends urged me to go to a tribunal for constructive dismissal, but I had enough stress to deal with, without confronting an aggressive and vindictive ex-boss in a legal battle. At least I had been given a month's salary, and was available full-time when Mick most needed me. The timing could not have been better.

We could spend a lot of time together, talking and trying to come to terms with this enormous change in our lives. We had no explanation for what had happened and considered some bizarre possibilities. Mick, who had strong psychic powers suggested it could be a ghost he had encountered in our cellar. We had a basement room with a stone slab and on one occasion when Mick went downstairs he heard the sound of a knife being sharpened, and felt a great evil power. In a struggle of wills he demanded that this spirit should leave the house, but it was an encounter which left him shaken. "I think the ghost may have taken his revenge and cursed me," he said.

I countered, "Do you think someone with a grudge against you has made a doll and is sticking pins into its ears?"

"Maybe it was the crystal which broke at our wedding," Mick suggested. "I told you that it augured bad luck." The absurd ideas and imaginings that we indulged in show how bewildered and overwhelmed we were by the situation. I thought of us as Babes in the Wood, wandering alone and helpless in a hostile and frightening environment.

Mick sat listlessly in the lovely May weather we were enjoying. "Hold me," he would say, "just take my hand." He needed lots of tenderness and physical contact to enable him to cope with the new situation. Touch was now his most important sense. Initially friends called to see him, but as his hearing got worse they became embarrassed and drifted away. I suppose they didn't know what to say. After all, it was a bereavement.

"How lucky it is that I am out of work," I said one day. "I think it was meant to be. I can now stay at home and be your guide and companion."

"On no account," Mick replied. "You must get out of the house and have a life of your own. You mean well now, but you will eventually feel imprisoned and unfulfilled. Besides, you have a family to support and it wouldn't be much fun living on benefits."

So I agreed to look for a job. After spending two or three weeks at home supporting Mick in the first days of his deafness, I initially did temping through an agency. Just as I started this, I had a phone call from British Gas inviting me for interview, and I began work there as a software technical author in June. The people and the environment were pleasant and relaxed after the frenetic and hostile office of my previous job. They were understanding about Mick's condition. This made it much easier to cope with work, the family and the special needs of my husband.

At the end of June we spent a family holiday near Oban in Scotland. My daughter Linda had finished her 'A' levels and my son Andrew his 'O' levels. Linda was going to live in the USA for her year out, working as an 'au pair' or mother's help to a family I knew. This was to be our last holiday as a family before they started leaving home. For four of us it was a magical week. Almost the height of midsummer, it was daylight until eleven or later. The weather was unbelievably good with blue sky, blue water and bright sunshine for seven days. We took the boat to Mull and Iona; we explored Glencoe; we enjoyed the beaches and the lochs.

One morning we set off at six and drove north to Fort William, zigzagging round crystal sea lochs beneath brilliant skies. The three children climbed Ben Nevis while I stayed with Mick. It was a memorable holiday, full of contrasting happiness and melancholy. It was a delight to be with the family, but I watched helplessly the sadness which settled over Mick like a cold mist, as he struggled with new and uncomfortable hearing aids, frustrated by the loss of beautiful sounds around him, fearful for what lay ahead. As I caught the voices of the family coming down the mountainside I knew Mick would never hear them properly again.

I was worried that Mick was getting no support. A private audiologist that we consulted mentioned the Link Centre for Deafened People in Eastbourne. It was set up to help people come to terms with sudden deafness, and ran courses for those affected together with their spouses. It was the only organisation of its kind in the country. When I contacted them they kindly arranged a customised visit for Mick and myself in December 1989. They had never helped anyone who was deaf and blind, but were willing to try.

The director, Rosemary McCall, a wonderfully caring and gentle woman, founded the Link Centre after a career in audiology. When we arrived, she whisked Mick away to talk to him alone. I had become very protective. This was the first time he had talked to anyone in an official capacity without me since he had gone deaf, and I was left in a state of anxiety wondering if he was all right. Rosemary and her assistant, Lorraine Gailey (now the Director at Link), were the first people to show any interest in Mick's difficulties, the first people to understand.

They arranged bed and breakfast for us at a local guest house and during the day organised meetings and activities at the Centre and elsewhere. They allowed lots of time for Mick and I to talk individually about our situation. Taking Mick into the rose garden, Rosemary encouraged him to use his enhanced sense of smell. She suggested the possibility of research and writing articles about the sense of smell. This might make a positive contribution to the literature available to blind people.

We met Ken Willard who, as a prisoner of war, had been tortured by the Japanese. As a result of his war-time

Touch Me Please

experiences he had lost his hearing. He too had loved music and could no longer access it. His own sufferings made him a kind and understanding listener. Escorted by Ken we visited St Dunstan's College, run by the national charity that provides rehabilitation, training and lifelong care for blind ex-Service men and women. The items and activities they showed Mick included woodworking tools and picture frames; up-to-date kitchen equipment; exercise bike and rowing machine in the fitness department; a special program to use on his own computer; and basket work and stool making. We felt there were some real possibilities here. Since only servicemen were eligible for admission to St. Dunstan's, they could offer nothing for Mick, but the instructors gave freely of their time that afternoon to demonstrate and assess. The Link report of our trip states: 'On his visit to St. Dunstan's he played their Steinway piano, giving pleasure to some of the residents. This was only for a short period because his impaired hearing interfered and made him "dry up".'

June Leaman, the special social worker at Link discussed possible ways forward for Mick. He was advised to register his dual disability so that when the proposed legislation came into force he would be able to apply for Mobility Allowance. We were both urged to consider alternative ways of communication, in anticipation of the time when Mick could not hear speech. Finally we had a relaxation session with a specialist teacher. The team at Link gave us encouragement and a little glimmer of hope. Perhaps the future was not entirely black. Moreover, they really understood our situation. For that alone we will be forever grateful to them. We subsequently visited Eastbourne several times.

From the start Mick was sure he would go totally deaf. At first, I refused to accept it and thought his fatalism was self-prophesying and would indeed bring about

Coping with the Silence

deafness. I suppose I was in denial. We travelled far and wide in search of a miracle cure. We tried local healers and some further afield. On two occasions we drove all the way to Matthew Manning at Bury St. Edmunds. Healers who claimed to have cured all sorts of illnesses failed to help Mick. Some laid on hands, others treated a lock of hair or used crystals, but nothing worked. I persuaded Mick to undergo a dangerous and extremely unpleasant fast, urged upon him by some caring and well-meaning friends of ours who were naturopaths. I really believed it might help. Years later Mick talked about his anger – unexpressed at the time – about what he felt I imposed on him. Looking back I can see that it was a stupid idea.

Perhaps even more stupidly, we acquired some magic spells from a local shop for witches and warlocks. I can't remember how we found the address, but we arrived at the shop which was entirely black without any windows. Eventually someone responded to our knocking and we were admitted to an Aladdin's cave, where we browsed and asked for help. There were witches' candles, powders and potions of all sorts. The only thing missing was the smoking cauldron. We returned home armed with the spells which we hoped would expel any malevolent spirits from our home. Making sure the family were all out, we placed raw onions at strategic points around the house, and recited incantations. In addition, Mick bathed in purifying pink powders to drive away the (supposed) evil. Perhaps the spells didn't work because it was all rubbish; or maybe they failed because we were not truly convinced, and laughed at the incongruity of them. Whatever the reason Mick's hearing continued to deteriorate.

Magic and faith healing aside, we had to be practical and Mick must attempt to build a new life. How was he to fill his days without music? Tactile activities were the

Touch Me Please

obvious choice. We ordered several games from the Royal National Institute for Blind People (RNIB), such as Scrabble (which Mick has always hated and still does), Cluedo and Monopoly, braille playing cards, Solitaire, Drafts, Chess and Othello. We purchased an exercise bike and rowing machine to provide much-needed physical workouts, but these were never popular and in due course fell into disuse. And Mick started reading braille books sent by post from the National Library for the Blind at Stockport.

We also bought a few braille books – some poetry and the New Testament – which I thought would give Mick some pleasure. It was delightful one day to hear him laughing loudly. He was reading the Sermon on the Mount and all he could think of was Monty Python and "Blessed are the cheese makers" from *Life of Brian*. So his wonderful sense of humour, although buried deep, was still there and irrepressible.

We managed to arrange some pottery at a further education centre in Leeds. Mick was taken there and back by taxi. He created some attractive coiled pots and a couple of (accidentally) asymmetrical jugs which I treasure and use to this day. He made an interesting spiky little cat for Linda, whose real cat Heathcliff was abandoned to our care now that she was in the USA for her year out. Most, if not all, of these activities were therapeutic and filled in some time, kept him occupied. But nothing could compensate for the absence of music. He yearned for it, his soul ached for it. He woke mourning its loss every day.

Next to music, what Mick loved best was the computer. I had just acquired an Amstrad with two floppy disk drives. We took this back and had a hard disk fitted, and Mick purchased a speech program to enable him to access the machine. We visited Dolphin Speech Systems in Worcester in July 1989 to talk to them. Mick set about writing a book on his life so far, which has been on-going for more than twenty years!

But we believed that soon he would be unable to hear the speech synthesiser. We had to plan for total silence, and embarked on a fund-raising effort to provide Mick with specialist equipment, consisting of a computer with a braille display (the Libra), an optical character recognition (OCR) scanner (these were in their very early days), and a braille printer. We sent letters to friends and acquaintances; to organisations and rock bands; in fact to everyone we could think of. People gave donations, arranged sponsored walks and held fund-raising events. Amazingly, money flooded in. Friends at our Quaker Meeting were particularly generous and we were uplifted by their support. We were immensely moved by one lady who had lost two sons in a car crash and yet showed Mick a deep sympathy. We were able to get Mick set up with the Libra and peripherals before the last vestiges of his hearing disappeared. He embarked upon a new interest which gave him many challenges and lots of hope.

Some Friends also gave generously of their time, visiting Mick at home, and taking him out for walks ("Woof, woof" Mick used to say) while I was at work. Peter D was a wonderful help for many years, and then Geoffrey took over. Each Tuesday he marched Mick at vast speed across to Roundhay Park, round the lake and back home. Elizabeth and David took him swimming at a local sports centre every Wednesday morning. Godfrey told him about his early life at sea on the great sailing ships during the First World War and his role as first mate on the voyage of Mayflower II in 1957. He talked about the Cutty Sark for which he was a consultant for the rigging. He brought along navigational instruments and aids to show Mick, and made him a large tactile die. Life was difficult, but it would have been a lot worse without these

Touch Me Please

good people.

As well as looking for a cure, I believed that Mick needed counselling. He tried many counsellors over the years. Some used their usual techniques of careful listening, relaxation and deep breathing, affirmation and being positive. Some, unfortunately, did very little except take the money. None of them enabled Mick to grieve.

Throughout the year we were kept busy with clinic visits for tests and fittings for hearing aids. By the end of 1989 Mick could hear very little. Added to his loss of music and the growing problems of communication he was plagued by tinnitus: bells, whistles, roars and rumbles which made it hard for him to sleep. He would never lose this unpleasant sound effect; the tinnitus was to be his companion forever. He was only 39, and we thought wistfully of the words of the Abba song:

> *"Who can say what we'll find*
> *What lies waiting down the line*
> *At the end of eighty-nine..."*

MICK: Sunshine Home

I can feel the wind of the past, blowing gently against my cheek as I sit in the warm sunshine in our garden at home. Today I was reminded of the enormity of what has happened. Pat took the call when the BBC phoned to ask if I would tune their piano. I have worked for them for nearly fifteen years, and now I have to let them down. I'll have to get used to this sort of thing; there will be lots of my regular customers ringing me and I will have to put them off. I just have no idea where they should go to get their pianos tuned, and it hurts badly that I can no longer tune them myself. I suppose I am trying to escape from the pain of the present by looking back to a time when I was happy. This wasn't very often in my case. The balmy breeze reminds me of sunshine days... Sunshine Homes, where blind babies were educated during the forties and fifties.

I had an inauspicious beginning. I was due in November 1949, but was born at the end of August. My life was so despaired of that the Catholic priest was called to give me the last rites. My twin, Janet, died minutes after she was born. I was a tiny wisp of life weighing only 1lb 7 oz. This has been hard for my friends to believe when they gaze on my solid bulk – an acorn grown into an oak. Indeed, you can climb my north face or take sunny holidays on my southern slopes. You need a coach tour to encircle Mount Gerwat, and a space probe to photograph my other side.

Being born premature was to shape and influence the whole of my destiny. It was to make a huge difference to my life for it caused my blindness, common to premature babies until two years after my birth. I suffered from retrolental fibroplasia, caused by the administration of excessive oxygen. Within a few years the cause of this was diagnosed and a remedy found. It came just too late for me. My life was, naturally, different from most from the start, because I depended on senses other than sight, and came to know and understand the world around me without seeing it. I started school at the age of two, much earlier than other children, at Sunshine Home at East Grinstead, where I spent four happy years. Since it was a boarding school a long way from my parents I didn't get home at weekends. The staff at the Sunshine Homes were known as Nurses, which may account for my tender attitude towards that profession throughout my whole life.

As at most boarding schools for the blind, we kept pets, including goats, rabbits, hens, dogs and cats. There was a great emphasis on animals and the touch and feel of them. The pets were tame and good with children. There was an old beach donkey called Nutty. This beautiful animal would happily accept pupils climbing on his back for a ride, and ate literally anything. One day after a cookery lesson there was a lump of raw dough left. I decided to give Nutty a little treat and see if he would eat it. Sure enough straight down into the bottomless pit it went, with a loud slurp-slurp. Nutty consumed the piece of dough almost in one gulp. It was pleasant to ride round and round on Nutty's back on a summer evening, stopping while he nibbled the grass.

Another feature of the school was the kitchen garden. Here, where cabbages, lettuces and many other vegetables grew, was the chicken run. Feeding and stroking the chickens was so fascinating that a few years later I pestered my mother to let me have some baby chicks as pets.

One of my pleasures was to feed the dogs on a once

a week rota with the other pupils. There were two beautiful dogs called Jessica and Jemima. Jemima was a boxer and belonged to the Sunshine Home. Jessica, however, was a mongrel that lived with the head mistress, Miss Clarke. Nurse Pat, who was responsible for looking after the dogs, would take one of us down to the room by the boiler house where the dogs' dishes were kept. Jemima used to try to steal Jessica's food but never achieved this, since Jessica was the bigger and stronger dog. There was no tinned pet food in those days. Bits of meat unfit for the pupils to eat were put through a turn-handle mincer which had a round bowl-shaped aperture at the top and a flat deep dish underneath. Nurse Pat used to give severe warnings about putting small fingers too far down the opening at the top. I used to love to turn the stiff handle. There was a little nut which adjusted the stiffness. At the same time food was put out for the many stray cats.

On a visit to the boiler house one day I cut my knee on a sharp coal scuttle. Returning slowly up the steps, feeling a little miserable, I suddenly felt a cold wet tongue licking the cut. I stretched out my right hand and felt Jessica's soft fur. Her warm, slightly rough coat felt comforting to stroke as she licked the wound clean of all the blood.

The heat from the boiler fire fascinated me, so much so that one day in my over eagerness to reach it, I pushed one of the boys accidentally down the steps. Luckily little Christopher was not hurt, but I was, quite rightly, severely reprimanded and punished. The boiler room was probably where I developed my fascination for anything dramatic like fire, heat, gurgling or hissing water pipes, and most of all, thunder storms. All these things seemed to be an outlet for the anger which even then burnt within me. During those far-off days, of course, I had no idea of its cause but later came to realise that it was due to lack of affection

Touch Me Please

from my family and inconsistency in what I was told was right or wrong.

Being curious and adventurous, I had some wonderful experiences in the Sunshine Home and the lovely Sussex countryside around it. One day, with my friend Janet, I left the school gates to find out where the road was. Many times I had smelt the petrol of passing cars, drawing me like a magnet, since I had never ridden in a car before. It wasn't a very busy road, but Janet and I found the closed gates a challenge.

"Do you know how to open the gates Mick?" Janet asked eagerly.

Wanting to impress, I boldly stretched out my hand towards the wooden gate. Though it was tall, the steel lift-up hasp was half way down, well within my reach. With a push of the right thumb the heavy steel bar lifted upwards and one of the gates swung outwards of its own accord. It was a challenge which we had met successfully and once through, we set off along the road. Leaving the pebbly drive, somewhat resembling a beach, our little feet trotted happily along the edge of the tarmac. Both of us jumped and skipped joyously, saying we would find our way to the farm a little distance from the school. We were so carried away in our excitement that we failed to hear the heavy boots of the gardener as he approached us speedily from behind. The first sign of his presence was a gruff voice saying "Come here" in a strong Somerset accent. Mr Friend, whose character belied his name, followed up this exclamation by boxing our ears soundly. My head whistled and sang for a good five minutes afterwards. Meekly, in tears, we were led like whipped pups back to the home. We were probably in danger, but the over aggressive handling of the situation by the gardener was typical of much of the treatment meted out to us pupils during my school days. Of course the real culprits were the staff who failed to make the gate child-proof.

A similar incident occurred on a Sunshine Holiday in Mumbles, when I was just five. All of us were staying at Miss Clarke's house, a large beautiful building with an extensive garden, containing a rockery. Never having seen a rockery before, I was fascinated by the different shaped rocks. How splendid it would be to use them to make a flight of steps. I proceeded to pull up the rocks one by one. I was quite carried away and had extricated four or five dozen rocks when I heard a loud voice from behind.

"What do you think you're doing? What DO you think you're doing?" My arm was grabbed roughly, and I was dragged indoors. "Do you realise I'll have to put all new plants in that rockery now?" screamed Miss Clarke. "I'll teach you to spoil gardens. You won't do it again after I've finished with you."

She laid me across her knee, pulled down my shorts with one swift movement, and proceeded to smack my bottom hard. Responding to the sharp, stinging pain I stretched my arm backwards after the second smack to try to prevent the hand descending again. This only increased the ferocity of the blows raining down on my posterior. At that point two other nurses came into the room, and Miss Clarke delighted in telling them what she had done and why. I felt demoralised, humiliated and miserable. Why, instead of smacking me in that way, had she not explained what a rockery was. It would have been so much easier, and would have been enough to prevent me doing such a thing again. Why, indeed, had we been left unsupervised for so long – long enough for me to dismantle a whole rockery? I often thought the way I was treated must have been the root of a lot of my views and opinions in later life. If I had been given proper explanations for some of the things that annoyed people I would not have harboured such long-term resentments.

Touch Me Please

Apart from this unfortunate incident, the holiday was a wonderful experience. The beach and the sea were fascinating. It was fun to walk in bare feet across the crinkled sand. I asked Miss Scrivener why it was rippled this way. She explained that the sea wrinkled the sand when it came in. As we walked towards the sea I heard for the first time the surf breaking gently on the shore. Something came over me which was to last for years afterwards, a sense of awe, a sense of mystery, and complete open space. The smell, the sound, the feel of the water as we walked in up to our chins was an unforgettable experience. Mesmerised by the constant movement of the sea I asked, "Does the sea ever stop?"

"No" Miss Scrivener replied, "never."

The summers seemed warmer then, and lasted longer than summers today. The Sunshine Home had lovely grounds with a small swimming pool about ten yards long. It was filled by lifting a grate in the ground and turning a little tap. Steps led down into the pool and we children used to sit there in the cold water if the weather was hot, or else we would try to swim. I was always fascinated by water, right from my earliest day, although I did not learn to swim until I was six or seven and had moved to my next school.

One particularly hot summer evening, a rather bizarre event occurred. We were in our little shorts sitting in the conservatory long after bedtime because of the exceptionally warm day. One of the children suggested a dare. "I bet you wouldn't dare take your shorts off and go into the garden."

While this challenge was being made the nurses were outside talking among themselves. The first young lad to remove his shorts only got as far as the door and ran back fearing he might get into trouble. Being the adventurous sort, I decided to take up the challenge. I took off my shorts and felt the scented air around my naked body. This was unheard of in those far-off days. I felt an inner thrill and exhilaration at doing something taboo. I walked through the door and down the gravel path which hurt my bare feet. I could hear the nurses' conversation. Instead of the expected hostile reprimand I heard giggles and squeals of laughter. "Has he gone? Is he really doing it?"

I continued towards the swing, settled myself on the rough wooden seat and started to swing vigorously. More peals of laughter floated across from the nurses. The warm summer air caressed my skin as I swung higher and higher. After a time I heard footsteps approaching, and through the laughter a nurse spoke. "Come along, now, the game's over. Let's have you indoors." She took my arm and I felt terribly daring, having achieved this unthinkable feat without any repercussions.

Summer was also the time for school outings. One day we went to London Zoo, where we were able to stroke the animals, particularly in Pets' Corner. The llamas were the best, for they seemed massive and had an unusual smell, and long furry coats. The most vivid recollection from the zoo, however, was the talking scales where a loud voice announced "You are three stones five pounds."

Quite near our Sunshine Home was Maharajah's Farm. There were regular visits here, and we all loved to stroke the cows, and enjoy the experience of them being milked. Often the cows urinated onto the concrete floor for what seemed a tremendously long time, which we found highly amusing and would discuss among ourselves.

At the fire station we had the opportunity to feel the fire engines. The sheer size of the whole vehicle as we walked round, touching, examining, was unbelievable. "Do you want me to start the engine children?" asked the fireman cheerfully. There was an enthusiastic chorus of

Touch Me Please

"Yes please". As the engine roared into life I cried out in fright at the terrific noise. I felt a fool in front of all the other children, but I couldn't help it. The kindly driver stopped the engine immediately and comforted me, inviting me to climb inside to feel the hoses and the seats in the cab and, best of all, to enjoy a demonstration of the wonderful radio system.

The school provided an ideal environment for learning through play and experience, encouraging initiative and free scope with careful guidance. My friend Graham and I heard that if you rubbed two pieces of wood together you could make fire. We sat all day rubbing vigorously to start our fire. Of course the staff were very careful to make sure we didn't have the sort of wood which would ignite or produce sparks.

My interest in pyrotechnics became a little over enthusiastic one day, when I decided to find out how a fire worked. I was standing in the classroom with a barrel full of spills. There was a bar heater on the ceiling above me and I wanted to make the spills ignite so that I could hold one and smell it burning. As I could not reach the heater the only way to achieve my purpose was to throw the spills up at it. I was caught in the act by Miss Clarke. As a punishment I was summoned to the phone and told there was a fireman who wanted to speak to me. I was really frightened, but was forced to go to the phone. I can never forget the trembling in my legs as I climbed the stairs. The man told me never to do such a thing again, and said that I had to be good for 'Mrs.' Clarke. His silly mistake in her title stood out in my memory. When I timidly promised I would never repeat the exercise he said "Right-i-o", an expression I had never heard before.

This was not quite the end of the story. Wandering down the staircase, with legs feeling like lead, I was quiet for a full three minutes. Suddenly I felt cheerful. I was the only child in the school who had actually spoken to a fireman, and I bragged about it to all the other children.

My mother sent me a parcel containing all the things needed for growing plants: container, earth and a packet of seeds. Nurse Scrivener helped to prepare the little plastic pots with drainage holes by putting clinker in the bottom. The plants were put in a safe place, watered carefully, and left to grow. Unfortunately one of the children accidentally knocked the tray containing the pots off the shelf, so the little seeds never reached maturity. I was deeply upset, and could not be fully comforted, even by Miss Scrivener.

Another outing was to the water mill which was actually operational and ground flour. We were able to feel the paddles on the wheel. One day the activity class constructed a model of the water mill from lengths of steel and wood. It had a handle which turned. Taking straw from an old thatched roof, placing it between the lengths of steel, and turning the handle, I firmly believed that this provided the basis for shredded wheat, a cereal newly on the market, which then required final processing at the real water mill. Later that day, as if to confirm my belief, Miss Clarke came back from the water mill with a packet in her hand.

"There we are," she said, "I've taken the box of thatching straw to the mill and look what they've done for you." She handed me the packet. "They've made some shredded wheat." I really believed it had been produced at the water mill. I was so happy that I trotted round school telling everyone, "I told you they could make Shredded Wheat."

Another model made in the same class was a mock-up gramophone. At that point I had never had a gramophone of my own to work by myself. That particular day each one of us was asked what we would like to make, so I

Touch Me Please

chose a gramophone. At the home we possessed one of the old free-standing wind-up grams. The smell of the felt on the turntable has always stuck in my mind. I remember this particularly because I had the honour of putting the arm on the record. Of course, with my mock-up model I could do this any time I wanted, and not have to wait for the teacher's permission.

An old tobacco tin lid was used as the turntable, a long pointed stud for the needle, a bit of felt cloth was put across a wooden case to make a speaker, and two small pieces of wood were used for the volume and tone knobs. I made a bit of a fuss about this because the knobs were square and could not be made perfectly round. Nevertheless, they really turned.

As if this wasn't enough, after the model was completed, the teacher asked if I would like to try it to see if it worked. A round piece of plastic was found, rough on the top to resemble an old 78 rpm record. I lifted the arm and placed the model needle on the record. To my amazement music started playing. As I spun the record round and round the music continued. I leapt for joy, turning one of the knobs to the right and to the left, and the volume of the music went up and down. I tried the other knob and the same effect occurred with the tone. I was fascinated and believed my model was really working. Only later did I realise that the teacher was playing the school gramophone.

We were encouraged to keep our personal belongings or those things especially dear to us in our "treasure boxes". Each of us was supplied with an old tin box and these became symbols of our individual personalities and interests. If we were naughty then we forfeited our "treasure boxes" or some of the contents, or we were not allowed access to our sweet tins. This was a dire punishment indeed.

I look back nostalgically, as the memories come flooding back, to a time when the world was full of sounds. Those early innocent years were probably my happiest.

The Silent Ordeal I must Face Alone

Article published in the *Yorkshire Evening Post* 30th November 1989

I look fine, quite healthy in fact, if a little overweight. What's the problem then? No one understands, that is the real problem. I have been blind from birth, and am used to that, but now I am profoundly deaf. I've heard all the old jokes about deafness, and even laughed a little at them. Now it has happened to me. Until May this year I was one of the most respected piano tuners in Leeds. As well as loving my work it was a point of contact for me, a way of meeting people. All this is now a thing of the past. I cannot begin to explain the sense of loss at the total curtailment of my career and abilities.

Let me dispel one or two myths about hearing. It is not like a volume control on the radio which just gets quieter and quieter. When I can hear speech with both my hearing aids up full, most people assume there is not much wrong. A favourite comment is "Well you can hear me." What they do not know is that the quality of the hearing is severely impaired with lots of frequencies missing, sounding like a very cheap radio with the batteries three quarters gone. Sounds are distorted, making it difficult to distinguish between them, and consequently it requires great concentration to make out speech.

If you have no sight and very little hearing it makes life very lonely, silent, and altogether strange. There are many problems. First there is the difficulty of communication. In a pub or any place with background noise the hearing aids pick up the noise and nothing else. With normal hearing the brain automatically suppresses the background and picks out the voice you are trying to hear. Being profoundly deaf, this is one of the things I have lost. At best I hear the odd word, and have to say "Pardon?" all the time.

Second, I am virtually a prisoner at home. It is dangerous and exhausting to try and go out alone. One of the prime factors in getting around for totally blind people is hearing. It is their guide and their saviour.

Apart from the hearing loss I no longer have a sense of direction. Hearing aids pick up sounds from two directions only. At a road junction I can't tell which way is clear. If anyone comes to offer help I can't hear them because of the noise of the traffic. Then sometimes, I am not sure whether someone is speaking to me or not. I hear the voice but not the words. I dare not reply in case they are not speaking to me, so often people think I am being rude or ignorant and walk away.

Thirdly I should mention the attitude of people I have known for a while. If I ask them to speak slowly, and explain why, they often make some little meaningless remark and run away as if I had the plague or something. Maybe they are embarrassed or don't know how to handle the situation. Many have promised "I'll come and see you some time and take you out," and other such things. Of course they all have their own lives to lead and in no way do I expect them to be at my beck and call, but the occasional invitation from old friends, customers or the landlords I used to work for would be appreciated.

I believe I would have had more sympathy and help if I had lost my legs or been physically immobile. Such conditions are obvious, whereas I look fit, so no one really knows how difficult life is.

Social services and other organisations are so overstretched they say they have no time to help me. They

Touch Me Please

did, however, give me a form for claiming my Severe Disability Allowance, for which I become eligible after being unable to work for six months. During all this time I have had to depend on my wife to take me places and finance me. I have always been, or tried to be, financially independent. Now this has become impossible.

The greatest loss of all is my music, which meant everything to me. Now it sounds out of tune. Being a piano tuner, my brain is highly trained to detect wrong notes, but my ears are giving my brain all the wrong information, for everything sounds horrible.

As if all this is not bad enough, I have to cope with tinnitus, a continual noise inside my head sounding as if the showers have been left on in the changing room at the swimming baths. This is with me day and night and can make sleep difficult.

The specialists have told me that there is no hope of any cure or improvement, and things are slowly getting worse. I live with the knowledge that I probably can't play or tune ever again. Imagine how painful it is when old customers ring me up. May I appeal to people to stop and think a little? Some of them, when I have explained why I can no longer tune their piano, ask indignantly "What am I to do now? Who else do you know who can look after my piano?" Let me say to all those who have not yet rung, if there was any way I could continue my career I would not hesitate to do so. The inconvenience of looking for another tuner is slight compared to the burden I now bear. There have been exceptions of course, and to those people I say thank you with all my heart and especially to my wife.

I have written this on our computer using a speech synthesiser. It cost our remaining savings and a loan but has been a lifeline. I hope there is some future for me out there, perhaps in computers. All I ask is that I be treated like a normal human being and not cast aside like an old boot.

PAT: Rehabilitation

At the same time as attempting to fill Mick's leisure time we pursued official channels for help. First we approached the Employment Service for assistance and spoke to a Disablement Advisor. She ascertained that the RNIB Rehabilitation Centre in Torquay undertook work with deaf-blind people. Mick was offered an initial assessment at Manor House at the end of January 1990. It was almost nine months since he had started to go deaf.

He could not travel alone, so the Disablement Resettlement Officer (DRO) organised train tickets for us both. I well remember the depressingly wet day we travelled from Leeds to Torquay. There were so many hold-ups on the way that we arrived about three hours late. I had planned to accompany Mick to Manor House before returning to Leeds later in the afternoon. I abandoned him at Torquay station to the protection of another traveller, and hopped back onto the train for the return journey, getting back to Leeds around midnight, tired and concerned about how Mick was feeling.

I need not have worried. All the staff at Manor House were immensely kind. It turned out that the Centre Manager, Mr Hewitt, had taught Mick to tune pianos at the Royal Normal College for the Blind at Albrighton Hall near Shrewsbury many years earlier.

The report on the initial assessment included an amusing section on Activities to be Avoided: "Climbing ladders, working at heights and any working environment where audible warnings are given". Mick really enjoyed his stay and wanted to return to Torquay for a vocational course. But Mr Hewitt felt that Henshaw's College in

Rehabilitation

Harrogate, which has a Deaf-Blind Unit, would be a more appropriate place for further training. He felt that Manor House was "not equipped for effectively meeting the needs of people with dual sensory impairment". So it was over to Henshaw's and Mick's social worker in Leeds, with the hope that he could be undergoing rehabilitation there by Easter 1990.

In late 1989 a visit was arranged, through Social Services, to the National Deaf Blind League at Peterborough. Mick and I travelled there by train with Mr Moody. At Rainbow Court, the specially designed flats for deaf-blind people, Mick talked to others who had also lost their hearing and sight. Patrick advised him "Do not grieve for what you have lost". So Mick kept a stiff upper lip. This was bad advice and he suffered for years because he did not grieve at the right time, and subsequently could not let go. The hurt was repressed and buried deep inside.

One of the main purposes of the visit was to assess the value of Hasicom, a means of talking to other deaf-blind people, through a modem connected to a computer. Unfortunately, it wasn't possible to see it that day; a technical hitch I suppose. Apart from plying us with quantities of coffee, they introduced Mick to the deaf-blind manual and we started to learn and practise it in preparation for the time when it would be our chief means of communication.

We tried various other methods of talking to each other. For example, you can't use finger spelling when you are driving, so we felt very isolated from each other on long car journeys. We learned the morse code and rigged up a gadget which could be tapped at one end and had a vibrating box at the other which Mick could receive. In theory this was for use where the hand language was not possible, but I am afraid I never got proficient at it.

Meanwhile, we paid a second visit to the Link

Touch Me Please

Centre for three days at the end of February 1990. After further conversations they noted that we were 'far more relaxed' after the 'depths of despair' we had experienced following Mick's 'traumatic hearing loss'. They made four recommendations for the future: a computer programming course in a local technical college; a correspondence course in computer programming; training in the use of a knitting machine; and creative writing.

Nothing was arranged at Henshaw's. Adrian Cox, the social worker from Manor House, was tireless in his efforts. He accompanied Mick to an interview in Harrogate, and attended two case conferences in Leeds. Much correspondence passed between Leeds Social Services Department and Manor House. We were not sure if Leeds Social Services were stalling. It was finally acknowledged that 'due to the complexity of Mr Gerwat's special needs it was most unlikely that the type of "package" he requires can be put together in his home area'. So Mick returned to Torquay for a further period of vocational assessment from 6th March – 11th April 1990. The staff pulled out all the stops. They made extensive enquiries about other provision. Whilst several agencies could offer fragmented assistance "it appears that nowhere can he obtain a comprehensive and well co-ordinated programme". So they agreed to take him on as a special case primarily to evaluate his potential for paid employment working with computers.

They could not have been more caring. They listed several subsidiary aims. They hoped to provide a professional psychological/counselling service to help Mick come to terms with what had happened. He certainly needed something like that. They took him to the beach to hurl stones into the sea in an attempt to express his anger and frustration. They agreed to look at his mobility and help to make him as independent as possible; to review his communication needs and help him develop non-auditory methods of communication. They aimed to provide extra staff, so that Mick could have individual support and a personal interpreter. They promised to provide specialist access technology equipment, and to help Mick to be involved in the social and leisure activities at the Centre. They said they would provide an Action Plan when the course finished and a Resettlement Service "to ensure a positive future". Finally, they hoped to involve his wife and other people throughout the course to make sure they knew what was happening, and to help their involvement in Mick's future.

When I visited Mick at Manor House for the first time they extended their kindness and concern to me. I remember Adrian Cox asking "And what about you? Are *you* getting any support?" – a question which reduced me to tears.

When he was much younger Mick had a beautiful Alsatian, Bridget. Because of his mobility problems Mick applied for another guide dog. After assessment at the Guide Dog Centre he was turned down because he could not hear traffic. It was simply too dangerous to depend entirely on a dog.

Mick paid a third visit to the RNIB Rehabilitation Centre from 10th September – 15th November 1990, and a fourth and final visit from 8th January – 1st February 1991. Their course plans had to be constantly modified as Mick's hearing deteriorated to the point where he used large body aids. He was mainly relying on the hand language at this point. Using the telephone was impossible. Although he could use a typewriter and send a letter to me, I could not write to him, at least not a personal letter, although any handwritten or typed communication could be read to him. The only way to talk directly – to express any personal thoughts – was in braille. Mick had a Perkins

Touch Me Please

braille machine which I learned to use inadequately. But at least we could keep in touch. This situation, like so many other experiences Mick had, emphasised the importance of communication. Without it you cannot be part of the world.

The main thrust of Manor House was to assist with communication, mobility and computer studies. He gained a good grounding in various IT applications, and his intention was to learn programming and work from home. He had applied for, and been accepted on, an Open University course which was due to start during February as soon as he returned to Leeds. The report of Mick's final course at Torquay concluded with an Action Plan:

'Mr Gerwat should pursue his courses of study via the Open University... After he completes his courses he should work with his DRO (Disablement Resettlement officer) and the RNIB Small Business Unit to establish himself on the home workers scheme.

'It is essential that Mr Gerwat and his family receive support from the Local Authority. Without appropriate input, much of the valuable progress is likely to be lost.'

Manor House could not have done more. Even after Mick's course had finished, Adrian Cox continued to campaign on his behalf. We were sad to hear that the Centre was closed in July 2004. We do not know how we would have managed without them during those dark days.

Adrian arranged for Simon Birtles, a Small Business Advisor from the RNIB, to visit Mick from time to time when he travelled north. Simon was a lively young man with a great sense of humour, who established a good rapport with Mick, and gave him a lot of practical help and moral support over several years.

After the personal attention and the busy days of Torquay Mick found it hard to adjust to a lonely existence back home, even though he was embarking on a challenging OU course. I was out at work during the day. Apart from the few loyal friends who visited him or took him out, he was isolated. We had hoped for practical support from Social Services, but nothing happened. Michael Jennings, Head of the Deaf-Blind Unit at Henshaw's wrote to Mick's social worker repeating that "Henshaw's College would be happy to provide support as and when required by Leeds authority".

Adrian organised a holiday for us at Palm Court, the RNIB hotel in Eastbourne, so that we could spend time relaxing together and be refreshed after the strain of the previous months. We spent a week there at the end of May 1991, where we enjoyed the wonderful swimming pool at Eastbourne, visited a vineyard for wine tasting, took a boat trip to Beachy Head and, of course, took the opportunity to call in at the Link Centre. While we were in the hotel I clearly remember overhearing one guest, newly blind and alone on an upstairs landing, calling out in a panic because her husband had left her briefly to fetch something. I was on the point of going to reassure her when her husband returned. Mick was never scared like that, having been born blind. One would imagine that silence and darkness together would be very frightening. He can never know what is going on around him. But I can't recall any occasion when Mick showed fear.

Adrian was shocked that Leeds were still not providing anything for Mick, and asked Tony Astom, the Director of the RNIB Vocational and Social Services Division, to write to the Director of Social Services in Leeds expressing 'his grave concern' over the handling of Mick's case. Adrian travelled all the way from Torquay to talk to us at home, and eventually a special case meeting was held in Leeds. This was attended by representatives from Social Services and the Deaf Centre, by Adrian and another member of the Manor House staff, and representatives from the National Deaf Blind League and Henshaw's College. It was awesome to sit in an august gathering of some twelve officials, haggling over what to do for Mick, urged and prompted by Adrian, though I found it galling that social workers and Deaf Centre staff were expressing their concern and ingratiating themselves, whereas they had failed to do anything for us for two years.

The outcome was funding for one day a week at Henshaw's College in Harrogate, where Mick mostly used a knitting machine, with a bit of computer studies thrown in. Enthusiastically, we bought a knitting machine at home, thinking Mick could churn out fantastic garments, but this was premature, since he wasn't actually taught much technique. The knitting mainly consisted of pushing the carriage back and forth; all the difficult bits were done by the teacher. He did, however, produce a couple of lovely sweaters. The computer studies did not really materialise. Mick discovered he knew more about computers than the teacher. On the whole, we felt this provision was 'window-dressing'.

Following this meeting Mick also started attending the Deaf Centre, but they had no young totally deaf-blind 'residents' that Mick could identify with, and they hadn't time to give him any attention. Unable to join in Bingo and similar activities, Mick spent the day reading a braille book which he provided himself. When we first met he had always said he wanted nothing to do with the world of the blind. He enjoyed a 'normal' life mixing with sighted people. It showed how desperate life had become that he was willing to sit on his own, chiefly ignored, in a day centre two days a week. It was much later that his computer skills were recognised and a unit for teaching computers to deaf-blind people was set up.

Rehabilitation

Once Mick was back in the daily routine at home, after work I would spend the evening with him. We had by now accepted that there was very little we could share and enjoy together. Social occasions were very difficult because of communication problems so we tended to make excuses or avoid them. In the early days I didn't visit friends often because Mick needed company. For us there could be no theatre or cinema, no radio or television, no music. Before Mick went deaf it was never quiet in our house; there was always music. Now we left the family to their media entertainment and found a quiet room. We might play one of the many RNIB games, or talk together about the day. At first I could talk to him if I sat close. Later, I had to spell the words out on his hand.

Andrew, a young community volunteer who lived in our neighbourhood, used to visit Mick one evening a week and help him with the computer. This was much appreciated, and Andrew was missed when he finished school and went up to Oxford.

For me life was still restricted but there was much to enjoy. By the middle of 1991 I had moved from British Gas to a subsidiary software company they had set up, with improved benefits and good prospects. I also derived much solace from the family. I believed my only real satisfaction in life from now on would be gained vicariously through my children and their achievements. Linda was now at Cambridge and I enjoyed taking her and fetching her home each term.

But Mick was desperately unhappy. He was trying so hard to rebuild his life and not to be a burden on me. He talked little of his feelings, he hardly ever complained of tinnitus, but he was changing. His old extrovert personality was shrivelling and he was often listless and unmotivated.

MICK: Early Life

We lived near a pub called "The Gom" in the rough end of London. It was a closed community where you were only accepted if you had been born and brought up there. Outsiders coming into the area were treated with wary hostility. Our family of four lived in a little through-terrace house in Mossington Road, near the old Surrey docks. As you went in the front door, you wiped your feet on the mat. On the left was the front room with a coal fire and a radiogram. This was my private retreat where I would go away and hide. The front room was my little domain. We had an old piano which was thrown out when I was around five, although we obtained another one years later.

My parents had installed some bells, and when meals were ready, or when I was required for anything else the bell would ring to summon me from the front room. Along a little passage, past the workroom, down a tiny step and through the door into the kitchen I would go. I turned the big, round plastic handle to open the door. On the right of the room was the boiler-cum-fire. At the front of the boiler was a door which pulled down, and on the top another door where the coal was fed in. This boiler heated a big tank. Water systems and pipes intrigued me, probably originating from the boiler room at Sunshine Home. I loved to hear the water gurgling through the pipes. I used to beg my mother to turn the water on downstairs so that I could listen to the tanks filling up.

On the left of the room was the table and three big wooden chairs with curved backs and thick wooden seats. The door into the scullery had a metal handle. In the

Early Life

scullery were an old gas cooker, a chair to put the washing-up on, a cupboard, a pot sink, and a bath. Yes, the bath was in the scullery. I used to play at the sink for hours, amused by the anti-splashers fitted to the taps, the rubber tubes which I could twist to direct the water anywhere I chose.

To the left of the sink was the back door which led into a little yard. This was rented off to lorry drivers for parking. So we had big lorries permanently in the yard secured by a large pair of tall wooden gates. We had no garden, but I used to spend hours wandering round the yard, or exploring the remains of the old air raid shelter. A wooden post held up a small lean-to porch where I loved to sit and watch thunderstorms. They thrilled me.

Back in the kitchen, against one wall adjoining the scullery door was an old settee; an armchair was against the door which led into the small passage and into the front room. Just before you reached the front room you passed my father's workroom. It was his exclusive domain and I was never allowed into it, having to be content with standing at the door and listening to him at work. He was an electrician and very good at his trade.

When I was three or four my brother, who was eight years older than I, used to play traditional jazz on our gramophone. It was an old electric one with a large square pick-up. The arm weighed about a ton and the steel needle, of the same type used in old wind-up grams, screwed into a tiny socket in the centre of the pick-up. I was very scared of this music because of the clash of the instruments. When my brother realised this he tormented me by turning up the volume.

Ron frequently teased and frightened me. He used to look after me when my Mum was at work. Sometimes we made little tents in the yard, but he obviously resented this responsibility, and vented his displeasure on me. He had an air-gun with which he used to try to shoot cats. One day he shot me in the leg with it, but made me keep quiet and not tell my mother by using dire threats of further torment. Obviously I was a nuisance to him.

On another occasion we were out in the yard where the lorries were parked. There was a device which I used to call a platform raiser but it was, in fact, a forklift truck. Ron sat me on the narrow platform stretched between the forks where I had just enough room to sit, then pumped it up. He called to me from below "You're thirty feet in the air. I'm off to have my lunch now." I had no idea how high it was, but I was forced to believe him. I pleaded with him to let me down: "I'm frightened. Please, I want my lunch."

"Every time you say that you'll be up there five minutes longer," he sneered. With that he abandoned me. When he eventually released me I stepped off the platform holding back my tears to deny him any further satisfaction, and crept indoors for a late lunch.

"I suppose you're going to cry now," he teased.

"No I'm not," I said defiantly, and I didn't.

As Ron grew older he developed an interest in cycling, progressing to scooters, and of course, he started work. What relationship there was between us – and there wasn't much – gradually diminished.

When I was five I was given my very first radio, which was a Vidor. If you closed the lid when the radio was still on there was a bleep to remind you to switch off. It had a felt backing on the lid upon which was embossed the name of the model "Lady Anne". It could run from mains or batteries and could be switched from one to the other very simply. Radio Luxembourg played all the latest records at night, and I spent many happy hours listening to these. Sometimes I used to lie awake in my little bedroom with the radio on until 11 o'clock. I loved my Vidor and enjoyed radio programmes for years, not only

Early Life

music but drama serials. At one time "Journey Into Space" was extremely popular.

When I was very young I had a craze for electricity and fiddled with plugs and switches. My father warned me that the electricity would say "How do you do?" but undeterred, I poked my fingers into a socket to find out exactly how it would 'speak' to me. The answer came very painfully and sharply, with the result that my electricity craze came to a swift halt.

From the time when I was a small child crazes have dominated my life. Even now, a craze sometimes rears its ugly head. What are crazes after all but bursts of ego. They come and go, they are transient things that last for so long, then vanish in the wind like a storm or freak wave upon the sea of life. At one time I was keen on gardening and planted seeds in profusion. Mum tipped a barrow load of soil in the yard on the site of the old air-raid shelter. I planted nasturtiums, pansies and some highly scented flowers. Besides flowers, I grew some watercress which I ate in sandwiches. The garden, however, disappeared one day while I was at school. Without permission the people renting the yard just concreted it over.

I had a craze for some sounds: echoes, ringing bells, cymbals and drums. I didn't know really why I liked these things; I just did. Then came light. This was strange because I don't think I could actually see light but I felt it. It had a strange effect on me. I loved to stand in front of car headlights when they were on and simply put my eyes up against them. The sun was another craze. It seemed to pierce my mind, to shine forth relentlessly.

Then came the sound of water flowing through pipes, falling rain and especially thunder. This still fascinates me. Storms were a real craze of mine. I loved them. There were never enough of them to satisfy me. I tried with my hands to feel what was flashing through the

Touch Me Please

sky. I thought I could feel the thunder and the lightning. Having never had sight, touch seemed to be the only way I could find out what was real, what anything was actually like. Thunder seemed an outlet of aggression, a release of feeling, booming, roaring, relentless. My mother was frightened of thunder, but I loved it. I would pester her, "Is there going to be a storm?"

After that was machinery, anything that did things: wind-up toys, gramophones, wireless, train sets and anything mechanical. How did they work, what made them understand the principal of movement or be able to work out, however crudely, what to do next? All these were questions in my mind that I longed to have answered. The big problem was, no one seemed to take the time to explain these things to me and I had to try and find them out for myself. This unfortunately involved opening things to find out how they worked, and this inevitably caused me some problems and got me into a great deal of trouble. If only people had just spent a little time trying to explain how and why, I would have been satisfied. There were exceptions. I remember my Uncle Sid (he wasn't really my uncle) explaining to me how a fridge managed to know when to turn itself off at the right temperature. To me, this ability was wonderful.

When I was about six I was spellbound by the ticket machines used by the bus conductors. There were two types: the simple punch type, where you had a ticket with a small hole in it, used right up to 1968 in Leeds, and the more complex machine that could print tickets of any price. This latter type fascinated me, so much so, that I kept asking on the buses if I could touch the machines. One conductor was so sympathetic that he promised my mother he would talk to the headquarters and see if I could have one. We didn't believe this would happen but, lo and behold, an official actually came round to our house

Early Life

and presented me with one. I can remember my brother was rather jealous and kept it for himself. It was a great collectors' item. Whatever happened to it? Who knows?

I came to love chiming clocks. I wanted to know how the clock knew when it was time to chime. This was much more difficult to find out. Grandfather clocks were something that opened up at the front and when I was very small, I could stand inside and find out how they worked. This got me into a lot of trouble. At the Sunshine Home where I first went to school, they had a wonderful grandfather clock with a really distinctive chime. How did it know when to chime? I tried and tried to find out. Frustratingly, the hands were hidden behind glass and I wanted to feel them to see if I could find out what time they pointed to.

From the age of four, I learned how to tell the time feeling model cardboard replicas of clocks but this wasn't the same as actually having a clock of my own. This I was destined to actually have later that year. A braille clock was given to me by the Ford car company, who bought presents for every child at our East Grinstead Sunshine Home.

Magnets were my next big craze. These fascinated me. One could hold and balance them on top of each other and make them 'float' in the air. I wanted a magnet so strong that it could attract metal from a long distance and bring it towards me through the air. This never happened but I did have a vast array of different shaped magnets in a large case. I kept this collection for years and years. Now, I would love to have it to play with again.

Flying, space and outer space was another of my crazes. I was always trying to reach beyond, to find out what was on the other side at the end of the street, behind the shop, beyond the building. It was my belief that beyond all of these points there was a wonderful land if only I could find it. Because I had no sight there was no evidence to disprove this. From an early age, I firmly believed that there was a real world underground, which I eagerly wanted to access. I even gave it a name: the "octangle". Heaven knows where I got that name from but it stayed with me for a long time. I think everyone thought I was a little bit mad.

Another question that puzzled me was, what were clouds? What was this "sky" the sighted world went on about? I had no notion of what it might be. I heard people talking about fog and mist. Could one actually feel fog? Was it a solid that stopped people from moving forward? I knew that sighted people got lost in it, so what was it? I could smell it of course but why couldn't I feel it, if it had the power to stop folks from going out? I found this hard to comprehend.

I was captivated by any form of drill or compressor. In the mid-fifties, there was a lot of building going on, new flats and apartments after the ravages of war. Near our school they were building blocks of flats. I remember being fascinated by the little dumper truck that used to take the cement from the mixer to where they were doing all the concreting. I always called this two-stroke truck a twug twug because of the noise the engine used to make. My poor long-suffering Mum had to look for the person driving this twug twug. I actually managed to climb aboard it and rev it up causing the two-stroke engine to go faster and faster.

Chickens were another craze. I pestered the life out of Mum until we got some. I remember their names as if it were yesterday: Peter, Paul and Jenny. They gave us some lovely eggs. We had them for a year or so, then Uncle Jack took them away and the next thing I knew I was eating them!

In 1959 I hankered after greengages. I can't think

why. My obsession was so bad that one day, in the middle of a lesson, Miss Anderson the head matron, who was extremely stern at times, brought one into the classroom for me saying, "Right, you've been going on and on about these. Now here's one and I hope we have heard the last of them."

Space, clouds, fog, magnets, light, the sun and wind – all were fascinating to me. The sea was another mystery and a craze of mine. I wanted it to stop and re-start just like a car, but of course it never did. I had dreams of it stopping, as if it was being turned off and on like a tap.

My parents generally indulged most of my crazes, and for my part, they gave me an interest which diverted me from other concerns. It did not strike me as unusual at the time that my mother often took me out, my father occasionally, but my parents never took me anywhere together. They always went separately. There was also a lot of shouting in the house, which I couldn't understand and managed largely to ignore because I spent most of my time at the Sunshine Home.

Life was innocent and happy then. I was aware of music during these early years but I had yet to realise its importance for me. I was unworried, knowing nothing about the cares of life, or the problems that I would have to face. Provided I had my toys and all that I needed, that was fine. There was no need to be concerned or to think about the future. At East Grinstead I was surrounded by happy, kind, affectionate people. The cares of adulthood were going on around me in other people's lives but I didn't even notice them. It wasn't until later years that they began to filter through the protective barrier of childhood innocence. All of us have the same experience at some time or other. The problems of the world, of coping with the harsh realities of life, began, I suppose, when I changed schools at the age of six.

PAT: The Cochlear Implant

Mick moved through aids of different strengths until he wore powerful body aids. Eventually, in 1990, these too became useless. We had started planning and preparing for the worst well in advance of this situation. As his hearing deteriorated it was more and more difficult to communicate with him. At home we learned the deaf-blind manual, which involves spelling out each word on the person's hand, and became quite proficient by the time we were dependent on it. Long before Mick was completely deaf we had to rely on it in busy places and noisy environments where background noise made it impossible for him to hear speech.

Soon Mick was isolated from people, apart from professionals who worked with deaf-blind people, and a few good friends and relatives who took the time and trouble to study the manual. It consists of a sign for each of the twenty-six letters of the alphabet, so isn't too onerous to get to grips with. But it still requires a willingness to put yourself out a little bit. For most people this is too much. Some are embarrassed by the tactile nature, especially men, and draw back from physical contact.

Mick had always been extrovert and gregarious. When he could hear he used to strike up conversations with anyone – on the bus, in a shop, in a pub or waiting room. He had a knack for breaking the ice; in public areas he soon had everyone laughing. Now his situation was pitiable. Even if he could get out to the pub on his own he was unable to chat to people when he got there. His courage and enterprise were amazing. In the early days of

The Cochlear Implant

his deafness, if I was out in the evening, he sometimes got a taxi to take him to a bar in town. Once deposited on a bar stool he would take out a card showing the deaf-blind manual alphabet. More than once he successfully got into conversation with other people, 'hearing' them through letters on his hand, and on one occasion, much to my surprise, even being chatted up by another woman who offered to take him out.

When Mick finally abandoned the most powerful hearing aids he was enveloped in a world of total silence and darkness. We could communicate, but of course it was slow and tedious. The deaf-blind manual was certainly useful for keeping in touch and passing on important news, but it wasn't ideal for discussing philosophy or debating the political situation of the day, which Mick would have hated anyway. It was inevitable that Mick became isolated. Now that he had neither music nor communication, he struggled to remain positive. I could see his personality changing. He had found self-expression playing the piano and listening to the music. He had always revelled in company and cheerful banter. That life was gone. He withdrew into himself and became a shadow of the lively person he once was.

Throughout our relationship we had never had the full range of communication techniques that sighted people take for granted. Mick could not see my facial expression, we could not exchange meaningful glances. I had learnt this early in our relationship but Mick had always known how I was feeling and how I felt towards him by the tone of my voice, whether it showed enthusiasm, tenderness, frustration. Now he had nothing to go by and physical touch was all important – a squeeze of the hand, a quick hug, an arm round his shoulder, holding hands, touching to show I was near. Otherwise he was in a vacuum.

Touch Me Please

Where the situation allowed, friends could talk to Mick through a computer. We attached his new braille computer to the old Amstrad. You could type into the Amstrad and Mick could pick up the text on the braille display. He was a good touch typist, but of course he didn't need to type back because he could speak. There was a cute little machine called the Alva on the market at the time. It had a braille display at one side and a tiny keyboard at the other. It cost about £4000. Simon Birtles arranged for Mick to have one on trial for a week, and we took it to Quaker Meeting. Several people talked to Mick through the Alva. Moved by Mick's plight, Beryl, an elderly lady from our Quaker Meeting, bought one for him. This meant that anyone could now communicate with Mick if they wanted to, without learning the deaf-blind manual. Beryl was a wonderful example of the generosity and kindness of Friends.

Once he was unable to hear his own voice Mick showed various signs of stress and difficulty. He began to stammer, although he had been a fluent and very competent speaker before. Whereas he had always been loud, now his voice became breathy, like a whisper and he was unable to correct it. Being the kind of person he was, Mick tackled the stammer and overcame it. He found he didn't stutter when he sang, so he sang as often as he could, mostly when he was alone in the house, so we didn't have to put up with his altered voice, which no longer sang in tune. After a little while the stammering stopped.

We had heard about the cochlear implant, first invented in Australia. It consists of a string of tiny electrodes implanted in the cochlea, designed to receive sounds and interpret them as the normal ear does. The sounds are picked up by a tiny microphone, converted to digital impulses and transmitted from the external

The Cochlear Implant

processor to the electrodes. Since there are only twenty two electrodes as opposed to the million channels existing in the healthy ear, the sound picked up is very primitive.

At first Mick thought his hearing would never be so bad as to need that. However, as the audiometric tests continued to show a deterioration, we asked Mr Fraser if he could refer Mick to Manchester Royal Infirmary (MRI), where they were embarking on an experimental programme funded by the Government. Adrian Cox from Manor House once again came to our aid and wrote to Mr Fraser in July 1991 expressing his concern about Mick's health and state of mind, and urging a prompt referral to the implant team. Nowadays many hospitals offer cochlear implants as part of their routine surgical programme, but it was much harder in the early days of this new technology. Professor Ramsden in Manchester was an old friend of Mr Fraser, so in due course a letter was sent.

Our first appointment was at 9 o'clock on a Monday morning in January 1992, which meant an early start to allow for the M62 traffic jams on top of the moors, and the slow journey from the motorway through the rush hour build-up to the city centre and from there to the hospital. A friend had suggested the best route and it was nerve-wracking on the first occasion, since I didn't know the way and we wanted to be on time. We made it by the skin of our teeth.

Mr Ramdsen explained that Mick would need to undergo tests to see if he could benefit from an implant. If the cochlear hairs were damaged, an implant would help, but if the auditory nerve was damaged it would be of no use. We were anxious to get an early appointment, but there was a long waiting list. Luckily I had some health insurance through work, and they agreed to pay for Mick to attend MRI privately for tests. We spent a couple of days in Manchester. Since none of the medical staff knew the deaf-blind manual, it was really useful for me to be there as an interpreter. It was a nervous time. As they inserted a needle to test the response of the auditory nerve we held our breath. We were immensely relieved when the tests proved positive. Both ears were suitable for an implant. Mick was finally on the list for surgery. At last we had hopes of lifting Mick out of the silence to a more normal life, but to our dismay the health insurance, having paid for the tests, refused to pay for the operation, so there was nothing for it but to wait impatiently.

Simon Birtles was anxious on our behalf. Once Mick was on the waiting list, he wrote to Mr Ramsden early in 1992 and again in June enquiring about the time scales. He pointed out that Mick was finding it difficult to retrain, and "becoming increasingly depressed and introverted". Adrian Cox also wrote about his concerns over Mick's health. The RNIB were prepared to look for funding for a private operation if necessary.

Mick finally underwent the operation in November 1992. It had taken almost a year from our first appointment with Mr Ramsden. This was a relatively short period (at that time), influenced I am sure by his special needs and the support from RNIB staff. Naturally we ourselves believed that someone both deaf and blind should take priority over the merely deaf. Again I stayed at the hospital, acting as interpreter, even going into the recovery room to speak on Mick's hand as he came round from the anaesthetic. He was in hospital for a few days, then we went home to wait for the 'switch-on'. This was when the external processor was attached and programmed, having allowed time for the scar and tissue to heal. We set off again over the M62 just before Christmas, excited and full of anticipation. Wouldn't it be wonderful if I could talk to Mick normally instead of using

The Cochlear Implant

the hand language.

Paul, the chief audiologist, connected the microphone and processor to Mick's head. This is held by two magnets: one implanted with the internal receiver and one external. Then he connected the processor to a computer and began the long process of tuning the implant. This involved taking each of the electrodes in turn and establishing the loudest and softest volume, and the highest and lowest pitch that registered. The session was filmed, and the whole implant team showed immense interest by popping in and out when they had time. Mr Ramsden was very keen to see the outcome. The efficiency of the implant depends, of course, on how skilfully the surgeon seats it deep into the cochlea. How would Mick find it when he was switched on?

He had been strongly warned not to expect too much. After the lengthy programming process was finished he was disconnected from the computer, some batteries were placed in the processor and he was launched into his new world. He was bitterly disappointed. He put on a brave show in front of the professor and the implant team, joking about how 'bubbly' it was, like being underwater, but his heart sank to think that this was his hearing from now on. It was so primitive, so lacking in tone. He said it was "like burying you in a jellyfish".

Nevertheless, it was a miracle. As we sat in the waiting room after a lunch break I read to him from a magazine about a trip to the West Indies on a banana boat and he was able to follow most of it. This is very rare among implant users. Most people take weeks to learn the new sounds and use lip reading to help interpret what they hear. Mick didn't have that option. He had to make the most of it, or remain in isolation.

There were several follow-up sessions. As Mick's

Touch Me Please

brain adjusted to the implant the processor needed to be fine-tuned regularly during the first few months. This period of our lives involved many journeys over the Pennines. He made good progress with the implant and was soon able to hear speech, provided he was in a quiet environment. This opened up lots of possibilities. He could use a speech synthesiser again with the computer. This was good news because braille machines are hugely expensive and the Libra was temperamental. It also opened the door to further training if we could find something suitable.

What was totally impossible was music. The implant did not recognise any musical pitch at all. Mick made several attempts to access some of the tracks he loved so much, but it was useless. So he was condemned to live without his music forever. Confucius said "Music produces a kind of pleasure which human nature cannot do without". This belief is frequently expressed. For many years I used to feel cross when people said glibly "I couldn't live without music". I thought, well some people just have to! Mick used to get angry with the people who would forever talk about music when it was clear he could not access it. Even one of the social workers – who really did nothing for him – used to visit him just to quiz him about the rock bands he had worked for. This was like rubbing salt in the wound. It was, without doubt, the cruellest thing that could have befallen him. He once said he would rather have been paralysed from the neck down, as long as he could have listened to music. But he picked himself up and started all over again with his painfully restricted life. At least things were much improved now.

Right from the start Mick knew that he would be able to do much better with two implants than with one. Over the years he often asked Manchester if they could offer him a second one but without success. It was always a dream, a hope, that we could raise enough money to pay for a second implant, but it was to be a very long wait.

Computers: lifeline to the world

Article published in the *Yorkshire Post* 2nd March 1992

The computer has many uses, but I wonder how many people depend on it for their sanity and their communication with the outside world, using it as their lifeline. I was born totally blind but this was never a problem for me. There are many things one can do being blind.

I chose piano-tuning for my job. I worked over the years for many people in the rock, classical and jazz worlds including Elton John, Queen, the Rolling Stones, Stan Tracy and many others. All this came to an end two years ago when I started to go deaf. My deafness increased so rapidly that I knew the time would come when I would no longer be able to hear.

What to take up next? Ever since my very young days reading science-fiction books, the computer had fascinated me. Now I turned to it as a means of, at first, filling the lonely days without work. Initially I used a speech synthesiser to work with the computer. In my early days I used my wife's Amstrad which I had bought for her.

Before long, however, I had to face the fact that I would soon be unable to hear speech. My wife, Pat, and I embarked on a campaign to raise money for a computer with a refreshable braille display.

There is absolutely no financial support for people who find themselves in my unfortunate position; the only way to get this equipment was to buy it ourselves. In the end we raised £15,000. After considering for a while, we settled on the Libra, a computer with a braille display built in and which is reasonably small. We bought a modem and a teletext box, a reader scanner for translating books, and a braille printer for putting the material into braille.

What then were my needs? I needed a contact with the outside world, I needed to be able to communicate with the general public and I needed an intellectual challenge. The last came first. Having learned the basics using the speech, I then turned my attention to the other needs. All this was not achieved easily as we came up against lots of problems both technically and also through lack of concern initially by the outside world in general. However, now I have all the equipment working well. My computer has an 88-MB hard disk; I have a number of programs including Wordperfect 5.1 and Norton Utilities. There are also applications for my braille printer and the scanning facility. The scanner works like a photocopier and digitally scans the text, after which the software formats it in either ascii format or for a wide range of word processors.

Now that I am totally deaf, my computer is the only way I can make contact with the general public (unless they know the deaf-blind manual, which very few do). Through my modem I am on two networks. One is Hasicom, the network especially for the deaf-blind. This is good but very limiting as it is only a very small system. The other network is Cosy, the Open University network. It is my intention to take a computer-programming course with the Open University. I had started to do so as I was going deaf but my deafness came quicker than I thought it would. The problems of brailling the course were colossal but now we have, through the RNIB, managed to arrange for its brailling.

Choosing a communication program was easy as I had one called Datatalk provided with the modem. For a

Touch Me Please

deaf-blind person there are problems accessing menus with a highlighted bar. One can now get braille displays which show up the highlighted text but this came too late for me. I find Cosy very fulfilling as there is so much of it. In my isolated and silent world it is like a breath of fresh air.

Another essential thing is to be able to keep up with the news and events of the outside world. For this we bought a little box which accesses teletext. This box, by Micro-projects, is like a modem box in appearance. One connects the box to the serial port as one would a modem. There is software provided with the teletext. It has all the usual functions of teletext, so that I can hold pages and read them. This is especially useful when using the braille display.

One extra feature is that I can save the text from the screen in ascii format, after which I can run it through my braille translation software and print it out in braille. There are a few problems with this teletext but there are no error messages in the program so one is left in the dark if something won't function. Another problem is controlling the teletext pages; it is like trying to train a dog. I wish also that one could access the sub-title pages. They go by so fast, not giving the braille time to register the text. I wish they would scroll up and then I could use the program to save the text of programming on television.

For the last week I have been evaluating an Alva braille carrier. It has a very small keyboard and braille display which has the facility of picking out highlighted text. I can use it as a terminal with either the Libra or my wife's Amstrad. Most important of all, it enables the general public to talk to me. It runs for seven hours without needing charge and is small enough to carry around quite easily. I can use it as a terminal with my PC

Computers – Lifeline to the World

and I can also put small programs on it. With my Alva I will be able, in some measure at least, to talk with anyone I meet. I will be one of the first in the country to have one of these computers and I hope it will widen my horizons as far as possible.

Without my computer and all the equipment I now have, I would find life impossible. My computer equipment is a lifeline to me; it has made the difference between total isolation and keeping in touch with people and the outside world.

MICK: North House and Problems at Home

When I was six I moved from a secure, sheltered Sunshine Home to a school which took boys up to the age of ten. This was North House in Wimbledon Park. We were so near the tennis courts that we could hear the scores, although at that time I had no idea what they meant. The school was much nearer to Bermondsey than the Sunshine Home was, which meant I could go home every weekend. This turned out to be a less happy arrangement. I think from this time I began to grasp, very slowly, the realities of our family life.

Being at home gave me the chance to get to know my parents better. Dad wasn't a person you could assess very easily. He was a genius when it came to electrical equipment. At first he worked for an independent company which went out of business and subsequently gained employment with the London Electricity Board. I came to realise, however, that he was a strange person, who said some very odd things to me. If I went near a drain he would say, "Be careful you don't get hydrophobia" which of course was impossible. I only discovered much later from a relative of mine, that my parents were never married, but my father had been married twice before, on the first occasion to a wonderful woman who died young. He then married again, but it was an unhappy relationship which, I think, ended in divorce. How he met my Mum while he was working in the fire service is an unsolved mystery, but they were not happy together, and it is an even greater puzzle why they stayed together so long.

North House and Problems at Home

Sometimes on Saturday afternoons when my Mum went to town, Dad used to look after me. He was a mysterious person whom it was difficult to feel close to. He would often wander round the house singing at the top of his voice about odd things that did not make any sense. Sometimes, referring to the little baker's shop near our house, he sang in a tuneless monotone, "Hansell's bread, Hansell's bread." Some of his topics of conversation were ridiculous. He used to imitate the sound of sawing Christmas trees, and talk about Jack Hayward in Meerworth Woods. At other times he would call "Look out, here come the Bow Street Runners".

He told a distasteful story about bakers' noses dripping into the dough as they worked, to give the bread a salty taste. My Mum told me, although I do not know if it is true, that he spent some time in a mental hospital. From his behaviour I could well believe this. Not only did he talk of these things himself, but taught me to recite them, much to my mother's annoyance. I always called him my Dad, and he accepted the role, but I learned later that he wasn't really. There was another man around, who was my natural father and my mother's boyfriend. He continued to show affection and devotion to my mother throughout her life, although she treated him abominably. So things were difficult for Dad. Years later he was able to talk to me about the unhappy position he was in. He didn't want to leave because it was his house, and I imagine he stayed also for my sake. I suppose life was pretty cruel to my Dad.

My Mum's background has a very shady side. Her parents were in India for a long time as part of the British Raj. My grandfather was in the army. My grandmother, who was strict as anything, often talked about the occasion she met Queen Victoria. Granny would tolerate no deviation from her will. I found out how true this was when she looked after me on occasions. I stayed with her sometimes during the school holidays when Mum was at work. I am sure it was due to her totally rigid attitude that my mother's life took the path it did.

Mum was the eldest of twelve children, and general dogsbody with the household chores falling to her. She would often tell me that at the age of eight she had to be up at six in the morning to scrub the fire grate. In an environment such as that it was no wonder she became embittered and rebelled against all parental authority. Like lots of women of her age she went into service at the age of 14. This had disastrous consequences as she was seduced by an older married man. As a result a child was born, a girl who would be my half-sister although I never knew what happened to her, or even her name. From what I understand my mother moved to live in Brockley. Of course she was totally disowned by my grandmother, and the rest of the family were forbidden to speak of her.

These tragic events did not end there. She went scrubbing floors and taking any job she could. There were many different men in her life at this time, although I have never found out the entire truth. She must have felt unstable, insecure, and unwanted. Continually she was at odds with her brothers and sisters over one thing or another.

She was living with my father in 1941 when my brother was born. Dad claimed that he was not his child. This period of my mother's life is still shrouded in mystery, but I think she took Ron to Leicester, maybe to escape the bombing. Being pushed from pillar to post with her little child up and down the country, taking any job, living in squalid rooms: all must have fanned the fires of her resentment and bitterness. Her sister Violet, or Auntie Vi as I called her, talked to me long hours about my mother: "I'm certain that if Vera had not fallen in love and been pregnant at such an early age her whole life would have been totally different."

Auntie Vi was the only member of Mum's family who understood what I was going through. The trouble was that if genuine affection was shown to Mum, the anger, like a canker, had eaten in so deeply that just when she could have grasped the affection she always found some fault with the person trying to show it, blaming them for her own shortcomings. By the time I came along the canker was well rooted.

My Mum's relationship with me was a love-hate one. One day she would buy me an expensive present, the next she would push me round the room, pull my hair and push me up the stairs. I well remember on many occasions being shaken until my very insides were feeling dizzy. Never in the whole of my life have I ever heard anyone who had a shout or a temper like she had. The viperous, venomous tone in her voice would have cut through tungsten. One moment she would put her arms around me and tell me I was all she had in the world. Within an hour she would be telling me if I didn't behave she would put my head in the gas oven.

Truly, the poor woman needed help but would never get it. In those far-off days counselling or support centres did not exist. With such unpredictable behaviour it was difficult for me to know where I was with her.

One Sunday afternoon I was playing my gramophone in the front room when it developed a severe hum for no apparent reason without any tampering on my part. From out of the kitchen my Mum screamed "What the hell do you think you're doing? Grrt you little swine." She tore into the room and grabbing me by the arm dragged me into the kitchen. Throwing me into a chair she snarled "Git down before I knock you down. All I do is pay out, pay out, pay out for you, nothing else. I'll take your gram and smash it to pieces, that's what I'll do. Then you'll have nothing to listen to, will you, WILL YOU?" With these last two words my Mum grabbed my head and banged it repeatedly against the back of the chair.

My mother first met my real father while she was a waitress in a cafe. He used to visit me and buy me presents. I always called him Popsey when I was young. Later I referred to him as Nunc. Strange to say, it was many years before I even knew his surname. One of the tragedies of this situation was that I had to constantly lie, making up stories to tell my father about where I had been with my mother. Mum told me that if I didn't do this I would be taken away and put in a home. The thing about lying is that it is like a climbing plant. Once the seed takes root it copiously multiplies and if you are not careful, you end up believing in the lies yourself. I am certain in my own mind that this contributed to my inability to face up to difficulties directly.

I remember the morning I moved to my new school very clearly. My mother took me. My father rarely took me anywhere, but I had in my mind his strange warning about drains when I went to see the headmaster. I talked to him of this concern about hydrophobia. He seemed both embarrassed and annoyed, asking me in a somewhat severe tone what I meant. I paid for my indiscreet babbling in the usual way – a vicious scolding – when my mother parted from me in the school grounds.

It is funny what paltry details one can remember. As I entered the dining room for my first meal I noticed that the chairs we sat on were leather covered, with studs bordering the sides and back. After I had finished my dinner I felt hungry and wanted some more. Turning to one of the pupils I said, "Excuse me Ron, how can I have some more?"

"You put your hand up," he replied, "and my name

North House and Problems at Home

is not Ron."

I had inadvertently called him by my brother's name. Fortunately it did not prevent me obtaining a second helping.

I was put into Miss Garling's class, where each desk had its own unusual little inkwell with a sliding top which opened and closed. Jean Garling was a lovely but firm person. One of the highlights of the week's lessons was on Monday afternoon, when she taught us about 'Roots and Shoots'. This involved keeping plants in little bottles of water. I put an acorn into one of these bottles from which long roots and shoots grew profusely. I asked her how long it would take to grow into a real tree. "You will be very old before it grows into a big tree," she said.

Her firmness showed itself fairly soon after I started at North House. I have mentioned my fascination for water systems. I loved to hear the toilet tank filling up after I had pulled the chain. One morning I could not sleep very well. I went to the toilet and pulled the chain four times, just to hear it filling. Unfortunately this was located not far from Miss Garling's bedroom, and I was suddenly harangued: "Do you realise it is five o'clock in the morning. How dare you wake me up at this time? I'll see you later." At assembly that morning I was paraded in front of the entire school and had my legs firmly slapped for waking Miss Garling up.

When I was only just seven I was learning to read. Looking through the alphabet I came across what I believed to be a word. Excitedly I said to my teacher "I've found a word 'def'. Look I can read my first word."

"No Mike, that's not how it is spelt" she replied. "It is d, e, a, f, deaf. It means you can't hear a thing and have to wear hearing aids like little radios."

"I want hearing aids, I love radios, I could hear the snow falling then".

Touch Me Please

Miss Garling roundly rebuked me. "Don't say that again. Can you understand what it would be like not to hear? You would not be able to talk to anyone. If I hear you say that again I will punish you." With a crestfallen face I said "Yes miss."

I also recall doing arithmetic during my first term at North house. I couldn't work out all the figures being thrown at me from all directions. In those days, blind people used things called Taylor Arithmetic frames with star-shaped eight-angled holes, and metal type. These were like a flat board with row upon row of holes. There was a tray along the side of the board which held "types", lead pillar-shaped objects about a quarter of an inch long. On one end they had a small groove and on the other there were two dots. The groove fitted into the hole and you could fit it at several angles from 1 to 9. Turning the "type" over you had the two dots. Again, there were several angles, one for zero and others for multiply, divide, add and subtract. There were probably others but I forget them now. You had to put the numbers in columns representing tens, units and so on.

This was extremely complex for an impatient seven year old. I banged my hands on the board and declared in a loud voice "Why can't we have a machine that does this for us, that can work out sums!" Once again I was pulled to the front of the class by Miss Garling and made to stand in a corner for the rest of the morning. "You do the sums yourself, machines can't do them for you!" she told me.

I must have been thinking about all this because that night I had a strange dream. I was sitting in a round chair. I had a large board in front of me filled with an array of knobs, levers and buttons. It was wonderful; each one I pressed did something different. One announced dates, some blew perfumed air at me, some allowed me to fly, some produced food and so on. All I had to do was

North House and Problems at Home

manipulate them. From the time when I awoke next morning I began to have a fascination for anything that was technical. This started with radios, progressed to short wave radios – they used valves way back then – and years later, in 1962, I was given my first tape recorder. I have already mentioned about fridges and machines that turned themselves off. I just wanted to know how things worked and to interact with them.

There was a long break in my acquisition of gadgets while I pursued my career in piano tuning. Then stereo came into my life in 1972 and stereo radio in 1980. Next came talking clocks in 1981. The BBC bought me one and I called it the droid. In 1983 I had my first talking calculator. So I finally had the last laugh on Miss Garling. I could do sums easily now, any amount of them. How I wish I'd had this while at school.

Charles John, born in Swansea, was the man who for eight years cast his large shadow of influence over my life. As headmaster of North House and later – after Mr Peppit's retirement – as headmaster of Linden Lodge, he had ruled over all of us with a rod of iron yet gloves of silk. This small, very insignificant looking man, who for years had suffered from severe stomach ulcers, possessed a weapon mightier than physical strength could ever be. This was his voice. I have never known anyone with a voice that could command, cajole, frighten, soothe, calm or amuse like his could. He ran a policy of fair but firm justice throughout the school. Every new boy was told on arrival, "You play ball with me and I'll play ball with you. Cross me and I'll come down on you like a ton of bricks."

There would always be a testing point with every boy where he would show us just what he meant. I had my baptism of fire when I was only seven and a half. I had been playing with some stones in the bushes and had started throwing them at the school fence to hear the hollow sound of the wood. I was carried away with this activity when I felt the lobe of my ear being gently pulled by a cold, firm hand. I knew without any prompting just whose hand it was. As in most schools, many wild tales abounded about the severe punishment Mr John meted out to wrong-doers, for even the most trifling of misdemeanours. Frighteningly exaggerated accounts of leather straps, shoes, slippers, and a long cane were convincingly related to all new boys. At that age I fully believed every one of them. The feel of those rough cold fingers on my earlobe brought forth terrors of such things happening to me. In a deep, low, threatening voice, sounding like a fully grown bear, Mr John said, "Have you been throwing stones at that fence?" His question was repeated three times with five second pauses between repetition. During the pauses I managed to squeeze out a weak "Yes sir."

My hand was grasped and I was led down the long path towards his house. During that walk pictures of the lashes I was about to receive – at least six, if not twelve – vividly flashed across my mind. I visibly began to shake, my heart rate almost doubling with every second. I was led through the door of the house, and seated in an old armchair in the kitchen. Mr John proceeded to turn towards the sink and wash his hands. The familiar pause, another of his effective weapons, now ensued.

Eventually he asked "What have you got to say for yourself? Why were you throwing stones at that fence?" I stammered that I didn't know, and awaited the fall of the slipper, the lash of the strap, or the thud of the shoe, which must surely descend upon my posterior. The fear grew so strong that I asked, "Are you going to leather me sir?" He gave a little chuckle and said, "What do you think I am? You and I are going to fall out of friends quickly if I don't see you growing up a bit. I'll let you off this time, but next

North House and Problems at Home

time..." At this point he opened his arms and gave the most almighty clap I've ever heard. With that loud clap came a tremendous sense of relief and he led me back along the path into the school grounds and left me. I had passed through the test shaken but unscathed.

Once a boy had passed through the test Mr John's attitude changed completely. Though still firm if you stepped out of line, he was warm, understanding and considerate. He always had time to listen to what you had to say as long as you didn't waffle. He gave firm and final judgements on everything, but was as gentle as a lamb if you were upset or in trouble. He was the father figure I had never had in my life before. With him behind me I felt capable of facing anything or anyone. I owe a great deal to Mr John for helping me through difficult times while I was at school. The tragedy was that for a long time I was unable to tell him how unhappy I was and how much I was bullied. He strongly disapproved of people "whining" as he called it.

After a while at the school, since things were not happy at home, the standard of my work dropped markedly. Not understanding the reasons for this, the staff at first punished me. Eventually one of the teachers came to the conclusion that something was wrong. Indeed, things were horrific at home.

I remember one incident as clearly as if it happened yesterday, although I was only seven. I had heard my Mum and Dad shouting at each other before, but had been unable to understand why and what it was about. It was breakfast time on Sunday. In our house we always had egg and bacon for Sunday breakfast, a meal which I relished enormously. I was summoned from my retreat in the front room by the bell, and made my way down the passage and into the kitchen. I sat expectantly on a big wooden chair at the table. My parents were in the little

Touch Me Please

scullery. I could smell the bacon and hear the fried bread sizzling in the pan, but I could also hear the angry voices of Mum and Dad as they shouted at each other. This was not unusual, so I tried to ignore the commotion. However this was impossible for I heard my mother snarl: "I swear Gus I'll take this kitchen knife and I'll kill you with it, I'll kill you, I'll kill you!"

I heard the cutlery drawer sliding open and the clash of metal as my mother searched for the knife. Taking it out she brandished it at my father.

"Put that thing down." His voice was urgent and harsh. "Don't be so silly. You won't kill me."

"Wouldn't I, wouldn't I?"

As she said these words she crept forward. Then my father picked up a weapon. I heard the scuffling, the drag of feet, the thuds as they hit each other, the occasional clash of a knife blade against something hard. Knowing my father's strength, I sat petrified, scarcely breathing, terrified lest a knife should sink into soft flesh, imagining my mother bleeding, dying. Suddenly there was a loud thud as my mother fell to the floor. She was crying and threatening to go to the police. I had never heard or experienced anything like this before. I was horrified both by the violence and my inability to understand what was happening. I was desperately afraid that one of my parents would be hurt.

Then there was comparative calm: my father was silent while my mother sobbed quietly. Time seemed to stand still as I hung tense within a vacuum, wondering what would happen next. I heard Mum scrambling to her feet. There was a clatter of plates and she entered the kitchen bearing my bacon, eggs and fried bread. Still sniffing, she set my breakfast before me. I loved bacon and eggs, but I could not eat anything. Dad came into the kitchen and we all sat, silent, strained. Mum asked me if I wanted my breakfast. My voice came thin and scared, "No thank you." This was my first inkling of the hard and bitter world outside.

Similar incidents followed, but that was the most piercing, the most traumatic. I felt shocked, in total incomprehension. My concept of Mummy and Daddy was shattered. Before that the rows and the shouting had been in the background and I had shut them out of my mind. Now, there was no way I could continue to do that. I realised for the first time that Mummy and Daddy were not perfect, did not like each other, in fact HATED each other.

I wanted to talk to my teachers and ask them about the incident. Why did Mummy punch my Daddy? Why did Daddy attack my Mummy? I knew in my childlike way that something was very wrong, but I needed someone to explain it to me. The rows continued, and with the upset they caused, coupled with the move to the new school, my work deteriorated. I developed boils and sore lips which reflected the inner turmoil I was suffering. It was nervous reaction. Then came the jumping fits. If anyone made a sudden noise I jumped. While eating my tea I would recall a particular incident and jump. It was an involuntary action I had no control over. Everyone at school thought I was being silly. Even my own mother did!

I spent a lot of my time at home in the front room listening to music on the gramophone or radio. My music was all I had left to cling to. If Mum and Dad had a row I simply escaped to the other room and kept right out of the way. At this time I started to rock. I still do it today when I listen to music or hear a rhythm. People have asked me if there is something wrong, if I need treatment. Way back in those lonely days I just got immersed in the music as an escape and I rocked for I had nothing else to comfort me.

Touch Me Please

The various manifestations of my anxiety and unhappiness continued. Eventually, the school staff realised that shouting at me would not make me sit still, that the situation was serious, caused by nerves and beyond my control.

Meanwhile, a boy called Ted Rose, who later needed psychiatric treatment himself, along with his friends, wanted to get me into trouble with the mistresses and matron, for no other reason I suppose, than I was a new boy and it was an amusing pastime for them. They made it appear that I wet the bed, which at this time was untrue. They fetched a mug of water and poured it into the bed in the night. I suspected that they were doing this, but was unable to prove it. One morning, however, I was awake when I heard Ted tell his accomplice, Rory Heap, to fetch the mug and pour it into the bed.

Naturally, the staff frowned upon bed wetting, and took a poor view of my feeble excuses when I tried to explain what was really happening. There was quite a storm at the school, and my mother came down specially to discuss the matter. I was summoned before Matron and reprimanded for my short-comings. It was a dirty habit and it was wrong. I was taken to Mr John, the headmaster, forthwith, who threatened me with a beating if there were any more incidents like last night! Despite his harshness, Mr John was a very humane man.

Eventually the staff believed the story about the water, but the affair triggered off in me a fear and a chain of events leading to later incidents. I think that experience was another factor which contributed to my inability to face problems until they are no longer avoidable. I would rather shelve difficulties than come to terms with them, and only tackle them when I am face to face and there is no escape. This weakness was to have a marked effect in my later life. Had I not feared and been unable to handle

North House and Problems at Home

problems, things might have been very different in my personal life.

The school put me in touch with Maudsley Hospital specialising in the treatment of nervous disorders, and I was sent to a psychiatrist called Mr Rodrigo. With him I played with plasticine. At the time I could not understand what he was trying to do, but in later years I could see the purpose behind some of the activities. He was focusing my mind on play to enable him to casually explore my family situation. I went to see him regularly for about a year and it seemed to be helping. My mother was always taken away by a lady called Mrs. Secombe, whom I recognised by her squeaky shoes. In most hospitals the staff wear leather-soled shoes which squeak on the polished floor. Mrs. Secombe's shoes squeaked amazingly loudly. I was puzzled as to why she always took my Mum away, but I found out much later they used to ask her questions about the family set-up at home, I suppose to give the psychiatrist some kind of clue to my state of mind. The cleaners' shoes used to squeak a lot too. I would sit and listen as people passed by, guessing the difference between the nurses, the cleaners and the patients, guided merely by the squeak of their feet.

Although the psychiatrist was helpful, the situation at home, which was the root cause of my problems, did not improve. I was becoming more aware of the hatred and aggression within our house. When the investigations into my situation were getting too close to the truth for my mother to face, she decided to terminate my treatment.

Life at home was made bearable by our next door neighbours who ran a cafe. I used to know them as Uncle Sid and Auntie Rose. Way back from my very earliest days they befriended me. They were always kind, and Sid was like a second father to me. I believe he understood me better than anyone else, right from an early age. Rose was

Touch Me Please

loving and affectionate. It was Uncle Sid who installed the bells that used to summon me to breakfast and it was they who gave me my first experience of riding in a car. It was a large, well-upholstered Humbler Hawk which moved smoothly and quietly and was magic to ride in. Their bacon sandwiches were the most delicious on the planet.

Later, when I had settled into my new school and felt happier, I had no wish to go home at weekends and tried to stay at school as often as possible. Things at home were no better. One of the worst aspects of my life was having to lie to my father. I had to walk a tightrope between my mother and her boyfriend on one hand, and my father on the other. My loyalties were being torn in two. My mother's boyfriend, Nunky as I now knew him, gave me generous presents and we had great fun together. His biggest problem was that he himself used to lie to my mother. I found myself constantly caught up in this triangle. How could I be expected to know what the word truth really meant when all three elements of the triangle claimed that I was telling the truth. At times there were as many fierce rows between my mother and her boyfriend as between my mother and father.

I found out later my Dad had full knowledge of what was going on, although I didn't know this at the time. Ironically there was a time when my father and my mother's boyfriend worked together, and they both respected each other. Dad would blame my mother for the affair entirely, and not Nunc. Nunc himself often used to say to me he wished he could get out of the whole thing.

"What stops you then?" I would ask, to which I received no reply. It wasn't until long afterwards that I found out for definite that I was his son. The tragedy was that his own wife was dying of cancer through these years. Many a time my mother threatened to ring her and tell her where Nunc was. Never in the whole of my life have I ever

North House and Problems at Home

known anyone with a more jealous streak than my mother. It was evil in its intensity. In fits of passionate rage during one argument with her boyfriend she was going to stick my head in the gas oven and kill me. I puzzled at this reaction, the only conclusion I could come to was that as I was Nunc's son this produced a threat to him. I had to work this out much later; at the time it just seemed like a nightmare to me. I said to Mum that my life was important and asked her "Don't I have a right to live?" She said there would be nothing I could do about it if she made up her mind to do it.

At weekends my father used to go down to his brother's farm in Maidstone. This gave Mum and Nunc the opportunity to spend Saturday afternoons sitting on the settee together watching the wrestling. My mother used to swear at the television, giving the wrestlers evil advice on what to do to each other. One day I walked into the room to get my steak pie and chips bought from the local fish shop. The Telfords pies and the massive portions of chips stick in my memory. After I had finished I walked over to the settee to sit down. Putting my hand out to find an empty seat I made a startling discovery: the large bulbous shape of a woman's breast bare to the world. I also felt Nunc's arms around my mother's stomach. I stepped back in amazement, suddenly fully realising the extent of their relationship. My mother shouted to me not to be rude, and hurriedly changed the subject, discussing the wrestling with Nunc. The shock must have shown on my face because Nunc said in a whispered, hoarse voice, "See what you've done now, Vera." Mum hissed at me, "You shut your mouth and mind your own business, and don't ask questions about things you don't understand. We are not all tin gods and it's about time you learned it."

At a later stage Dad used to take me with him to my uncle's farm. Though my Dad was mighty strange

Touch Me Please

company, I enjoyed these trips. Auntie Clara and Uncle George were kind to me in their own way. They had a few weird ideas about how I should be, seeming to think that I was incapable of doing anything myself, and talking to my Dad about me, rather than speaking directly to me. They used to tell me imaginary tales about the animals on the farm, thinking I would be stupid enough to believe them.

One unpleasant incident happened when my uncle George forced me to stroke a large bull, of which I was frightened. However, as I grew older they became kinder. I spent many a happy weekend helping to milk the cows, sitting in the warm sun in the hayfields. My Auntie Clara's farm meals were something to be desired. She had a philosophy that everyone should eat well. Being a farm, all the meat was absolutely fresh, all the sausages were home-made, and the taste was out of this world. We used to have delicious unpasteurised full cream milk on our cereal.

PAT: Learning to Have Fun

It was often hard to be positive about life as Mick's hearing slipped away. I tried to be cheerful and to spend as much time with him as possible, but draughts and dominoes were poor substitutes for music. Conversation gradually became difficult. But, however grim the outlook, life had to go on, and there was a world out there. Little by little we began to look outwards and mix with others, although there was a limit to the 'others' who were willing to meet us half way.

Our first holiday abroad was in August 1990, courtesy of Inland Revenue. I found I had a tax refund since I could claim a married person's allowance and transfer Mick's Blind Person's allowance to myself, from the date of our marriage in 1988. I asked Mick to choose where he would like to go with this unexpected windfall. He wanted to visit a volcano, since that was how he felt – a great pressure building up ready to erupt. We plumped for Sorrento, with Vesuvius on the doorstep, and took a package holiday which organised our flights and accommodation.

On the first morning, there were welcome drinks and a guided tour of central Sorrento. Mick was mainly dependent on the hand language by now, so we stuck out like a sore thumb among the other travellers in our group. But Mick's enthusiasm and sense of humour impressed everyone. He kept interjecting humorous comments during the introductory talk, unable of course to hear how loud he was. Throughout the week we kept bumping into other people from the group, whom I rarely recognised, but who always recognised Mick. They would ask amiably

Touch Me Please

how we were enjoying the holiday, much as people fuss over animals and children, as if Mick were a lucky mascot.

The weather was almost unbearably hot, and our hotel was without air conditioning. Often when we got back to our room I lay on the marble floor, as it was the coolest place to be. During the week we took an official tour to Vesuvius and Pompeii. Mick could smell the volcanic smoke and almost feel the underground rumbling. It was very hard work at Pompeii, since the guide's words had to be spelt out letter by letter on Mick's hand. Amazingly, one man from the party approached us and offered to share the interpreting. How lucky it was to find someone – at that very time and place – who was proficient in the deaf-blind manual, considering how rare this skill is. How grateful I was to have a break and rest my arm, particularly since I felt hotter than ever before in my life as we traversed the baking hot stone roads. Much of Pompeii is tactile and Mick lapped up the commentary; here was something he could really enjoy.

We also took the local bus to the Amalfi coast, where the road clung precariously to the edge of the cliff, with a sheer drop plunging to the sea below. We walked down hundreds of steps through the town of Positano to reach the beach far below, sensibly returning by mini-bus from sea level. On another day we took the boat to Capri, strolling to Tiberius's Villa through cool green walks. In the pleasantly cool evenings we enjoyed a meal and a drink and soaked in the atmosphere. It was a good holiday, and we began to feel there was something to enjoy together after all, despite the limitations. A holiday abroad gave Mick the chance to enjoy warm weather, to taste different food and sample the local wine. He loved swimming, so we always booked a hotel with a pool, which was safer than the sea.

Another year we visited Crete, where Mick much

Learning to Have Fun

appreciated the history of the Minoan Palace at Knossos. It was in Crete that I almost lost Mick. We took a bus ride to Rethymnon and found we had not taken our swimming gear. It was a gorgeous day, so Mick went in the sea in his underpants. He is a strong swimmer but of course has no sense of direction. He could not hear people on the beach, nor does the Mediterranean have much in the way of waves to give an indication of where the beach is. I watched him getting further and further from the shore and began to worry. I was calculating how far he would need to swim to reach the African coast, and pondering exactly which shore he would be washed up on.

I asked a delightful elderly lady if she could swim after him and bring him back, which she willingly did. She described herself as a 'geriatric back-packer' who arrived with a rucksack and found a room where she fancied. She then offered to lend me her swimsuit so we could bathe together. So the day turned out well after all.

Mick was always interested in the history of the places we visited such as Malta, where he could appreciate the old buses and the narrow atmospheric streets of the ancient medieval capital, Medina. He was always keen to try new experiences and during our holiday in Corfu went paragliding, demonstrating no nerves at all.

Through visits to Henshaw's College, which had a Head Office in Manchester, Mick was introduced to the Deaf-Blind Fellowship (DBF). Derek and Hilary, who lived in Greater Manchester, worked tirelessly to raise funds for subsidised holidays for deaf-blind people from all over the country. Many of the clients lived at Rainbow Court in Peterborough; some lived in the north-west; Mick, I think, was the only client from Leeds. Our first trip with them was a weekend in Gloucestershire, followed by a Christmas party at a hotel in Wilmslow.

We found it extremely hard to adapt. Most of the

Touch Me Please

participants had been born deaf-blind, although many had some vision which enabled them to use sign language. We were entering a new world of the disabled and found communication difficult. I remember we both felt particularly miserable at the Christmas party. Although the dinner was delicious the disco which followed was unbearable to Mick. We could not understand why deaf people would want music as a background. All Mick could hear was a discordant sound. While others danced and mingled, we sat sadly withdrawn in a corner. They must have thought us a gloomy pair.

Over time, we came to understand that most of the clients had never heard music properly and therefore the rhythm and sound gave them pleasure, and an opportunity to dance. And in due course Mick, too, was able to mix with the others and dance to the distorted sound, and appreciate the rhythm. We enjoyed the Christmas parties for many years after that, until Hilary was too ill to organise them.

The Deaf-Blind Fellowship arranged an annual holiday, usually in June. Since my children were successively sitting exams in May and June until the youngest reached 18, I was not able to go with Mick. Luckily, some good friends agreed to be his guide. Geoffrey accompanied him twice, and Janet took him to Tunisia, where he experienced a camel ride and a trip to the desert. He came to much appreciate and enjoy these holidays, although it always remained difficult to get on friendly terms with most of the participants because of the communication problem.

In November 1995 we both went to Tenerife with the DBF, staying in Playa de las Americas. My initial impression was not good. I disliked the huge urban-like sprawl of holiday complexes, the rows of rowdy Irish bars and English breakfast cafes, the cheap entertainment in the

Learning to Have Fun

hotel. Here was tourism on a grand scale; I thought it was tacky and was determined I would not enjoy it. Nor did I for the first two days, suffering it with a superior air. Mick said I was a complete misery. On the second evening of our visit the hotel ran a competition to find the happiest couple. We were sitting sedately with a large group of DBF holiday-makers, when couples were invited to come forward. Being extrovert and very fun-loving, Mick was eager to take part, but I hated any kind of exhibitionism and my shy nature recoiled from any public display. I am not quite sure how or why I eventually succumbed, but I gave in to Mick's wishes and gingerly presented myself for the slaughter.

The next half hour was unbelievable fun and taught me that if you really let your hair down you can have a good time. Mick came into his own, exuding humour and finding expression for his repressed personality. I had to do very little – just be his sidekick. With his subtle double-entendres (like referring to the G-string on the piano) he had the audience rocking and of course we won the competition. We were presented with several bottles of champagne which were distributed liberally among our party. I am not sure that Derek and Hilary totally approved as they said very little about it. But I was very glad I had agreed to take part because it meant so much to Mick.

From then on I enjoyed the holiday immensely. I found the promenade walk to Los Cristianos was delightful, as were some of the lovely fishing villages and coves we visited by boat. We went out for a day dolphin-watching and the crew actually took Mick into the water at our earnest request – a thing they never did – so that he could have a chance to feel the dolphin he could not see. Going up Mount Teide was an unforgettable experience. We were surprised by the temperature change and the

Touch Me Please

lack of air.

Through Simon Birtles we were in touch with Beryl and Nuala in the Small Business department at the RNIB headquarters. In 1993 they were organising a trip to Strasbourg for blind people who ran their own businesses, so that they could lobby their Euro MPs for fairer conditions and more help. Although Mick was not working, Beryl felt it would be helpful for him to go and put his case, since he was resentful at the lack of government support.

We travelled by coach and enjoyed the opportunity to meet up with the other travellers and hear about their working lives. One delegate made large easy-to-see or tactile games for visually impaired, which were marketed through the RNIB catalogue. Carolyn was entirely blind, but painted pictures from memories held from her sighted days. Some delegates were in education.

None of them except Mick, as far as I recall, had any hearing problem. By this time Mick had a cochlear implant but was totally dependent on the hand language where speakers were out of range. During the lobbying session he kept up with the various questions of the delegates and the responses of the MEPs as I translated everything on his hand. Very bravely he stood to make his own contribution and movingly described how his life had changed and how little support he had received. He particularly drew attention to the fact that he could receive no benefit of any kind for six months. It must have been like speaking in a vacuum, since he could not see or hear anyone present. Later, we were able to meet and talk with Michael McGowan, the MEP for Leeds. (Predictably, nothing whatsoever resulted from this meeting.)

I think Mick gained considerable respect from some members of the party. Anyone who is blind and relies heavily on hearing must comprehend the horror of going

Learning to Have Fun

deaf as well. Being Yorkshire by adoption Mick believes in calling a spade a spade, and doesn't have much time for politically correct expressions such as 'visually impaired' to describe total blindness. I remember how we offended one member of the party who spoke about Mick being hearing impaired (as if he just needed a hearing aid) and I said that was not true – he was totally deaf.

After the formal sessions were over we had the chance to take a boat trip on the canals and explore the lovely town of Strasbourg. In reality, I could appreciate it, but nothing had any meaning for Mick. Never having enjoyed lovely views, he had always experienced the world through the conversation of companions, sounds of laughter, water lapping, traffic roaring, birds calling, the banter of the shop keepers. Now there was nothing, except the warm sun, food and drink. As someone once told him philosophically, at least he could still enjoy a beer. That was very true, but there is a lot more to life than beer. And it is easier to philosophise about it than to endure it.

I particularly recall a visit to a swimming pool, perhaps at the end of the visit, or on the way back. This was something Mick could really enjoy. A strong swimmer with lifesaving skills he was fun to be with in the water and I relaxed as he 'saved' me round the pool. I could see that Beryl from the RNIB was moved and delighted that this was an activity we could share and enjoy.

As we were preparing to travel home Carolyn presented Mick with a beautiful picture which she had painted herself. It was a lovely gesture and the painting still hangs in my house today.

When I started my new job with British Gas Mick was just going deaf. I found my colleagues and the management sympathetic and understanding. It was not until 1991, when a small subsidiary software company was

Touch Me Please

set up and a group of us moved from BG to work for the new company, that a social life developed. We would arrange meals out, particularly at Christmas, and everyone showed a desire to be friendly with Mick and to communicate with him. Gillian learned the hand language and talked to him enthusiastically. We began to receive invitations to homes, and this became easier after Mick had the implant. We loved visiting Gillian and David, and two friends who lived in Skipton. We could enjoy a meal and a drink and in a quiet environment Mick was able to keep up with the conversation if we sat moderately close together and the numbers were small. He was able once again, in a limited way, to fulfil the outgoing side of his nature through social interaction.

We also found interesting places for him to visit. He loved trains, so on one occasion when we stayed with my sister and her husband in Coventry we went on the Severn Valley Railway, which was delightful and had a preserved railway station that was fairly tactile. Years later, for his 50th birthday, I booked lunch for the four of us on the North Yorkshire Moors Railway, and we drove to Grosmont for the round trip to Pickering and back. This involved eating the starter and main course on the down trip, and dessert and coffee on the way back. He also enjoyed boat trips if we went to the seaside.

We found that museums were very willing to provide exhibits which he could handle, if we asked them in advance. He had an excellent visit to Eden Camp where the curator brought out lots of WW2 display items, such as officers' fine quality great coats and the comparatively rough uniforms of the rank and file; various weapons from the period; fire-fighting equipment, gas masks for adults and babies, and a range of ration books.

At the Royal Armouries in Leeds they provided things like beautifully wrought and decorated swords and fine chain mail from around the world. Then they took him to the menagerie and let him feel one of the large horses, showing him the broad back and the fetlocks. He held a peregrine falcon on a gloved hand and with the other stroked its feathers. With a bit of forward planning and a willingness to look around, we found we could sustain Mick's interest in a variety of subjects and we managed some good days out.

Life was certainly improving – a bit for Mick and a lot for me.

MICK: Linden Lodge

In 1959, during the hot summer when plums were 2d. a pound, Mrs. Wills came into my life. Cynthia Wills had been a nurse and was in her fifties. I called her Pilly because nurses dispense pills. She undertook the night duty at North House, looking after the boarders at the end of the school day. I thought the world of her. When she was around her affection for me opened my heart for the first time in many years. Months later, while stirring the Christmas pudding, I wished earnestly that she could be my mother. In her company I felt happiness and motherly love for the first time, since I was deprived of it at home. At the tender age of nine I had no notion of any other sort of love, but it was comforting to be cuddled, and afforded motherly protection.

Along with my deep wish for more of Pilly's company, at this time I first discovered the real beauty of classical music, which spoke to me with a new intensity. I had been to concerts at the Albert Hall since I was four or five and quite enjoyed them. I was familiar with Coppelia, but now I heard for the first time a piece of music which seemed to me, and still does, one of the most beautiful compositions I have ever heard – Mendelssohn's Violin Concerto. The record belonged to Valerie Ager, one of the pupils. I was in the dormitory playing with a little game of solitaire which Mum had sent me when the music began. I lay there listening, emotion welling up in me. I found a beauty in that piece which is virtually unparalleled. It opened up a new world to me musically. Eventually tears ran down my cheeks; I cried at music for the first time in my life.

Linden Lodge

I continued to go to the concerts organised from school. These made me appreciate classical music with a new intensity. I no longer merely enjoyed music; it was a part of me and an expression of my soul. Music filled my life from that time on. Through the sixties pop tunes would jump out at me during emotional difficulties, through different romances. Music and my love life were always closely linked.

A popular radio programme of the time was "Where are you now?" with Wilfred Pickles, where he recalled old war memories. Some of the songs from that programme were very moving. Here again, the music made me cry, and I continued to be affected in this way as long as I could hear. I began to realise just how important music was to me. I had been taught quite a bit by Mr Deacon, a vicious, cruel man, who used to grab us by the shoulders and squeeze our shoulder bones. His unpleasant personality put me off learning music. I didn't take piano lessons seriously until 1960, when I moved schools once again.

I changed schools in September 1959, moving to Linden Lodge. A gradual system of transfer was intended to help the transition from one school to another. During the autumn of 1959 I attended my new school as a pupil, but slept at my old school.

Once again, all the boys were so much older than I, and I was frightened and alone. As a new boy at Linden Lodge I was taken in by the right-handed screwdriver, the left-handed sky hook, the glass hammer, the elbow grease, and the usual old tricks played on the new boys. I could take all that, but worse was to come. I was a victim of bullying and received the first of my many beatings from the other pupils in November. They would react to the most childish, stupid things sometimes. On this occasion, eight lads set onto me and split open my chin on a bar. Of

Touch Me Please

course I had to explain it to the teachers when I got back and if I revealed the true cause I would receive a second beating from my tormentors!

On another occasion, Rory Heap stamped with his full weight on my ear and head, so that I was quite ill and had to stay in bed for a couple of days, clutching my toy dog. The staff were concerned about me, and it was sobering to think that my hearing might have been affected at that early age. Rory's father was a kind man and talked to me a great deal about magnets when they were my current craze. When he found out what his son had done he was very cross about it, but by that time the damage was done. The regime within the school allowed incidents like this to happen, and along with the beating, this was the first taste of a very bitter year in 1960.

In the New Year I severed my link with the old school entirely. At the end of 1959 I said goodbye to Pilly for ever. I was due to leave North House on the Friday before Christmas. Mrs. Wills was on duty on the Thursday evening and it was our last chance to say goodbye. I remember her kneeling by the bed that night and saying, "I won't say goodbye I'll just say au revoir." Then she kissed me. I cried for hours afterwards because it was the most wretched moment of my young life and I could hardly bear to part from Pilly. I wondered how I could cope with the loss. I felt as if the world had ended. She had been someone beautiful to me. I thought as she left me of the day I was playing with the little push-along train. One of the nuts came loose and part of the train came off. The other boys said I would get into trouble with the headmaster. I explained to Mrs. Wills that it wasn't my fault, and she comforted and reassured me. Now at my new school I would have no one. She was out of my life and after Christmas I started to sleep at Linden Lodge.

Then the bitter year of trouble really started. It lasted

perhaps until September. There were a couple of thugs who set themselves up as bully boys. I was the 'new boy', so I was to be played with, dropped off tables onto my eyes, and thrown about the room. It was great fun and everybody enjoyed doing this to the new boy. I was pretty sensitive at that time. I didn't know anyone, and could not confide in any of the staff because they were all strange to me.

I had a couple of records which I brought back to school with me, but no one liked them and no one would play them for me. All this had a devastating effect on me because things at home were no better. My brother was in trouble because he had been sacked from work. My parents were constantly rowing. Things were very unhappy, but I had no one to talk to about my distress.

Meanwhile, I learned the hard way it doesn't pay to be cocky. I had a new Emerson radio to take back to school for the first time. I remember this little set very clearly, for the sound reproduction was excellent and I could obtain a wide range of stations, including Luxembourg, which put me into the top bracket in those days. I was delighted with it and boasted how loud it would play and how clear the reception was. For the first time I had something I could be really proud of! A lad called Michael Pearson, who was a little older than I, decided I was too cocky, too clever. He gathered a large crowd of pupils to march round the grounds after me chanting, "Let's think about Cocky, let's think about Gerwat!" It sounds silly now, but people following you day after day singing rude things about you, on and on, is a very distressing experience. Children can be very cruel. Just as water dripping on stone eventually wears it away, as the sea erodes the cliffs, pounding and ebbing, advancing and receding, crashing onto the rocks, never ceasing, always washing at the cliffs and breaking them up, so my fellow pupils wore down

Touch Me Please

my patience, my nerves, my energy. From that day on I watched my every word.

About the same time, whilst doing some woodwork, I accidentally sawed up someone's stilts, not knowing what they were, and was going to be beaten up for that. As we went into the dining room I was crying and was warned not to let the staff know what had happened. A kind-hearted nurse stopped me, however, and coaxed me gently to tell her why I was upset. "No one will hurt you," she promised, and I found myself, in spite of the threats of reprisals, pouring it out to her. Once again, when the staff knew what was happening, they dealt with bullying and sadism. I earned the name of "splitter" and was shunned for telling tales, but there was only so much I could take.

I was given a respite, but the bullies had no intention of abandoning me altogether. They bided their time, and were ready to pounce when the opportunity came. One of the boys, Graham Piper, had a Costa Brand radio of which he was very proud. There was quite a competitive spirit about the sort of radio you had. It was a status symbol. Looking back, I imagine Graham had left the radio on when he got into bed and run down the batteries, although he denied this at the time. Consequently, the obvious explanation of its failure to function one morning was that someone had been fiddling with it. Some of the boys liked to think they were good at detective work, and after lengthy discussions and considerations, it was decided that it must have been me. Before they could report me, however, they had to wring from me a confession that I was actually the culprit.

A young lad Brian (who paid more than twice dearly for what he did to me that night) decided to handle the matter. His dad worked in electronics. His father, incidentally, was a very nice man and his mother was delightful, but Brian was spoilt. Brian knew a bit about

Linden Lodge

how light bulbs worked and how to disconnect them. The first thing I realised was that a crowd of hostile boys were encircling me, questioning me, shouting at me about the Costa Brand radio. "We know you fiddled with the radio. We know you turned it on, and you're going to admit it. If you don't, we'll make you."

There was a shuffling of furniture and I gathered they were moving my locker. After some scrambling I heard Brian say, "Right, the bulb's out" and I was propelled forward and hoisted onto the locker. I could not guess what they meant to do with me, but I was scared, fearing being dropped onto my head, or some similar trick which I had frequently suffered from in the past. This time my hand was seized, raised above my head, and inserted into the light socket. Despite my efforts to pull it away it was held there with an iron grip.

"Did you break Graham's radio?" Brian asked.

"No, I didn't touch it," I protested, "I didn't!"

"OK" Brian ordered his followers, "switch on." A searing pain surged through me. I cried out, trying at the same time to pull my hand from the socket. Through the torture I heard Brian's voice, "Did you break Graham's radio? Did you?"

"Yes, yes," I sobbed. The pain ceased as my hand was released. It didn't take long to admit to the crime I had not done. No doubt any boy in that situation would succumb quickly enough. But in the longer term, this experience encouraged the weakness which had already taken root in my character. I would avoid facing any problem or situation just to steer clear of trouble.

Although I was suffering badly at this time the wheel was turning, and no one was immune from the mass cruelty of the boys at Linden Lodge. It was a fortunate boy who escaped torment completely. Brian, my torturer in the interrogation scene, received the 'Cocky' treatment some time later and I was vicious enough to join in the chanting crowd that dogged his heels.

Meanwhile, the investigation into the radio continued next day. It was decided I must have an accomplice, so they demanded his name, twisting my arm behind my back. I gave one readily enough – the first name that came into my head, which happened to belong to one of the older boys. He was fifteen or sixteen. When he found out that I had told stories about him he decided to gather a gang of older boys to beat me up. What a stupid, silly incident to make such a fuss about, but it seemed to me as if the weight of the world was upon me. Indeed that school community was the world to me, and from it I expected pleasure, hope, fun, confidence and companionship. None of these I found at first, receiving only bullying, isolation, fear and misery.

Fortunately for me, just as the gang had caught me and were ready to sort me out, a teacher happened to pass, and naturally asked what was going on. My tormentors made up a story which, thankfully, the teacher did not believe. I was taken into the pottery room, the door was shut, and I was safe. Here in this refuge I could pour out the whole story. All the bullies were rounded up and there was quite a storm in the school.

As it drew towards the Christmas of 1960 things improved slightly. I think the staff were beginning to understand what I was suffering and they started to be kind to me. They weren't unkind before, but now they were paying more attention and some of them were affectionate. I now felt, for the first time since leaving East Grinstead, a sense of stability and growing confidence. I enjoyed roller skating and playing cricket, and occupied myself a great deal of the time listening to my radio.

During the early sixties my brother was no company to me at all during my weekends and holidays at home. I remember once making him a good solid wooden tool box in my woodwork lesson. When I presented it to him all he could do was laugh. Mum rebuked him for this. His interest in motor bikes gave way to interest in girls. In 1959 he met Colleen, the girl he eventually married. Many a time I wanted to talk to him about my home life, but he never had the time to listen. He was too busy lying on the front room sofa, kissing and cuddling Colleen. When I sat in the front room listening to music he used to turn the volume louder than usual. At the time I didn't know why, but later realised it was to cover the rustle of skirts. Three or four times on an evening he used to ask me if there was anything on television I wanted to watch. That I suppose was to get rid of me so that they could get down to some serious love making.

Colleen seemed a nice gentle sort of girl, and I got on well with her at first. One day I went with them to help them choose some furniture for their house, but I felt that the only reason they took me with them was because Mum had spent ten minutes persuading them to do so. I felt continually on trial in their presence, never daring to put a foot wrong, being told all the time to keep quiet and sit in the corner like a naughty boy. Neither of them took anything I said seriously.

Meanwhile at Linden Lodge the crazes went on: wind-up grams, radios of any type, early tape recorders, short wave radio, police messages – one thing after another.

With the dawning of 1961 new horizons began to emerge for me. I started to realise - just slowly - about girls. That was the time of Miss Nesta Lake. She was a lot younger than Mrs. Wills, being only 29 while I was 12, so the age gap was decreasing. She was lovely, vivacious, and very tender-hearted. Once again, as with Mrs. Wills, I felt she understood me, but the trouble was I fell overboard for her, along with several other lads. I thought I was in love with Nesta Lake, but she called it infatuation, and I suppose it was.

Bernadette Stanley was our Catholic religious teacher. She was one of the old hellfire and brimstone brigade. We were told that if we sinned, when we died we would be burnt in the coals and fires of hell and live forever in torment. Vividly, with a great deal of relish, she described 'down below'. She was terribly strict, driving the Latin text of the Catholic mass into our brains parrot-fashion. I hated it. Every Sunday we were dragged off to mass at seven in the morning and what's more, on Communion Sundays, which occurred once a month, after putting us through the ordeal of confession on a Saturday, before which we were almost briefed on what sins to confess, we had to fast from 5 o'clock on Saturday evening until 11 o'clock on Sunday morning. If my stomach rumbled during the offertory, I used to get into trouble. On returning from one of these trips we pounced on our breakfast like rabid wolves. There was one tiny bonus to this, however. We used to demolish all the left over bread and honey and I loved it. As if this wasn't enough, every single feast day, and there seemed to be dozens of them (I never realised there were so many saints) we had to suffer a three-hour evening mass during the week.

There was a good side to Bernadette Stanley, however, as there is with everyone. She it was who started to teach me the ukulele, and that is where I was introduced to my first "meaningfully aware" folk songs. I should have been grateful that she taught me French, but many years later when I found myself alone and hungry in France I couldn't speak a word!

Much later, when I was deaf, I met Miss Stanley again. She had written to me after seeing my television programme *Is There Anybody There?*. She was totally different: kind, gentle and very regretful about what may have happened in the past.

"Oh Mike, I was a young prig back in those days", she told me when I talked about how we were treated at school, and she seemed genuinely upset.

About this time the incidents of fire in the school started. During 1961 fires were discovered in the toilets two or three times. The following year the number of fires increased, and there was some consternation amongst staff and boys as to who the culprit could be. Ivan Mortimer and some of the older boys firmly believed that I was the guilty person and determined to extract a confession from me. Unfortunately at this time my resistance was very low as I was going through a nervous period, and taking strong sleeping pills. The effect of the tablets was to further debilitate my mind and reserves, so that when they approached me I was easy prey for them.

I was unaware that during the interrogation a tape recorder had been switched on. As part of their campaign they promised to intercede for me and prevent my instant expulsion from the school if I confessed voluntarily and gave the name of my supposed accomplice. They harassed me continuously, wearing down my resistance until the only escape from their badgering was to admit that I was guilty. Once again I gave the first name that came into my head. My supposed guilt was recorded on tape. When I discovered what they had done I stumbled upstairs and wept bitterly, utterly miserable, feeling my life was at an end. I remember Miss Lake taking me with her to the headmistress, Mrs Bingley. She knew at once that I had nothing to do with the fires, and was extremely kind. All three of us talked throughout the night about all my problems, including the difficulties at home. I found them affectionate and sympathetic. As for the fires, the real culprit turned out to be one of my old enemies and he was

Touch Me Please

sent for psychiatric treatment.

The arson accusation was only one of a number of factors that caused me REALLY to start bed-wetting. The tension at home, the sleeping tablets, and a course of injections I was undergoing, all played a part in my mental and physical weakness. Miss Stanley was quite angry at first and said I needed discipline. Suddenly, however, without warning, there was a complete change in her attitude. She suggested the injections might be the cause of the problem. I remember Miss Lake, and even Miss Stanley, talking to me gently, trying to find out why this was happening. From this point on the staff became far more understanding, taking me aside and offering to talk to me for long periods. Sometimes Miss Lake put her arms round me. Sheer heaven! Maybe that was all I wanted at that time. I had suffered a great deal at the end of 1961, and had been deprived of love both at school and at home. Perhaps I just needed someone to care.

At that precise moment the school embarked on a production of Gilbert and Sullivan's *Pirates of Penzance*. This helped me to forget the recent nightmarish incidents, and to take my mind off Miss Lake for whom my passion was still uncontrollable. In the final concert we performed various songs which my parents recorded. The music was a wonderful tonic. I hold that operetta especially dear, and have always done so, because it marked the end of an era of misery, victimisation and absolute loneliness. It symbolised a new beginning, a new life, a fairer and a more just existence.

By the end of the year my infatuation for Miss Lake was beginning to wane because I worked hard at school and immersed myself in music. We were already planning the next musical, and intended to put on a full production of *The Mikado*. At the auditions I was the only boy out of the whole school who was picked for one of the principal

Linden Lodge

parts, and was cast as Pish-Tush. I was very proud of this. At first I was the understudy, but then it was decided that I should actually take the part. I tremendously enjoyed going along to the late-night rehearsals and singing through my part. As well as the solos we had to rehearse the madrigals and the choruses. Some of the words will always remain with me:

Our great Mikado, virtuous man
When he to rule our land began...

I was studying music at the same time, learning a Beethoven G Minor Sonata with George Newall, who began to teach me music in 1960. We worked on the Daneman in the typing room, and I was beginning to strike up quite a close relationship with Mr Newall as my love of classical music increased. George Henry Newall, that was his name. One of the silly things I remember was his age, for it was one year ahead of the actual year we were in, so that in 1962 he was 63. At first when I arrived at Linden Lodge we had a clash, which started when I fidgeted during a concert we were taken to. I was forced to write a four page essay on the concert. In actual fact I took the blame for the other lads messing about, but was too frightened to say so.

Mr Newall could be strict yet kind. It was he who taught the famous jazz pianist, George Shearing, all he knew. When I started music lessons, like all boys of my age, I was reluctant to practise properly. One day I was severely rebuked for this lack of concentration and was told firmly either I practised or I would learn music no more. From that day forward a total sea change came over the relationship between George Newall and myself. He, like me, had been blind from birth. Therefore he taught me all I knew by ear. We had tried learning by Braille music, but I found it so slow and impossible that I didn't have the patience with it. George had an incredible ability to

Touch Me Please

compose music. He wrote the scores for all Mr John's plays which we performed in school. By now, Mr John was the headmaster at Linden Lodge.

I clearly remember one morning George Newall was sitting at the piano during my lesson composing a song for me to sing in the school play *Ballyhoo*. The chords, tunes and sequences would flow from him like water from a tap. We became very close friends because he noticed and understood how nervous I was. Through him I learnt the beauties of classical music. He would devote half our lesson time to playing pieces of music and asking me if I liked this or that. The one bad side effect of all this was that all the other boys in the school called me teacher's pet because I believed in nearly everything Mr Newall stood for. It was certainly due to him that I acquired the ability to compose music myself and I actually enjoyed the challenge of learning new pieces week by week.

The tragic thing is that when I went to Shrewsbury College my musical education was stopped for over a year. When I did resume, a vital year was lost and I found it difficult to learn with a different teacher. There was an empathy between George and myself which I could never recapture with any other music teacher. It was almost as if we were musical soul mates.

In 1962 Ron and Colleen were married. This was a lively family occasion, with my Uncle Henry's band providing the entertainment. There was no such thing as a disco in those days. The wedding didn't mean much to me. My main interest was recording the service on my little Philips tape recorder.

In the summer of 1963 came the long-awaited performance of *The Mikado*. I was just thirteen, and there was so much activity, so much excitement that it seemed a new world to me. We enjoyed the trappings which went with it. Each morning Mr John read us *The Invisible Man* by

H G Wells, to keep us calm before the performance. How we loved gathering in the sitting room to listen to the gripping story. Mr John was an expert reader; we found ourselves completely lost in the tale, totally immersed.

The whole purpose of the performance was to raise money for a swimming pool to be built at our school. Vividly I can remember being made up by the make-up artist (who was our school secretary), the nerves and tension before going on stage, then most importantly, my own solo in the concert, feeling the dryness in my mouth just before I was due to sing, remembering the strict teachings and lessons of Mr John, telling me to throw my voice to the back of the hall. There was an exhilarating tingle at the end of each performance, knowing that just for once, the attention of the entire audience and my fellow performers had been focused on me for a few minutes, and that I had held them spellbound for that brief time. As part of the fund-raising campaign members of the cast toured the houses and streets within the neighbourhood selling concert and raffle tickets. Each house was packed out, including the two Saturday performances. The production was an outstanding success and raised over £5000.

With my new-found confidence and self-expression in music, my interest in other things, and my work in general, improved. I found science fascinating, and learned everything I could about chemicals. I joined the Braille Library in London and started to read avidly. This helped me to forget the things that worried me, and my nervous condition gradually improved. I very much enjoyed reading a space fiction story called *Rocket Pilot* by Philip St. John which I read again and again. It is an irony that I have now, after a long search, acquired a copy of this rare book and still read it 'again and again'.

I particularly enjoyed participating in the literary

Touch Me Please

and debating society which met every Wednesday for discussions. "Lit and Deb" we called it. We sat on the long benches in the gymnasium and discussed world affairs, such as the Berlin Wall, the name of which we transferred affectionately to our bread pudding. I was now able to play a full part in school life and found it rewarding and satisfying.

Pottery was another interest. Mr Robinson, my form teacher at the time, also took us for this subject. I found great satisfaction in beating the clay to knock all the air out of it. We had a potter's wheel at which I became the star pupil. To show us how a professional potter works we were taken to a large pottery in Stoke-on-Trent. First we saw the huge piles of clay stored in the yard outside, and were then taken to the department where the potters' wheels were. It was at this point that Mr Robinson mentioned to our guide that "Mick Gerwat here is our top pupil on the potter's wheel." I was gently pushed forward. My face glowed with satisfaction. A soft, gentle voice came from my right saying, "Shall we make a pot together, so that I can show you how we do it?"

Mr Robinson thought that was a splendid idea, so I was placed on a stool in front of the potter's wheel. I heard the gentle click, click of stiletto heels, combined with the subdued rustling of skirt and overall as the young lady came up behind me. A pair of cool, slender arms encircled my body from behind. Before this my mind was prepared to concentrate on the pot we were about to make. Now, as the sweet musky smell of her scent assailed my nostrils, I found myself slipping away into a fantasy world forgetting altogether the pot we had to construct. Both of her slim cool hands took hold of mine and gripped them firmly so that I could hold the clay. Her head and chin rested on my right shoulder so that she could instruct me what to do. I felt her cheek close to mine, soft and soothing. Involuntarily I began to tremble, my hands feeling unsteady. It was a vicious circle. The more my hands trembled the more she gripped them. There I was in front of the whole school totally unable to concentrate on anything but the wonder and joy of this new feeling which engulfed me. From out of the cloudy mists of my fantasies I heard Mr Robinson saying, "What's up with you Gerwat? You usually do better than this at school." I could hardly tell him that all my passions were being driven absolutely wild by this woman's presence, the young firmness of her body resting against mine. The pot was, however, eventually constructed and I kept it for many years afterwards.

My love for the radio continued unabated. Everyone had his own radio, and I was no exception. In the event of breakdowns we relied on Mr Davis, 'Taff' as we called him, to carry out repairs. We all loved Mr Davis who was a genius with radios. One morning he was found dead in his car with his dog lying across his chest. He had killed himself. Although I never found out the reason for his suicide, the incident upset me deeply. The car remained parked on the pitch at the bottom of the school grounds for a long time. I used to go down and feel it with that sense of helplessness which comes when one is close to death.

There were moments of fun and excitement too, particularly with the girls' school next door. We managed to meet girls in spite of all the difficulties meant to deter us. Mr John was very strict and pretty shocked if any of his pupils got as far as kissing a girl from the adjacent school. He entirely disapproved of "horseplay" as he called it. We had ways of circumventing his precautions. There was an alcove just off the main alley which was used for a quick "Hello", holding hands and a kiss. But beyond this there was a shelter which had a door, and this was reserved for

Touch Me Please

the more passionate embraces. The only way you could get to use the shelter with your girlfriend was to book someone for "guard duty". The guards listened out for the approach of teachers and there were various signals. There was, at the same time, a useful escape route from the shelter if necessary. We could have a whole ten minutes in the shelter when our turn came. I much appreciated being part of the system. The alcove allowed you five minutes, the shelter ten, and if you were trying to make up after a row you could have a whole fifteen minutes.

No dire accidents ever happened, and our physical explorations rarely went beyond innocent kissing and cuddling. At that time we hadn't had any sex lessons, and the older boys told jokes which we younger ones did not understand. They would ask me if I followed the joke, and I would laugh and pretend I had. Later, Mr H our science teacher, taught us some of the facts of life. Mind you, quite frankly, he was no example, although he was well-qualified to know something about the subject. I once fell over him when he was with one of his ladies on the lawn. He threatened to give me detention for disturbing him. When I made it clear that I would tell the headmaster the reason for the detention, Mr H shooed me away with a warning not to do it again. He took the part of the Mikado in our famous production. I often had to fetch him for rehearsals and never knew where or in what condition I would find him, for he was often occupied with a "friend".

As a welcome break from my family difficulties, I spent a pleasant week at Hopton Constitutional Holiday Camp as a guest of the Lions Club in the summer of 1963. Everything was paid for and we were given a little spending money. They were really good to us and I enjoyed the holiday immensely, although it was eventful. Walking along the edge of the cliff I stepped into mid-air and slid down the prickly gorse-studded dunes, landing forty feet below, and had to be rescued by a helicopter. My parents were rather upset when they heard about it later.

On another occasion I walked into the Ladies' toilets not being able to distinguish them from the Men's, to the consternation of some of the women there (as if I could see anything!). Despite these little hiccups I didn't want to come home. During that holiday the first wispy notions of the full possibilities of sex began to enter my mind. There was a wonderful lass nicknamed 'steaming Sue' because she had such vitality and passion. She was only seventeen or eighteen, so things were improving – there was even less discrepancy in our ages. We used to go out on a speed boat and she wore an incredible scent. As I realised how attracted I was to Sue I had my first ideas, my first inklings about the delights of the flesh.

The autumn of 1963 also saw the beginning of *Dr Who*, a new television series which was to have a great effect on my life. In itself it was only a silly serial, but like other things at the time which I was to cling to later, it was significant for me. I started to follow it but didn't think much about it until the following year. Then I suddenly developed an almighty crush on one of the stars of the programme, called Barbara. By now, at fourteen, I could understand the powerful urges of sex, the attraction of women. I dreamt up all sorts of wonderful situations and adventures in which I was involved. It used to put me off my class work, I was so lost in my fantasy world. The teachers used to lose patience with me. Whilst I was ostensibly working I was imagining myself in some voluptuous situation with this woman TV star who was forty something. Everyone told me how stupid I was to be so immersed in Barbara, but I could not help myself. The actress who played her, Jackie Hill, died of cancer in the 1990s. I was pleased to find out a lot about her from a programme I acquired many years later. Like Pat, she was

Touch Me Please

a Quaker.

In those days, there were no televisions at our school and I used to get Mum to record the programme if I was away from home at the weekends. This caused rows to break out, since Mum and Dad were fairly hopeless at technology, or at least recording things. Today I have all the old programmes broadcast those many years ago. How I longed for them way back then. It is ironic that now when I have only my cochlear implants to help me communicate, I can get any *Dr Who* programme I want, any *Star Wars* programme I want, and almost anything else.

In the summer of 1964 a dramatic event in my life occurred. The site of Linden Lodge school for the Blind was at that time at Bolingbroke Grove in Battersea. As early as my first commencement at Linden Lodge there were rumours of the possibility of building a new school within the grounds of North House, where I had been a pupil previously. Several target dates were given for the building of this school. After endless delays it was completed in August 1964. The gargantuan task of moving all the equipment and furniture from one school to the other was undertaken that summer. We were able to help a lot with the heavy work and the shifting of boxes, tables, benches and so on. We did this in long lines, led by those with partial vision – a risky undertaking. Lessons were suspended during the chaos of the move. The easiest way to occupy the whole school in one fell swoop was to read to us. Though this task was shared by several of the teachers, the main brunt of it fell on Mr John, the headmaster.

His talent for drama was outstanding and in the September of 1964 I was chosen to take the part of a pirate sea captain in one of his self-penned plays, *Ballyhoo*. While preparing productions of his own work, he was in his element, guiding everybody firmly but kindly to do exactly what he said. One amusing incident occurred during rehearsals. We were recording the whole performance on tape to keep for posterity, and one of the scenes had to contain a rioting mob. We all gathered outside in the grounds of the school and on orders from Mr John started shouting, screaming, cursing, stamping around. We were given certain phrases to say, such as "Down with the Queen" and references to swindling the Treasury. We needed about ten minutes of this while the dialogue went on above. Chog, as he was nicknamed, had forgotten to inform the neighbours around the school. The police sent four riot squads round, bells ringing. This added a much-appreciated dimension to our effects tape for the play, but caused Mr John a little embarrassment.

Even my part in *Ballyhoo* did not distract me from Barbara, my idol. I tried to find out if I could write to her, but I could not discover where she lived. There was no way I could contact her, and even if I could have done so, I didn't stand a chance. It was a quest, an obsession. Right through the summer I lived for Barbara. I was deeply emotionally involved. As school broke up for the holidays the teachers said to me, "For God's sake you've got to forget that stupid woman. It's affecting your work and your whole life!"

I used to have girlfriends at the same time. Jenny Firby and I went together for a year. Her parents had a big business and were very rich. Although Jenny was a nice girl she was Pisces and would have been no good for me, but at that time I enjoyed her company. But all along I had this craze for Barbara. I watched *Dr Who* avidly week after week right through 1964. In the autumn I met a girl called Barbara Mills. If anyone could kiss and cuddle Barbara could. I was fond of her, but she was flippant, flighty. Probably I was keen on her chiefly because her name was

Touch Me Please

the same as my idol's. I remember Barbara Mills with affection and sadness, for she died of a brain tumour when she was only twenty.

Throughout my school career it was obvious that I was not academic. I couldn't – and still can't – spell. I'm illiterate in that way, so it was really a question of pressing on and doing what I was best at, and that was music. Unfortunately, my parents refused permission for me to take any exams although I never knew why. This was a shame because my music was progressing quite well, and meant a great deal to me. As the winter of 1964 came, it was time for me to decide upon a career.

It was obvious that I could not type or anything like that because I was hopeless. I was almost sent to Heathersett for training in engineering, as I had an interview there, but my music teacher took me aside and said I could be a jolly good piano tuner if I put my mind to it. He showed me a bit of the inside of the piano, the shank and the check, the hammers, and some more details. I was enthusiastic but my mother opposed the idea because she had been told that piano tuning was a dead-end career and would not get me anywhere. After that I did not know what to do, or which direction I should take. Fortunately, George Newall held out and eventually won the battle and I was able to pursue my interest in music and pianos. Obviously Mr John had spoken to my parents and used his persuasive charm on my mother. One day the staff asked me, "Would you like to be a piano-tuner?" So I said, "Yes please."

PAT: Looking for work

Since pianos were definitely out, Mick really wanted to work with computers. The course at Torquay had given him some good basic knowledge, and they supported his plan to take an Open University course in programming. In the meantime, he extended his technical knowledge at home, once he was set up with the Libra braille computer. It was so temperamental and unreliable that it was constantly crashing or failing. He had to reinstall software over and over again, and learned a great deal about the operating system and trouble shooting. Whereas most of us feel like running a mile if the computer goes wrong, Mick actually enjoyed it and rose to the challenge, which was very lucky considering the problems that the Libra threw at him.

He embarked on the Open University module with great enthusiasm and optimism. This was in February 1991, before he had an implant, so all communication had to be through the braille computer. The RNIB were very supportive and gave a grant towards the cost of the course. As the weeks went by Mick found it hard to keep up and complete the assignments within the timescale. As the OU could not provide the course materials in braille, it was almost impossible to continue. The RNIB generously stepped in and arranged for the course to be transcribed into braille (courtesy of prison inmates).

But this was only one of the problems. The programming content of the course was quite old and difficult to grasp. The software that came with the programming was also very old with an old-fashioned editor that was difficult to use. We asked for more time,

Touch Me Please

which the OU granted. Once again Mick was struggling. Not being able to attend the seminars in Leeds he could not get help from a tutor. Even if he could get there, how could a tutor communicate? We put this problem to the OU, and asked for more assistance. His tutor, Rose, paid a couple of visits, but the individual support they could provide was inadequate for Mick's needs. Eventually, as he slipped further and further behind in the assignments, he concluded that the task was too difficult for him. He felt that he could have coped with more help, and that the OU failed him. At least they refunded the course fee, which was appreciated. This episode demoralised Mick. He had come back from Torquay with such confidence, and he hated to admit defeat. And it happened at the most difficult time – when his world was totally dark and silent.

Another potential career was horticulture. Looking at all possible activities, we had bought a greenhouse and grew tomatoes, cucumbers, aubergines, peppers and melons. Mick was conscientious about watering every day, but didn't have a strong interest in growing plants. Since I was busy with work and family I sometimes didn't get out to the greenhouse from one weekend to the next, so it did not receive the tender loving care it deserved. (It did, however, become a pleasant smoking den for Mick.)

The RNIB suggested that Mick could embark on a horticultural career. They put us in touch with a blind man in Derbyshire, who had built up a successful nursery. We visited him one hot summer Sunday. Everyone else had also chosen to visit Derbyshire to enjoy the lovely weather. After struggling through the traffic jams, we finally reached our destination tired, very hot and extremely thirsty. We were duly impressed with the setup at the nursery, and chatted about ways and means, but what we really longed for was a nice cup of tea, or even a drink of water. Alas, only the nursery tour was on offer. Mick decided he wasn't interested in that kind of work anyway, probably influenced by the discomfort we were feeling during the visit.

There was little possibility of undertaking any kind of training using the deaf-blind manual, but once Mick had a cochlear implant we started to consider the options. He could not hear well enough to participate in a normal classroom, but he could hear speech with special provision. He had an excellent sense of smell and very sensitive touch, so aromatherapy seemed like a good idea. We made enquiries at a local college to see if they could provide one-to-one tuition. Eventually funding was procured through the Enterprise Grant system and a tutor found for a ten week course in Massage. This involved theory of bones, muscles and circulation as well as massage techniques. A taxi service was organised to get him to and from the college, but the course materials were not accessible. Mick had to scan all the relevant papers, I spent hours correcting and formatting them, and then Mick printed them out in braille. This was all worthwhile when he gained the massage qualification, allowing us to work towards the next step.

Sandra was an aroma therapist in Rochdale. We travelled across the now very familiar M62 to see if she was willing to take Mick on. We were delighted when she agreed. Next we had to find the money, which once again was covered by an Enterprise Grant. We purchased a massage couch and during his course Mick had to undertake some practical work. There was no shortage of volunteers to come to our house for a free full body massage. Clients had to give their feedback and on the whole they were complimentary. Mick had a good touch, not flippantly light but powerful and strong. He had a knack for finding knots in the muscles and, although the treatment was often painful, he could iron out those knots and make you feel a lot better, as I know from my own experience.

His sense of smell enabled him to easily identify the different oils and his excellent memory meant he could readily determine the type of oil to use for each problem or occasion. The course got him out of the house, gave him something challenging to do and a feeling of satisfaction.

The examination did not go well. The examiner did not like Mick's style which was friendly and chatty. She commented that he was unprofessional and failed him. Mick was livid about her comment and the fact that she made no attempt to communicate with him personally. He felt she was extremely ignorant and showed a total lack of understanding for his situation. Sandra urged him to retake the exam but he refused. He was still able to carry on as a masseur. He had a few clients but didn't build up a large clientele. We were a little apprehensive about advertising. He felt uneasy about visitors calling during the day when there was no one else at home, as this was a security risk. He obviously couldn't see if they got up to anything, nor was the implant good enough to enable him to hear if anything happened. He was also wary about massaging women on their own in case of any false accusations. I was the main beneficiary of Mick's new skill and enjoyed it immensely. Sadly, the couch was not very strong and after a few years a particularly heavy client combined with Mick's strong action demolished the couch, and that was that! Moreover Mick was gradually putting on weight and his smart clinical tunics got much too tight. So the aromatherapy massage petered out as a career, although he still has the skill.

Good as his massage technique was, his heart had not been fully in it. His real love was computers. With the advent of the internet and e-mail he made lots of contacts and enjoyed communicating in the cyber world, since his physical world was so restricted. With the implant he could now revert to a speech synthesiser, which was much cheaper, rather than depending on a costly braille computer. In any case the Libra was becoming unusable. He now had his hands free for the keyboard instead of constantly moving them to read the braille display. Because the implant uses computerised digital sound Mick found it much easier to listen to his speech synthesiser than to a human voice. He could also connect the processor directly to the computer which was even clearer than trying to hear it with the implant's external microphone.

Contact with the National Deaf Blind League (NDBL) had been established late in 1989, and the director, Ann Barnett, was conscientious on Mick's behalf. She urged us to apply for Mobility Allowance, and to put pressure on Social Services for more support. In 1991, encouraged by the NDBL, we bought Mick's first external modem. He could now connect to Hasicom and talk to other deaf-blind people through the computer.

In 1996 the charity changed its name to Deafblind UK and appointed a new director. She asked Mick to edit *The Rainbow*, the magazine by and for Deaf and Blind People. He was excited to have this opportunity. It involved checking and collating articles and laying out the magazine ready for publication. Any material received in braille had to be typed up onto the computer. The icing on the cake was a small honorarium.

Whilst Mick was popular with the director and staff at Deafblind UK he visited Peterborough several times and in 1997 we received an invitation to the Buckingham Palace Garden Party along with other deaf-blind representatives from the organisation. As we entered the gates, crossed the great courtyard, climbed the steps and traversed the ornate gallery to reach the gardens at the rear of the palace I wondered what Mick would get out of the day. Milling around with hundreds of others we waited for the royal party to appear, unsure of whether it would be better to stand in one place or another. We found that the Prince of Wales was heading in our direction. Several people were already placed strategically for a brief audience with him. The secretary or equerry saw Mick's red and white stick and brought us forward, promising to do what he could to effect a meeting with the prince. He did so and Mick was delighted – and completely at ease – to chat to Prince Charles explaining how the cochlear implant worked, and how everyone (including the prince himself) sounded like a dalek. I was rather overwhelmed, but so pleased that Mick had been given this opportunity. We both felt that the Prince of Wales was warm and friendly. For the rest of the time we enjoyed the tea and I described the scene.

In 2000 Mick was invited to Peterborough to meet the Duke of York. The local paper described the event:

> Royal Visitor meets deafblind
>
> Michael Gerwat has worked with some of the legends of rock music. But the royal visitor he came into contact with yesterday will leave as long a lasting memory as any of them. Mr Gerwat was one of many deafblind people introduced to the Duke of York on his visit to Deafblind UK's headquarters in the city yesterday.
>
> Michael, who is editor of the charity's monthly magazine, has worked with the likes of John Lennon and Bob Dylan as a tuner of musical instruments. But yesterday's meeting was one of his most special.
>
> "I introduced myself and explained how I had lost my hearing 10 years ago" he said. "I told the prince about the cochlear implant I have had in my

ear and he seemed genuinely interested. He's just the same as his brother, Prince Charles, whom I have also met. I can sense people and he was a really nice man and warm. I have a lot of famous people to compare him with and he was genuinely very nice."

What wasn't mentioned in the newspaper article was the comment Prince Andrew made to Mick – he knew that his brother, Prince Charles, was told he sounded like a dalek!

We also participated in a visit to the Houses of Parliament to lobby MPs for more support for deaf-blind people. But our days in the limelight were numbered. Mick proved in the end to be too outspoken and strong-willed; he wasn't always the meek grateful disabled person that the officers preferred to deal with. When he disagreed with proposed changes to *The Rainbow* his influence waned and his contact with Deafblind UK dwindled. When the organisation was rebranded from the National Deaf Blind League the new emblem was a funny little monkey. I thought it was bizarre, but perhaps that said it all.

Because Mick was a fluent and persuasive speaker he was a valuable spokesman and ambassador for both the NDBL and the Deaf Centre in Leeds. In September 1995 he was invited to participate in a Cochlear Implant Open Day organised by the Link Centre for Deafened People, to speak about the benefits he had received from the implant.

Mick was also admired by the Manchester implant team. They were delighted that he could actually hear speech after switch-on (although to Mick it was so disastrous). They were impressed with his progress, and the use he made of the implant. We bought a Sennheiser transmitter and receiver to enable him to hear an individual who was some distance away, or swamped by environmental noise. This meant he could, for example, hear a lecturer who was willing to wear the transmitter. Mick called it the 'conch' because this shell symbolises speech and communication in the Buddhist religion. We used it sometimes if we ate in a pub or restaurant. He also plugged the processor directly into the RNIB talking book machine (braille books were now passé) and into our special BT telephone. He was so competent with all these gadgets that one of the implant team came to Leeds specially to make a film of the 'bionic man' to show to other implantees.

Early in 1996 the director of the Centre for the Deaf and Blind in Leeds acquired an old computer – the slowest in the world – which allowed Mick to escape from reading braille books all day. He had to take his own Hal speech system with him. With the general growth in IT, it was then decided to offer some computer training to the 'residents'. At last Mick had the opportunity to use his mainly self-taught skills to help other people. In 1997 he was set up with a new computer, a new synthesiser and access to the internet. He now had his own little unit where he taught his pupils first of all to touch type, then to use a word processor and, later, how to access the internet and e-mail.

This was, of course, voluntary, but by now Mick was receiving benefits which gave him a measure of self-respect and independence. As well as Incapacity Benefit he was awarded Mobility Allowance at the higher level, after attending a tribunal. He was one of the first deaf-blind people to receive this benefit following new legislation. Previously it had been payable only for physical inability to walk. At the tribunal Mick had to demonstrate that he was unable to hear anything outside, and unable to walk about without assistance. (Of course he could physically

Looking for Work

walk, but with no sense of direction, could not safely do so on his own.) The mobility allowance enabled us to get a Motability car, which was a great help to the family finances. In 1992 these separate benefits were replaced by the Disability Living Allowance which contains a mobility component.

In the very early days of his deafness Mick was very keen to find paid work. He applied to the University for a job brailling course material, but did not even get an interview. As time passed and the aromatherapy blossomed then faded, he settled for voluntary work at the Deaf Centre. Life seemed to be settling into a pattern, and we began to enjoy some good times.

MICK: College Life

It is September 1965. I have just arrived at the Royal Normal College for the Blind at Shrewsbury. Colleges of this sort were once called asylums which implies that blind people are insane, so the word "Normal" was added to the title.

At last it is time to leave the protected world of school. I am very anxious about this. I'm on the edge of the grown up world now and it frightens me. I'm standing in the conservatory of the college. I have two very large cases in front of me which have to be heaved upstairs to the "dorm" and unpacked. Everything is totally strange to me. I don't know my way about the place at all, I hardly know anyone either and the prospect of all this is extremely daunting. I'm looking in my case. Unpacking is something I've never done. So, where to start? I feel an utter sense of helplessness as I try and sort out all this mysterious mess.

It was a great disadvantage to me that my parents never seemed to have time to talk anything through with me, to talk to me about unpacking and where to put things. My mother was merely impatient about the whole thing. Dad really didn't care much one way or the other and made a meal out of reading me the form that the college had sent, laughing at some things and generally not taking things seriously at all. Let's face it, Mum and Dad didn't want me to tune pianos at all. They were doing all this reluctantly and hated the idea of me pursuing what they considered was a backward career.

What did they think I could do then? I thought of that excruciatingly embarrassing interview at County Hall where we blind persons were regally advised by

College Life

patronising fully-sighted "old farts" who had as little idea about blindness as a normal member of the public had. God knows where they got their so-called experience from. It was a favour even to speak to these folks. How subservient we had to be. "Dress smartly, stand straight, speak quietly and only when you are spoken to, let's not have any opinions please." This was the order of the day.

I thought of all this as I unpacked, making a pig's ear of the whole thing. I piled all my clothes in the wardrobe in a massive untidy heap. There are those who say I still do that today, but I think I've learned a little better since those far-off days. I still have a mental block about hanging clothes up though; folks despair of me.

Now I had to find out so much; everything was strange. I had my first lesson in growing up that very day. Up to this point, all our food at school, our drinks and so on had been put in front of us. There was a gradual move latterly to teach us about table setting and not just to have stuff put in front of us on plates as it had always been. Drinks, however, were poured out for us if they were hot. Now though, I had my first experience of milk jugs, teapots and having to put milk on cereal. I had never done this at home either, a great mistake on my parents' part I always thought. It was, I suppose, understandable but for me at this time, it was a real pain.

"Listen Fred, you are not at home with Mummy now, here you pour out your own tea and learn to grow up, we're not your parents and don't you forget it." This was said by a gruff-voiced "vision" person. The word "visions" referred to those students who had some sight. They were the aristocrats of the community. "Dims" – that's us totally blind folks – have no sight at all and the term "dim" referred to the fact that we could only see very little light or none at all. However, it can be imagined that the word "dim" was also used to denote our intelligence.

Touch Me Please

Fred? Did this gruff bloke who, I found out later, wet the bed, mean me? In those days, I was a timid, shy, rather pathetic specimen of a person. I freely admit it now and I had to be schooled in the art of toughening up. This was done the hard way, but more of that later.

It's an irony that this very same gruff unfriendly person wanted to learn the ukulele, something only I could teach him, so fate decreed that we would, in the end, become friends. This really opened the door to my being accepted in the community. Well, I soon learned to pour tea. I also had to learn how to spread butter, jam and so on. I've never been good at it and I still am not! This was made quite an issue by the PE master of all people, an army sergeant who, for a short while, worked at the college. I was unceremoniously taken into the duty room to be taught how to spread butter and jam on bread. It was actually quite an interesting experience because I wasn't the only one who had problems with this. I had, in fact, started a whole new set of lessons at the college. This idea spread and there were queues of folks learning "life skills" so my tea pouring did have some benefit.

It would soon be time for starting my course, for doing the job I had come to learn. Together with the process of becoming independent, developing a mature attitude to life in general, this new college environment was all part and parcel of the whole package. The shack, this place of learning, a long corridor with loads of single rooms each containing two pianos, was to be my home, my world for the next three years. The very first thing was the usual induction and advice about working hard and putting in positive effort if you wanted anything back. This lecture took up over half a day! Now our timetables were distributed. Magic, now I could really start to learn. The timetable became like a litany and eagerly we looked for any new and interesting things on it.

College Life

The day was divided into four periods, two in the morning and two in the afternoon. The two most boring items on this list were "PP" piano practice – this was boring because there was a hell of a lot of it and I had no one to teach me – and "study" which meant wading through huge tomes to learn about piano theory. Actually, this became fascinating. The trouble was, the room where we studied was so hot that one often fell asleep. There would be double periods of this study.

"CU" (chipping up) was the first stage of learning how to tune. What an endless task this seemed at first. Let me tell you, it should be used as punishment in old-fashioned prisons! Imagine standing for a period of over two hours in front of a stripped down piano. All there is is the back of the instrument and lots and lots of strings. The average piano has around 200 strings. These have to be tuned at first with a t-shaped implement. New learners had to use this as opposed to the normal lever shaped tool. T's as they are called are in fact very rarely used in tunings, usually only for instruments with loose pins. However, we had to learn early control of our wrists and had to build up muscles and strength for which these T's were invaluable, although we didn't think so at the time.

Well do I remember Mr Hewitt laughing his head off at my early efforts, my face looking strained, grimacing with every turn. He was helpless with laughter. "Michael, customers will think you're having a stroke or something the way your face looks."

After a while though, one can get used to anything. I actually came to love "chipping up". Then there were the repairs. I really loved this part of the job: learning all about the innards of the piano, what each part does, what to do to repair them. Then it was back to strings again. More blistered fingers making coils round pins with very thick gauge wire, blood flowing from grooves in finger ends, wire whipping up at you like a school cane, being poked in the eyes with the ends of wire. "You'll learn to be more careful won't you," Mr Hewitt (or Mr H, as we came to call him) used to say.

Leaning my trade as a piano tuner, I worked with, and came to love, pianos. Oh how I loved every aspect of what a piano was. I came to know them like members of the family, each piano having a definite character of its own. The Rolls Royce of pianos for me is the Steinway. This aristocrat was the favourite of my teachers. Mr Wilkins, our main tuning teacher, looked upon them almost as gods. This rubbed off on me somewhat and I grew to love them too. We had special lessons on how to tune, regulate, and adjust them. I only rarely came across one in my work but immensely enjoyed working on one when I had the opportunity. Everyone used to tease me about my obsession but I didn't care. I'd found the job I would do for the whole of my life, as I thought at the time.

Mr Wilkins was a master tuner and an expert repairer as well. He had a Steinway himself and I was privileged to play on it at his house once and his wife read a book onto tape about the firm and its history. To work with this man and learn from him, was both a pleasure and an experience. I learned all the most intimate details about the workings of a Steinway. He even took out the action from of his own piano for me to look at. Oh how I miss them now.

There were other less pleasant aspects to college life though. Bullying went on, usually the "visions" bullying the "dims". This was a real shame I always thought. This certainly had a distinctly political aspect. Labour, socialism and all it stood for, was god at college. Anyone who disagreed in the slightest was ruthlessly persecuted, and that included me. I'd had enough of this sort of thing back at my old school and I wasn't about to give in to it

College Life

now. It's all so silly when I look back, but at the time it was really serious to me. I remember being chased all round the extensive grounds, merely because I had different ideas from the other students. This was all part of finding out what the real outside world was like. I had to become tough, to learn how to protect myself. Due to this and my unhappy life at home, I was a nervous person and suffered greatly.

As a counter to this, on the advice of a kindly lad called Tom Lewis, I took to smoking a pipe which I did for many years. I used to sit in the corner of the student lounge in a comfortable arm chair looking like Gandalf the Grey with smoke rings pervading the air. The lounge had a wooden floor and an ornate fireplace carved in beautiful wood. King Charles II was supposed to have taken refuge in this building while on the run from Oliver Cromwell after the Battle of Worcester. The lounge was equipped with huge ashtrays on large stands. I gained a great deal of comfort from my tobacco smoking though I was never addicted to it. I could, at any time, take it or leave it. Tom Lewis and I became good friends. He was almost a father figure to me. It was Tom who gave me my first mobility lessons in Shrewsbury, taught me how to walk around the town, and went out with me.

There were the lighter sides of life as well. The "postie" or local post-office-cum-shop used to sell anything from sweets to steak pies. I loved the latter and used to wander up to the "postie" and get them, along with my tobacco or, later, cigars. I was told that, when you smoke a cigar, you mustn't take off the wrapping or the tobacco will fall out. Stupid me, I believed every word. I found out the hard way of course, when the thing almost blew up in my face, quite dangerous actually. Lads will be lads and I was a novice and had to learn from experience.

Funny things happened to me during my work as

Touch Me Please

well. One thing stands out in my memory. Lots of folks used to visit the college, parties from all sorts of backgrounds and cultures. On one particular day, a party of ladies was looking round the college. They ended up at the repair shop. I had been given the job of fitting a rather long string to an old piano. "Here's Michael, he's fitting a new string on a piano here" Mr H said to the ladies. Here I was, crawling under the piano, nose almost to the ground struggling with wire and hitch-pin to which the string fits. The ladies, wanting to see more, knelt like genuflecting nuns, their dresses rustling as they lowered themselves. I had one on either side and they were also feeling with their hands what I was doing. I enjoyed this very much, being a lusty young adolescent male.

It was at this point that the head of the college wandered in looking for the guests. "Where are our lady guests?" Mr Lidster asked. Everyone was looking round for them. Meanwhile, I was very happily getting on with my work, and then Mr H came over to me and said, "Aha, there they are, under the piano!" We emerged, all of us dust covered, a look of total innocence on my face. "Ah Gerwat, so that's what you get up to in your working time," Mr Lidster said. We all laughed and I was ribbed about it for the rest of my time at "quad" as we called it.

One aspect of growing up was taking up drinking. Nearly everyone did it and I was no exception. I remember my first night at a pub, the Royal Oak on Copen Hill. Mitchell & Butler's bitter was my poison. The tables had two layers. On the top we kept a glass of orange to satisfy the law while on the lower shelf our pint was stored. I felt on top of the world and finished the evening with pie and chips. I remember singing *Tears for Souvenirs* while having a bath after my first night's drinking. Thereafter our evenings out always finished off with the obligatory visit to the fish shop. Perhaps this just might have accounted

College Life

for my growing size.

Every time you left the college grounds, you had to book out and on return, book in. This was obvious because the staff had to know who was in and who was out. I wasn't eighteen and therefore shouldn't have been drinking alcohol. How long it seemed before I would be that magic age when I could go and have a drink without worrying about being caught. The landlords were very lenient back then, provided you didn't make any trouble of course. The college staff knew exactly our ages, so we had to defend ourselves against their questioning. Some were more alert than others. Strong mints were the order of the day. Of course any self-respecting staff member would be suspicious at once and the dreaded question "Have you been drinking?" would strike terror into us. I never actually got caught, even with the worst member of staff, Mr Ian Muerdoul, or simply Mr Doul to us. Gating was the lightest punishment for offenders. If you really misbehaved, then you were taken before the headmaster. I'm glad to say this never happened to me.

I enjoyed many a happy night out and life began to settle down to a pattern. I was loving my work and that first Christmas, I found a girlfriend. We met at the college Christmas concert. Dressed and made up as a black minstrel, I was playing the ukulele and singing all the old sing-along songs together with a mixed audience of students and the general public. Lin and I courted on and off throughout my time at college.

A weekly feature on our timetable was typing lessons. There were two typing teachers, first Mrs Madden, later replaced by Mrs Bird, a real stunning beauty by all accounts. We tuners very rarely saw Mr Doul, the senior typing teacher, since we were beneath contempt as far as he was concerned. "Tuners are no good and will never learn to type properly," he would

Touch Me Please

constantly say. Therefore we usually had Mrs Madden. All she did, was to give us long boring passages to type out from braille texts. She would then look at the results and tell us our mistakes. She never actually taught us anything, not me anyway. I had learned basic touch typing long before but again, I was mostly self-taught, a crime according to old Doul.

I was late back one night, no drinking this particular time but I returned, quaking in my boots. Doul had two stock phrases that he always used. "You have been taught, you know the rules." If you tried to put up any defence his reply was "Yes, I know, I quite agree, but you have been taught" at which point the sentence would be pronounced, the dreaded gating. So, no going out.

One day I had my first summons to the duty room to his presence. It was a Saturday evening and I couldn't think of anything I had done that I should be thus summoned. "You tuners, you can't type. I've told you this before, you know the rules, I've been getting reports of your work." What the hell was all this, at this time on a Saturday evening? I meekly waited for the blow to fall or some further criticisms.

"I don't know why I'm doing this, since you are only a tuner. Come to our room and have a cup of tea and we'll talk about your lousy typing." Well, this was unheard of. I meekly obeyed and in "our room" who should I find but Miss Hill, the matron. We had a rather pleasant hour talking about this and that, Doul telling Miss Hill all about how inferior I was because I was a mere tuner. I soon realised this was one big laugh and started, gently at first, getting back with one or two quips about typists. A great time was had by all and I left feeling as if I'd crossed a very important barrier. From that time on, I had several pleasant evenings with them both. I was further in their good books because I copied a tape of Doul's daughter's

College Life

wedding for the folks in New Zealand.

Time passed and I was moved on to tuning proper pianos, then finally came the milestone in Summer 1967, when I had passed all the tests to go on the "outside connection". This was work experience actually tuning people's pianos. By then, I had passed my 18th year and could lord it over the "under aged" newcomers. I only did this in a jocular way though. The outside connection was a whole new world, sending out appointment letters, having to type them out, for which I was under the direct tutorage of Doul himself. Oh boy, did he go to town, ripping out sheet after sheet with the words, "Wrong! Start again" followed by more ribald comments about tuners and their lot. Eventually the letters got completed.

This outside connection lark had several steps to be completed before we could actually go out and meet the customer. Setting the appointment date was only one of them. There were cards to fill in for the primitive hard copy database used in those days: name, number, shoe size, type of piano, record of previous visits if known, repairs history if any, cost of job, cost of any materials used, amount charged for job, for repairs or tuning, or both. Oh boy, then we had to type an invoice! This was mostly a waste of time since customers preferred to pay me directly. Then there was a receipt book with carbon paper in. This was before the job was done. We had to go through all this afterwards as well, plus review the report sent in by the customer! Yawns!

It's my first job, I'm setting off, no sat navs here, merely my tongue, to ask where places are. "It's up to you to find out where the customer lives, not them." This was quite a task involving phoning bus stations, train stations and the like. All this done, I am now setting off for the house. I feel confident as I arrive, I know my job and I can do it just fine. Now I'm at the door, hand raised to knock.

Touch Me Please

All went well and in fact it turned out to be much easier than I had imagined. So things began to settle down. I was out doing regular jobs now and gained a reputation for good work.

Things didn't always work out that easily though. On one occasion, a large-sounding dog hurled itself at the gate just as I arrived. I staggered back wondering what I should do. I had a mission and it must be completed. So I managed to pluck up enough courage to step forth through the gate. From out of the bushes bounded yet another dog and the two of them circled me, ready for the kill. Two! This was a bit much I thought. From inside the house came a voice shouting at the dogs. Then she called to me "Don't worry they are only being friendly." If this was being friendly, what would it be like if they didn't like me? In the end, I found both the lady and her dogs very friendly and kind. I returned there a few times as there were repairs to do.

Another wonderful advantage of working on this connection was the fact that one could get jobs working in pubs. There were 156 of them in Shrewsbury after all. There may have been more who knows. I would do the job then have a few beers. Mr H would give me these jobs last of all in the day, because he knew I'd have a drink afterwards.

I worked hard and it was soon time to go on actual work experience at Micklebergs, a Bristol firm. I have happy memories of this time. Previous students had not got on well with this course and were not very popular down there. I was expected to save the college's reputation by doing all the right things. I met the landlady, a lovely widow called Mrs Smythe, who was really kind and I liked her a lot. We spent many happy hours talking and she came to think the world of me.

As for my work, I learned a lot from old Mr Godfrey

College Life

who worked in the repair shop. At first, he was rather hostile to me and gave me all the worst jobs. After a time however, he began to have more respect for my skill. He too thought a lot of me as did Mr Haskins, the person in charge of the shop. Initially, he gave me the oldest rubbishy pianos to do, but he soon saw that I could make a good job of them, so I was moved on to the new instruments, or given the most difficult ones to sort out that other people had made a mess of.

I soon gained great respect throughout the firm. They had two bosses, Roy and Jack Mickleberg. Roy used to look after the wonderful museum of old instruments they had down there. Because of my reputation, I was allowed to look in and play all these old instruments one day. I had a wonderful time that afternoon.

It was near the end of my course now and I was preparing for the big day, my final exams or "Tiff" as it was called. On my last day at the firm, everyone came to wish me well, even the young lads and Mr Godfrey himself. They complimented me on my work and even Mr Haskins, not a man of many words, was complimentary.

Finally I was taken to see the bosses. I entered the palatial office of Jack, the really big boss. He enthused about what I had done and said I could always get a job down at the firm if I wanted one. I often wonder what would have happened had I done so. He gave me some money in an envelope. Let's face it, I'd worked hard for them but I had also learned a good deal about daily work. I felt on top of the world as I made my way home to Mrs. Smythe's for the last time. The following morning, she kissed me fondly. I noticed a few tears on her cheek. "You'll be happy, I'm sure, away from my nagging," she sniffed and I could tell she was really sad that I was leaving. I felt the same because we had got on so well.

I returned to college and prepared for the journey to

Touch Me Please

London to take the Tiff. Reports were sent in from Mickleberg's to the college and I was congratulated by both Mr H and Mr Wilkins. I was to meet Mr Wilkins many years later in different and difficult circumstances. He happened to live next door to some friends we were visiting. At the time I was over three quarters deaf. He offered to play a recital to raise money for the braille computer I wanted to buy. I clearly remember him saying that he didn't know how I was going to cope with the rest of my life without music and piano tuning. He said to Pat "Michael was one of the two top tuners I ever taught in all my years at the RNC. He had a natural aptitude and a great love of the job as I do myself."

    I was the only one taking the Tiff, so Mr H and I went down to London for the exam. Little did I know what would happen when we arrived there. He loved tennis and we listened to Wimbledon while travelling down to London. We stayed at the YMCA and after a meal, went out for a drink. "This is to relax you for tomorrow," he said.

    The day dawned and we set off for the building where all the pianos were. On arrival, we discovered that it was about to be pulled down! This really upset me because I'd come all this way to complete my work. I felt really sorry afterwards for the poor caretaker, who had been rousted out of bed. There was scaffolding all round the building and water was dripping everywhere. I felt so deflated, I had come through three years and I was ready now for the exam. Mr H was as calm and cool as a cucumber, soothing me and saying that I could still start work and come back to take the exam later. After negotiations over what seemed to me a very long time, we were allowed to enter the building and get on with the business of the day. Tuning was in the morning. I managed this without any problems at all. I had some

College Life

theory questions and answered these with ease. It was a subject I revelled in.

Before the exam, I had been fed so many tales, half-truths and so on that I was very apprehensive. Mr Little, the repairs man, was said to be a real terror. "He will trick you, give you a difficult task to do, an angled shank most likely or a string that goes under the covers!" These two things were at the top of the hard jobs list along with centring.

The afternoon came and lo and behold after I had replaced an easy new string, he actually gave me one of those angled shanks to deal with. Ah, but I had something that would defeat him. Little did he know that in my tool kit I had a brand new device, invented by Mr H for doing this very job. Mr Little was watching me to see how I did the job. "What's that you've got there?" he asked. I proudly demonstrated what it was. "How would you do it without that device though?" he asked. I knew the answer of course and proceeded to tell him. "But," I said, "I'm keeping this to take with me after I leave college." He accepted this and I completed the job successfully. He was impressed with the device as well.

At the end of the day, Mr Hewitt consulted with both examiners for what seemed like ages. He managed to find out that I'd passed with flying colours! We packed our things to return to quad. But before we did, he took me out for another drink, because he felt I deserved it after all the drama of the exam.

There was one final step to be taken before I could launch myself on the outside world. This was the interview at Barkers of Leeds. I had decided to leave home and settle up in Leeds, near my girlfriend Lin. I worked hard and prepared for my trip up to Leeds. The interview proved much easier than I had expected. They accepted me when they heard I'd passed my exams. "I'm going to

Touch Me Please

take you on trust," Mr Cockheram said. All was complete now and we returned to college for my last few days before I started at the firm.

I had one further thing to do. I had been chosen as best tuner and best student of the year. I had a cup and two prizes of money, a welcome thing I thought. Saying goodbye to everyone was painful in a way but I was full of hope for the future. I remember going out that last night celebrating with a few drinks. Old Doul couldn't resist a last shot in the locker. "Have you been drinking?" What did it matter? I answered "Yes sir." He put on his sternest voice. "You're gated for a month, you can't leave college for a month." We both laughed our heads off.

The next morning I was rudely awakened by students and old Doul, literally tipping me out of bed. I had an early breakfast and said my goodbyes. The gates closed behind me and I left the life of an adolescent student behind and was launched into the sighted world for the first time in my life.

Media Madness

PAT: I am standing at my own front door. It is locked and no one will to let me in. I have just got home from work and I'm tired and rather hungry. I am keen to see how Mick is faring today but I am an outsider and am not allowed to disrupt the TV crew who are still busy. I must wait on the doorstep until it is convenient for someone to move the equipment in the hall. This is the first day of filming a documentary about Mick and already I feel cross.

Mick has never been a stranger to publicity. In 1985 he was interviewed on Radio Leeds' *Day One* about his life and career. He had just completed a 'tuneathon' which involved tuning an old piano non-stop for three days and nights. He was working for three weeks a month in France at the time, and reading lots of palms. So he had plenty to talk about, and came across as his usual ebullient self. He recorded three songs for the programme, one of which he had written himself.

After his course in Torquay the local paper published an article about him. Simon Birtles prepared a press release to be sent out with Mick's own account of what had happened to him. Then Peter White from *In Touch*, the radio programme for people with visual impairments, heard about him and set up an interview from the Leeds studio. The programme had to be pre-recorded. We received Peter's questions in our tiny box room at the BBC in Leeds. Then there was a delay while I spelt them out on Mick's hand. Mick was so eloquent in describing his situation that the whole half hour programme was given over to him. It went out in 1991 and

Touch Me Please

snippets were included in *Pick of the Week*.

I also wanted to express what it meant to me, how our lives had been affected by circumstances, and how difficult it was to maintain my faith. I wrote an article for the Quaker weekly *The Friend*. This resulted in a flood of letters from readers expressing their concern and good wishes, and subsequently some visits to our home. People who initially wrote to us sometimes called in to see Mick if they were in the Leeds area. We remember particularly Tom Sutcliffe, a clergyman who was deaf, who came to see Mick before the implant and then afterwards. He and Mick communicated by typing 'both ways' on the two computers. He advised us that a sense of humour was the best way to cope with a difficult situation. Ronald Gill was a Quaker from Derbyshire. He had been a sailor involved in the Northern convoys to Russia during the last war. He edited the text of *HMS Ulysses* by Alistair MacLean. This was Mick's favourite book, which he had scanned. In the early days, scanners were not very accurate and a lot of work was needed to tidy up the text. Joan visited Leeds from Eltham, and she too offered to edit some scanned texts and worked on *Jennie* by Paul Gallico.

Mick got a lot of publicity when he completed his aromatherapy course. Thomas Danby College, quite rightly, were proud of the support they had given him, so an account of his achievement was sent to the local paper. In addition, he was included in Job Finder, a Yorkshire Television programme on the world of work. And so it went on, until we had built up quite a sizeable scrapbook of cuttings.

I pace up and down in front of the house, recalling the day when we had a call from a television producer called Lucy Jago. She wanted to do a programme for the series entitled *The Day that Changed My Life*. She visited Leeds to discuss the outline of a half-hour documentary to portray what had happened to Mick and the impact this had on his life. We were excited at the prospect of communicating in this way, and Mick hoped it could bring in some money for a second cochlear implant. Ever since he went deaf I have been Mick's support and guide, and we have shared everything. We are very close, so I didn't give it a second thought when all the plans for the filming were made without any reference to me, since I was at work.

Now, at last, someone is letting me in. I am horrified to see how they have taken over my home. The furniture has been rearranged and there are lights, cameras, boxes of film, enormous microphones and baggage everywhere. There is no prospect of preparing a meal. I suppose this is normal practice, but I feel angry that no one took the trouble to warn me about it. Mick looks delighted with everything. For him it is a liberation to be the centre of activity, to have admiring people around him, and the chance to verbalise how he feels. He seems to be intoxicated by the professionals around him, and I sense that he wants to keep it that way. He wants to do this on his own without my interference.

I feel like an intruder. I hardly seem to exist as far as the TV crew is concerned, but a few days into the filming they set up my own interview and I have a chance to talk about how things have affected me.

Some work colleagues are holding a barbecue in their garden on the Saturday and we are invited. I inadvertently mention this to Lucy, explaining that we will be otherwise engaged. She, however, feels this will be a great opportunity to film us socially and see how we manage among friends. The barbecue hosts are horrified at the idea and absolutely refuse to have their afternoon overrun. So Lucy sets up her own barbecue, driving us to a relative of her production assistant in Manchester (over

Touch Me Please

that dreaded M62 again). Here we are dumped for a couple of hours while the film crew go off to take some beautiful rural scenes. We are getting pretty fed up by the time they return for the filming. It is a long day and I feel irritated at being manipulated. Whilst our hosts are very friendly, we have never met them before. The whole set up is artificial, with them masquerading as long-standing friends. I wonder afterwards why I have agreed to do it. The whole incident has soured our relationship with colleagues at work.

There is, of course, masses of footage that isn't used in the final programme. My younger son, Chris, was interviewed in his bedroom. This, once again, annoyed me. The film crew invaded the attic without so much as a by your leave. People who have been burgled talk of their privacy being invaded. That is just how I felt during that week. The invasion of the attic could, perhaps, have been justified if Chris had been included in the film. I never saw the interview, I have no idea what he said, so the edited programme gave no indication that anyone else lived in the house except Mick and myself whereas, in truth, we were balancing family needs with those of Mick. I feel this is the most annoying thing about the film.

Certainly Lucy Jago sympathised with Mick's situation. I understand his passionate outpourings reduced her to tears. But he must have known she was not the only person ever to feel his pain. Lucy set out to present the view she wanted, as naturally any producer will do. Although she tried to portray sensitively what Mick had lost and the depth of his deprivation, she offended some viewers by including a lengthy session of Mick trying to access music, failing miserably, and expressing his grief and anger in a very emotional way with a generous smattering of bad language. I think she had her own agenda too, and showed an immodest interest in Mick's physical needs, understanding of course how much touch meant to him. She conducted separate interviews with Mick and myself. When we received the script and were preparing to go to London to see the programme before transmission, I was horrified to see how she had juxtaposed our words, spoken in different contexts, to imply an untruth. Mick spoke of his passionate nature and his need for physical touch. He emphasised how important love-making was to him. Then an extract of my interview followed, admitting that Mick's deafness had made the relationship more difficult. I had been talking of communication, pressure of work on me, not our sex life.

Mick had final control of what went out. I had no say in the content of the programme. I wanted the script to be changed to remove an insidious suggestion, but Mick was happy to leave it as it was. The night before our trip to London was one of the most unhappy of our marriage. We could not agree. We slept in different rooms, although to be truthful, neither of us slept much at all. I felt betrayed and rejected by Mick. No doubt he felt just as hurt as I did. By the morning we wanted to be reconciled. Mick agreed to ask for a change in the script, which was accepted by Lucy. The final insult to me was an invitation for Mick to attend the screening party in London, but without including me. Now what lay behind this do you imagine? He decided, thankfully, to stay at home and listen to the broadcast with me.

When the programme was screened in July 1996 it made an impact on many people, although some felt it was sentimental and over-emotional. It contained imaginative scenes of Mick floating in the water, or up in the clouds, a kind of dream escape from the misery of his earthly existence. But it enabled him to verbalise how his life had changed. "When I went deaf I lost me, I lost everything I had ever known, I lost an entire world... There is no world, no night, no day, nothing to relate to... I lost my mobility, I lost my dignity because people treated me as if I was a cuddly bear, or as if they didn't want to talk to me. They would run away because they couldn't cope with talking to me." He saw life as a prison, solitary confinement where he was 'dragged' around "like some useless piece of sacking".

There was an angry scene where Mick attempted to listen to his favourite Genesis track 'Entangled' on his Technics centre but grew increasingly frustrated. He said he could hear the words (because he knew them so well) "but I can't hear the guitars in the background, no tune, bloody nothing. I know what bloody well should be there, I know what it bloody isn't. It sounds like someone's done something rather terrible to the cat. Music is the greatest loss I will ever have. It's there yet I can't get at it. It's not fair, people moan about stupid little things, yet they've got music to listen to like this. To hell, no point in worrying about it. I've got to go on – if I want to. Something will help me go on. How can I explain to anyone how it feels? I can never get music back. It's blooming unfair."

The film was sold to other countries and Mick had a lot of feedback. One school in Italy sent some delicious pasta and Italian gourmet food. People e-mailed him from Australia. For a time he enjoyed celebrity status. Even Oscar Moore, the Guardian reporter, who wrote the moving PWA (Person with Aids) column, referred to Mick in one of his articles. As Oscar's sight failed he attended an RNIB training course and described his feelings facing a life without vision. He continued "When I got home I listened to a television documentary about a blind piano tuner who had now lost his hearing as well. He could barely conceal his angry frustration at his new affliction and I was humbled and appalled at my erstwhile snootiness."

It is good to have the film, and I often replay it to hear again in Mick's words what he has lost. On the whole it was worthwhile, but it created a chink in our marriage, the first damage to our close relationship. This is a pity because the whole event could have been handled more sensitively.

Subsequently there was a lengthy article in The Sunday Times Supplement which elicited a response from James McWhirter who offered to raise money for a second implant. Unfortunately he got waylaid by other interests and the fund-raising did not materialise.

But Mick did get something out of the experience in addition to the publicity. He had spoken of his love of *Star Wars* and how he identified with Obi Wan Kenobi. He used one of his quotes as a kind of mantra: "By striking me down you have made me more powerful than you can possibly imagine." As a last act of kindness Lucy obtained an Obi-Wan Kenobi robe from the BBC wardrobe and thereafter Mick was often to be seen sitting at his computer enveloped in voluminous brown sackcloth.

MICK: "Come on, you've had your say, and I don't mind, but surely I have the right to return serve." Pat and I had been talking one summer evening around Wimbledon time. "It can't hurt now, it's 17 years ago. You've said how you feel, now it's my turn." I said this light heartedly, but I found the whole event so hard to talk about, then and now. It's like lancing a boil in a way, because we had different views and at the time I was feeling really low.

It's worth looking at another event here as background. Pat and I had been trying to find different ways to get someone to take me out independently, so I could choose what I wanted to do. It is a fact that sighted folks who very kindly look after and support us, often have their own agendas, even if they may not realise it, about how our lives should be run. It's instinctive, something that is human nature. It's also human nature for some form of rebellion to take root in the person being looked after. Looking back now, I see many follies in the way things happened but at the time it all seemed right to me. It is only afterwards, with hindsight, that I can see things in perspective and realise how close to the edge Pat and I came.

How did it all start? Well, with a simple phone call actually. Lucy Jago, the producer mentioned earlier, phoned me and said she wanted to talk about implants and their effect. I told Pat about this. At the time there was no talk at all about any film being made.

Lucy came up from London one day and at first we discussed implants, what they were, how they had affected me, my life now that I was totally deaf and so on. She was kind and, I felt, sympathetic. I found myself talking about how it felt to be deaf and blind, my days of total silence. I then played a part of the radio series of *Star Wars*, where Obi-wan fights Darth Vader. This was the lengthened radio series which was far more explanatory. We had my large Technics centre then and the series was on an old cassette. The phrase "By striking me down, you have made me more powerful than you can possibly imagine" came up. It was at that point I found Lucy in floods of tears, literally weeping on my shoulder. "Michael," she said through her tears, "can you film all this for me, can you explain just how it all felt? There's far more in this than I could have ever imagined." I thought about this for a while. Yes, I must admit, I wanted to blast the public, I'd had enough of rejections, I'd had enough of social services thinking it would cost them too much to help a deaf-blind person get out of isolation, that it was too expensive. I felt bitter, I felt trapped and here was someone who was willing to let me have free rein, to tell it just how it really was. I did not want a nice tidy story here, I wanted to let go, to do just what Pat had always said I should do, but do it publicly and make it really hurt the viewers, wake them up, shock them!

I agreed I would do what Lucy suggested. I knew in my heart that if I got into long discussions about it, Pat would reject it out of hand, through fear. Bless her, she's very reserved. I know now, I shouldn't have gone full steam ahead, but I was feeling so imprisoned. Years earlier after the *In Touch* programme we had been offered the chance of going on Esther Rantzen's programme *That's Life* but were warned that, if we did, she would go for the jugular and hurt people and authorities to make them act and maybe it would backfire on us. Having discussed it, Pat was very nervous about going ahead. I was content to agree with her, I was happy about the success of *In Touch*, had plenty of reaction and at that time was thoroughly satisfied. Now though, here was another chance and I wasn't going to let it pass.

When Pat returned from work, I explained what Lucy had suggested but that nothing had actually been planned as yet, which was true. Pat was happy about this but obviously wary of how things would turn out. Since I didn't know the extent of what would happen, I felt I hadn't done any wrong as yet. After all no commitments were made and nothing was set in stone. I said Lucy was going away to consult with her bosses.

Later that month, she returned and we went for an afternoon drink to discuss what would happen. This time we discussed things in more depth. I explained how I could no longer hear music. After a couple of drinks, my tongue loosened and I became upset about what I had lost. It all spilled out, all the bitterness I felt against the world, against what had happened to me. Lucy I must admit encouraged me by asking me to explain how I felt inside. Her sympathy acted like a catalyst and I really let rip about it.

We got a taxi back to my home. After going inside, she said, again through her tears, "Michael, will you cry for me, will you really show just how you feel?"

"How can I cry on demand like that, it wouldn't be genuine though would it?"

We talked some more about filming what I felt. She had some ideas about shooting artistic pictures and so on. "Michael, this will be your real chance to say how you feel, how you are inside." Whether foolishly or wisely, I fell for this. It spoke to all my anger, all my inner feelings in a way I had never before experienced. All the counselling, all the previous experiences, all the things we'd tried had only been scratching the surface. Now I could really let it out and maybe it would help me and ease Pat's burden at the same time.

But what would Pat say if I told her all of this. It didn't take much guessing. This is where we were so very different in personality. I avoided talking about it when I should have put it to her directly, perhaps being firm but kind. We could have worked out a compromise. But if we compromised the whole thing would lose its punch, it wouldn't be allowed to run the angry course I wanted it to. I wanted this to hit damned hard, I was fed up with pussy-footing around things, this was the big one and I wanted it this way. If necessary, I would go it alone, this would be my project, my chance to say to the world, "This is how it bloody well is and I hope you like it."

All this is very painful to me now, as a Buddhist. I fully realise where I was misguided but at the time there was no stopping me. No way did I want to hurt Pat, but no way did I want to miss this one, no way did I want to let this chance go by. So the film was made. A lot has been

Media Madness

explained about those fraught days. I will only say that the section where I tried to hear the music was definitely not faked. I remember the day it was filmed. I was sitting in our sitting room, preparing to film this "drama bit" as I thought of it. Actually, I thought it would be a lousy flop and sound so fake it was laughable. How wrong I was. No one ever heard the full version of it because it had to be very heavily edited. I can't remember much of it myself now. I know I "lost it" as they say these days. Something inside of me let go, was released, was set free.

Lots of the film – swimming in the pool, the artistic filming, smoking my pipe in the greenhouse, the part where *Star Wars* is mentioned – was so emotional for me, so meaningful. I wanted it out in the open and nothing, nothing was going to stop me, not even my dear Pat. Of that I was determined.

Sadly it was this event, on top of all the rest, that drove me to try and kill myself. I felt the tension all along, through the filming, through the trouble over the script. I actually wanted it left alone, I felt it did say how I felt at the time. Isn't it always the way that you start "down the dark path" to quote Obi-wan and don't realise where it will end. The real trouble is that you can never foresee outcomes and consequences of what you do, the Karma of it all. I think, sadly, it laid the foundation stone for issues that arose in our later years. Though I was glad we made up after our disagreements, it left a chink, a crack between us.

On reflection, I was unwise in some ways, but I stand by the fact that, listening as best I can to the film, I think it achieved some good in many ways, despite all the problems it caused. I did get a lot of reaction, I did get heard.

MICK: A Bunch of Keys

I'm on the train, college life is behind me now, but as yet, it still clings to me like ivy. Mr Hewitt (no more college nicknames now) is on the train with me to see me settled in and then he will go, leaving me to my own independent life. How very small I feel now. I am no longer a big fish in a small pond but quite the opposite. We blind folks have always lived in our own communities, we have very rarely lived in the sighted world at all – only for brief periods when we were taught mobility but always under supervision and really, it didn't feel like the outside world at all. This world was a total mystery to me anyway. What's more, there would be no one to catch me if I fell, if I did anything wrong or things went astray in my work. I felt totally alone and very frightened. I could hardly show any of this to Mr Hewitt as we bumped, rocked and rattled our way northwards towards our destination, Leeds. It wasn't as if I'd left my parents on good terms either. They were totally against me living in Leeds and wanted nothing to do with me. My brother and family as well had turned against me and all because I wanted to make a life of my own.

Work would be the order of the day, hard work. I hoped the folks at this new job would be as friendly as they had been at college. The train seemed to get more rackety the further north we ventured. Finally, we arrived at our destination. "Let's go and find one of these lovely 'cafs' you're always going on about. Let's have a pint pot of tea and northern chips with something," Mr Hewitt quipped. Everyone had been ragging me at quad over the last few weeks about how conditions in the north were so

A Bunch of Keys

primitive, they had only just heard of the phone. I retorted that at least they had the first bleeping road crossings.

Full to the brim with home cooked fish and chips, bread and butter (you could cut yourself on the fresh crusts) and pints of tea, we started on the task of learning my way from Barkers, the music shop, to the bus stop for home. I had my toolkit with me and my white stick plus a few overnight things. We had sent the bulk of my luggage on by rail. What an eventful day it would turn out to be. Mr Hewitt took me to the shop door of Barkers, popping in to see the manager to confirm that I would be starting on the following Monday. It was Friday now and I had two days before I started work.

One interesting feature of Leeds is the arcades. You could go across Leeds from one side to the other without ever getting wet, it was said. I had to traverse three of these arcades, to reach the bus stop for Middleton.

Street furniture, as it is called nowadays, was rife back then. Displays of all types were scattered about outside shops, in the middle of pavements and everywhere you can think of. On that first day, I sent three different displays sprawling on the ground, to wit: one rack of shoes, one huge stall full of oranges, one armchair over which I measured my length, and when we visited the market, a whole stall packed with fruit and veg. I wasn't the most popular person in the city that day. Eventually, we boarded the bus for Middleton and what would be my digs for the next three years. It was a reasonably new council estate and to get where we wanted to be, there were flights and flights of steps. They weren't just flights, but there were long gaps between the steps, making it one of the hardest mobility challenges to deal with. Mr Hewitt said, "If you can manage these steps Michael, you'll manage anything." How right he was, and I soon learned to leap up them at break neck speed.

Touch Me Please

I was staying with relatives of my girlfriend, Lin. After the obligatory cup of tea, Mr Hewitt left the house. Oh boy, now I was really on my own. My landlords worked all day, so I was left alone to get on with my new life. I loved the beer up here, I loved the food, it seemed a wonderful new world to me on that first day as I prepared to settle in and start work. The little house had an inside bathroom, something I had never experienced at home in my life! Always, I'd been used to trudging outside into the back yard to an outside loo. Now, here was a room with an actual bath, and I had my own bedroom upstairs.

On Monday morning Lin's parents took me to Barkers to start work and then to lunch for that first day. I felt honoured and really thought I was set fair for a happy life with very few worries. I remember the first piano I tuned. It was an Ebach, made under licence for Barkers. I met Ivan Stanley Bath. This man was, I think, one of the most morose miserable men I've ever met. Even his own family wouldn't speak to him. He ate very noisily, had bad language and didn't like anyone, except the manager and old Jack, being the "god" of the tuning world as far as Mr Bath was concerned. It was the first day of Yorkshire Television going into colour and I clearly remember tuning a piano to be used for the performance in the opening ceremony.

Tuning on the road, having to find places, having to work with all sorts of different people, having to put up with every type of difficulty along the way, and working for a firm that cared no more for me than they would a dog, soon tarnished any illusions of the "happy life". At first, I did a lot of work in the shop itself, tuning pianos that hadn't been looked at for ages. There were all sorts of instruments and I really began to learn my job. Mr Bath, 'Old Misery' as I was soon to think of him, never once complimented me on anything I did, he just wanted more and more work. I worked a five and a half day week for a measly £11, rising to £12 after the first week, Wow, down on your knees and celebrate!

The first outside job I ever did was at the Lido review bar on Albion street. I had to go and collect a string to be sent away for replacement. I trotted off and found the bar, falling over a set of old arm chairs that were outside a second hand furniture shop that had caught fire the day before. It was rumoured it was for the insurance. I arrived and met old Tommy, who looked after the place. Basically, it was a strip club, pure and simple. I had to remove the string and then take it back to the shop. From that time on, I used to visit the bar once a week to tune the piano. It was a rather old baby grand piano, very small but I suppose suitable for what they required. There were juke boxes in those days, but for a club of this sort live music was the order of the day. The disco, though it did exist, was a rare thing back then.

Now things started to change. The manager realised that I could do jobs outside. He piled work onto me, giving me a bunch of cards which I couldn't read. I had to have them read to me. Blind folks today don't know they are born I can tell you. There was none of this equality stuff. If you couldn't do the work, if you didn't measure up to the job you were doing, out you went and no appeal.

I really worked hard over those first months, doing up to five, sometimes six, jobs a day travelling on buses everywhere. The manager almost smiled when he found out that, as a blind person, I could get a free pass; it meant he would not have to pay my expenses, a thing he very rarely did anyway. Even for the jobs outside Leeds travelling expenses were not paid after a while. Pound of flesh? Barkers got more than that out of me, they didn't even supply all the material I needed for work: string wire, felts, tapes and a lot of other stuff I had to have. I soon

Touch Me Please

became very bitter. I felt used and abused. I gradually put myself out less and less for them. I freely admit now, that if I could get private work and customers, I got them. I needed money like everyone else and I didn't see why greedy Barkers should have it all. Though I hated Barkers, I loved my work and met a lot of different people of all types, classes and nationalities. Stories tumble out of my memory like unpacking an old trunk.

Those early years brought me in contact with pub landlords, the university, the polytechnic (now the Metropolitan University) and ordinary houses. The pianos were as varied as well, from old wrecks to Steinways. All this was a learning experience. I remember going to Mulligans to do their piano. This was a place that catered for old time traditional music and served stews. What a place that was! I was upstairs repairing one piano while they had one downstairs as well. I was enthusiastic and revelled in my work.

One day, near my first Christmas in Leeds, I was walking along Boar Lane when my tool case burst asunder and everything spilled out into the middle of the main road. All the traffic had to stop for about ten minutes while we picked up all the stuff. Dampers, string wire, hammers, screwdrivers, felt, ivory key tops, pliers, cutters, saws, files, levers, jacks, glue, regulating tools and washers of every type and size scattered themselves like confetti all over the road. The police came and once again I wasn't popular in Leeds.

I encountered some interesting characters whilst doing jobs. Usually you would get cups of tea or coffee, biscuits, dinner even and beers, orange, but sometimes nothing! It was these "nothing" jobs that really annoyed me. You could bet that the hardest jobs gave the least reward. Often the poorest folks were kinder and more generous whereas those who had money were the

A Bunch of Keys

meanest.

Once I found a large bunch of white fivers under the keys of someone's piano. Being an honest person, I meekly handed them over to the lady. She paused. "Are you sure that's all there was? I don't trust you, I bet you've kept some for yourself. I'm going to report you to the manager of Barkers." I was shocked. How could I prove it one way or the other? "I should look in your pockets or bag, to make sure!" No way would I allow this to happen. In due course, I was called into the manager's office and accused of taking this person's money. From that time on, I really hated Barkers and all they stood for.

During the long bus strikes of 1970, I was expected to walk everywhere doing my jobs. They totally refused me any transport whatsoever. This really put the seal on my hatred of them. From that time on, I stole as many customers from them as I could. I suppose that was wrong but I didn't care. If they chose to treat me like dirt, why should I be loyal to them?

I was sacked one Saturday morning in 1972 with no notice at all, just chucked out. The blow fell when Lin was pregnant. I didn't know how to face the family. It was the greatest shame to be out of work. Eventually I told Lin's parents what had happened. I was depressed about losing my job and needed comfort and support, but instead I only received blame and harsh words. So bitter did I feel at the way I had been treated that I applied to an industrial tribunal for unfair dismissal. Hearing of my situation, my mother came up to Leeds for the first time since our marriage specifically to help me defend myself at the tribunal.

It was held in April 1973. Barkers had a professional solicitor and barrister. All I had was Mum. Barker's barrister took every word my mother said and placed it in a mixer, twisting every point of defence and smashing it to pieces like matchwood. Mum was upset and annoyed at the way she had been handled at the tribunal, I just wanted a peaceful life, and all Lin and her family wanted was for the affair to be stopped, and my mother to keep out of it. The result was that Mum swept out of the house, swearing she would never come to Leeds again while I was married to Lin. Apart from one occasion, she kept faithfully to that promise. Thanks to her support, however, I received compensation of £80.00.

Though the whole incident was hard, it was, in the end, the best thing that ever happened to me and I could look back on their meanness and petty tyranny as a bad dream thankfully ended. I was on the dole for around six months. Then a little firm called Melody Inn Pianos started up. They rang me to ask if I was interested in doing some work for them. I jumped at the chance for it meant I could come off the dole. They offered me a job for five mornings at £10 a week. The job not only entailed looking after the shop every morning, but also tuning and repairing pianos. They got their pound of flesh, but it was a job. I was promised commission on sales, but that was never put into practice. Moreover, they wanted to see my private tuning records so that they could keep the details of my few clients, which I refused to hand over. The one saving grace about that place was that they had a radio and when there were no customers in the shop I would listen to plays, music and stories.

Through all my twenty years of working – with some gaps – I had some wonderful experiences, all of which happened once I branched out on my own, after working for shops or dealers! These last folks were really the pits: little setups where money was the name of the game, selling pianos abroad, cheating old ladies and anyone else they could get away with fiddling. I hated them as much as I did Barkers. Everyone seemed the same, out to exploit me as much as they could. I liked best the jobs I got on my own. I met some lovely people and some of them became life-long friends. One even became my second wife eventually.

In the early days, I wanted a guide dog so I could get around much easier. At the end of 1969 I had an answer to my application. I was invited to the guide dog centre at Bolton for a month early in 1970. I was quite apprehensive about this, wondering what it would be like, but when I arrived at the training centre I had a lovely surprise. I was given my own little room with a radio, and the Social Security paid me something to live on for the duration of the course. I was given a beautiful alsatian called Bridget.

My month at the training centre was an experience in many ways, not least in my contact with the girls there. I was totally inexperienced sexually having attended a boys' school and a segregated college as well. The presence and friendliness of the kennel maids opened my eyes to possibilities. Although the friendships I cultivated were purely platonic, I enjoyed the company so much I didn't want to leave at the end of the month. However, I was very proud of Bridget when I took her home.

She made a great difference to my life. She came with me on journeys to customers' houses which helped me enormously in my travelling, but she was also a bit of a tie because I wasn't allowed to take her to certain places. I loved her, she was an extension of me, though customers didn't always think so. The Alsatian breed wasn't popular in those days. There had been stories in the papers about children being savaged by them. Today, it's Rottweilers, back then it was Alsatians. This was unfair on me because it meant I could take her hardly anywhere when I went out. Today, things are so much easier for owners of guide dogs but back then, they were regarded with mistrust and suspicion. I well remember Lewis's, a large department

Touch Me Please

store in the centre of Leeds who actually collected for Guide Dogs, refusing me entry to their cafe for a meal. I contacted the guide dog centre in Bolton where I trained, and told them about it. About a week later, I was passing the shop when a member of staff sprang out from the doorway and almost begged me to come in and have a coffee in the cafe. It was, of course, ridiculous if the dog's presence denied me access anywhere, since the whole point of having her was to get about! Customers at home, clients in the cinema and the small dealer I was working for, none of them liked Bridget.

Mind you, I had some funny experiences with her. She loved water and would plunge into any stream, puddle or river with aplomb. She had real spirit. At the end of my training, we were in the park with my trainer, Mr Wright, a wonderful man, who had looked after Bridget ever since she was a puppy and really loved her. He was making the dog 'sit-stay'. I had to walk away and the dog had to stay exactly where I'd left her. This was just too much for Bridget to cope with. There was all this lovely open land to run about in and she had to keep still. For a moment or two my will held firm but in the end she succumbed to her natural instincts. She took off at a great rate. Mr Wright stuck out his leg to stop her. 100 pounds of racing dog hitting a single human leg can have only one consequence. There was a terrifying crack and the next thing I knew, poor Mr Wright was yowling on the ground in great pain cursing the day he'd ever met Bridget. "They made the mould when they made you," he said afterwards. I felt really awful about it.

I was working for the Cairn hotel in Harrogate where there was a conference of WD and HO Wills, the tobacco firm. Dinners were being laid out on very low tables right next to poor Bridget. Let's face it, even the best trained dogs, faced with this temptation would give in. As

A Bunch of Keys

I tuned on, unbeknown to me the waiters were putting dinners on the tables. Bridget was tied to my leg, so the dog couldn't wander around the room and annoy anybody. There was, however, a low table near her. Several times the waiter put a plate on the table. Why he didn't see Bridget sitting there, heaven knows. The dinner would disappear down that mighty gullet and the waiter, thinking he hadn't put anything on the plate duly refilled it. After a time though, the truth dawned on the staff. I felt a tap on the shoulder "I think your dog's very hungry." With a sinking feeling I apologised profusely and offered to pay for what she had done. "Oh no, it's no problem at all, I just thought you should know." The waiters and staff were dog lovers and they gave Bridget and myself a lovely dinner. That greedy creature ate it as if she'd had nothing. On another occasion, I was working at the Grand Theatre. Les Dawson was appearing and Bridget took a liking to him. I remember him saying "Watch out, she'll have my bacon sandwich in a minute."

Bridget also proved to be a real tippler! I remember working in a local pub in Leeds. It was evening and after I had tuned the piano we were all having a lovely time. Let's face it, didn't I deserve a drink? Sitting with Bridget tied as usual to my leg we were drinking and talking. A slightly slurry voice said, "Hey pal, what about a pint for the dog?" Before I could stop him a dish was put down and filled to the top with, of all things, cider. With great relish, Bridget lapped this up in no time. Everyone was a little merry by this time as I was myself. "Oh, she's very thirsty, don't you ever give your dog a drink pal?" Another pint went into the dish. This disappeared as the last one had done. I didn't know it, but people kept filling the damned dish.

The next thing I knew, I was having to take poor Bridget outside for a much needed loo visit. With legs splayed out in all directions, staggering, and giving an extremely expressive drunken whine, she stood and peed for about five minutes. I wondered at how much a dog could hold, it seemed to go on for ever. Everyone had followed me outside and laughed their heads off. It wasn't so much of a laugh though because I had to get home.

    I tried setting off but it was hopeless. Poor Bridget staggered and wobbled and swerved all over the pavement uttering very long complaints between a bark and a yowling whine. She kept trying to jump up at me but couldn't hold her balance. One of the patrons took pity on me and took me home. On arrival, we had to stop outside the house while another five minute pee was dealt with. I got her inside and she promptly fell asleep. Never have I known such loud snoring. I was disturbed three times in the night for more pees! The next morning she was very reluctant to leave her bed. She whined and keened, obviously suffering a doggy hangover.

    When I started working at Melody Inn Bridget had been with me for four years. My employers did not like her in the shop, and many house customers refused me entry because of my dog. There was a press campaign at the time because a baby had been savaged in its pram by the family Alsatian. I began to lose work because I had Bridget. I made a very difficult decision and on September 19th 1973 someone from the guide dog centre came to take her back. I missed her sorely. She had been a wonderful companion and guide to me. At first I blamed myself that I hadn't trained her properly, but that was untrue. It was simply that she was unacceptable to other people. I heard she went to a really good home, but she would never work as a guide dog again. I had to let her go because I could not afford to lose work. I never had another guide dog and had to get about to jobs as best I could.

PAT: Plumbing the Depths

By the mid-nineties Mick had been deaf for six years and we had tried pretty much everything that might help him: hospitals and faith healers; charitable organisations and Social Services; computer studies and aromatherapy; braille books and tactile games; even exercise equipment. There came a time when we couldn't think of anything else and Mick reached that awful point when he realised that this was as good as it was ever going to get. He was an extrovert shut off from everyone around him. He was a musician no longer able to play or listen to music. He was imprisoned in the house except for the occasions when friends took him out. He had tried to make a life without music but it had been so much part of his life and his soul that he began to feel he could not go on. He became more withdrawn, a complete contrast to the fun-loving, cheerful and extrovert personality I had married. He had never properly grieved for the loss of his hearing, and the suppressed grief was affecting him.

I, too, was feeling particularly low. I was missing the music which I had denied myself. I felt it was too unkind to listen to what Mick could not enjoy. Moreover, I could not really enjoy it myself. I got too upset. I asked the GP for some help and he organised six sessions of counselling. It was amazing how much difference this made. Just being able to talk about it lifted a burden. The counsellor suggested that I should listen to music in the car on my journeys to and from work. I realised that depriving myself could not help Mick in any way. It did not make music accessible to him, nor would he want me to suffer when it wasn't really necessary. So I began to listen

Touch Me Please

occasionally to Classic FM in the car but it was many years before I could actually go to a musical performance. The first one was an Abba tribute band, but I didn't enjoy it. I just wanted to cry because some of the songs had strong associations with Mick and our early days together. It took years before I could go to an opera or concert and enjoy it. I could only do that when I learned to completely block off what had happened to Mick. So gradually I came to enjoy music again.

But Mick had no such opportunity. He had been buoyed by the television crew and the excitement of making the documentary. I think he had high hopes of a big financial response to fund a second implant. But when everyone had gone and nothing really changed he sank into a depression.

He was feeling particularly low when we had a Ukrainian visitor staying with us. This naturally involved showing her some of the local tourist sites. We visited the five rise locks at Bingley and walked along the canal. Mick was very quiet and uncommunicative. The next day, Saturday, we drove to Haworth and after going round the Bronte museum we wandered the cobbled streets and explored the old-fashioned shops selling soaps, pegs and traditional household things. I could not elicit from Mick a spark of interest in anything. He just trailed round with us looking sad and withdrawn.

That night when he came to bed we cuddled and he mumbled something about going to sleep in my arms and never having to wake up. I was almost asleep and continued to drift off until I realised there was something in the way he said it that sent a sudden alarm like an electric shock shooting through me. Instantly I was wide awake.

I spelt on his hand, "Mick, what have you done? Have you taken some sleeping pills?" He was sleepy but replied "A few."

"How many have you taken Mick?"

"About six."

"Are you sure? Did you take more?"

It seemed he had taken more but I couldn't ascertain how many. But what should I do? Was it a dangerous or lethal dose? Would he simply sleep it off, or should I ring the emergency services? They would not appreciate an unnecessary callout. If it was a lethal dose would it be kinder to let him sleep and let things take their course? It seemed more compassionate to let him die as he was so unhappy. I struggled with this dilemma for a few moments but decided I could not let that happen.

I had a vague idea that I should keep him awake, so I shook him and talked to him and tapped his face. I dialled 999 and requested an ambulance. Since Mick rarely wore his pyjamas I had to get him into them before the paramedics arrived. This was a struggle as by this time he was drowsy and a dead weight. Chris came home at some point and he helped me to dress him and keep him awake. Mick was just able to stagger out to the ambulance when it arrived, supported on each side, and off we went in convoy, ambulance then me, to St. James's hospital. They didn't need to pump his stomach but monitored him until the early hours of the morning when we were allowed to go home to bed. We had very little sleep as they made an appointment to see the psychiatrist on Sunday morning. Our young visitor was abandoned to the TV and a range of videos she was thrilled to have access to.

Mick saw the psychiatrist alone and perhaps it helped to pour out his troubles. He had been prescribed pills to help him sleep and some for depression but, unknown to me, he decided to stop taking the latter. Apparently he should have come off the medication gradually. Stopping suddenly can cause severe mood swings. But the psychiatrist recognised that it was something more than that and arranged for the community psychiatric nurse from Mind to call on him. The nurse was very helpful and suggested that a carer be found to take Mick out once a week, and so another Michael was introduced to him and became his guide-companion on a regular basis. This meant Mick could go out for a drink and a chat independently of me; it was something he could decide for himself and the arrangement seemed to work well. There was a good rapport between the two Michaels.

What really helped Mick to face the future was finding Buddhism. He had been seeking a spiritual dimension to his life and had hoped to find it with Quakers. Friends had been immensely supportive when he first became deaf, but later, as he struggled to find meaning in his life, he felt that one or two had not shown sufficient understanding. When he spoke of deriving strength from Obi Wan Kenobi and of possibly wearing his robe to Quaker Meeting, he had been told that would be inappropriate.

He had often been fascinated by what he had heard about Buddhism and when a staff member at the Deaf Centre talked to him about his Buddhist faith it was a natural step for Mick to go along to a Buddhist meeting with him. Almost at once it seemed right for him. He soon gained more composure from meditation, and the idea of karma gave him at last an explanation for his suffering. He felt he was paying for some wrong-doing in the previous life, maybe even in this one, and the hope of a better life in his reincarnation was a consolation that helped him bear his current situation.

In a relatively short time he 'took refuge'. Attending Buddhist meetings, whether at an evening event or a weekend puja, gave him the chance of a new life outside

Plumbing the Depths

the home. Above all he had regular meetings with the lama who helped him understand and come to terms with what had happened. From this point on Mick was able to cope much better. The restrictions were just as bad but his mental approach was stronger. He was able to accept his lot more patiently. Now there was a spark which enabled him to get as much as he could out of his limited life and to look for new opportunities.

MICK: New Beginnings

By 1976 Lin and I had two children. We enjoyed our daughters, but it was hard work at home. Bringing up little children when you have no sight at all makes for interesting new challenges. Right from the start, our little ones were bottle-fed. In those days, there was no easy SMA ready-made milk as there is today. It was all powdered. It had to be stirred with a fork to get out all the lumps. Because neither of us could see, it was almost impossible to make sure all the lumps were out. The little teats got blocked up time and time again.

Nappies were no joke either. There were no simple shaped disposables around, we had to use the old terry towelling ones. I remember those pins with the tops that clicked into place. I think my fingers were like pin cushions by the time I'd finished. The process didn't end there either. The nappies went into big square buckets filled with very hot water and Napisan. But first we had to hold the corner of the soiled nappy down the loo – many's the nappy I lost down the Leeds sewerage system.

Sorting out the little clothes so they matched was another difficulty. As they all began to grow, there was the problem of spoon feeding, a messy job at the best of times. I perfected a method in the end, using my fingers to make sure the spoon found their little mouths.

Once on their feet, Claire and Joanne were as "wick" as any fox. From a very early age, they knew we couldn't see. I well remember Joanne saying "I'll detik I'll detik" (get it) and throwing objects ahead of her, knowing that we couldn't see where they were. She would then pick them up again and throw them further away from us. On

New Beginnings

one occasion Joanne or Claire got hold of the box of matches and actually lit one. Luckily I managed to find it and snuff it out in time.

Once they began to talk more, they used to do some really cute things. Taking my fingers, they would try and get me to feel the pictures in books. It took a lot of explaining to them that I couldn't actually feel the pictures. Once they were a little older, Joanne and Claire used to describe the pictures on tinned food. I well remember Joanne saying on many occasions "mixture" which meant that there was more than one thing in the tins.

All little ones run off at some time or other. This really was a problem. The family suggested we put reins on them to keep them with us, or bells on their clothes. I strongly resisted this idea; they were children not animals to be herded. I can understand their reasoning but I hated the thought of children with bells on them.

Joanne was a gorgeous child, very sensitive and caring. She thought a lot of me. She had a generous nature, always seeing the good in people. She was very discerning in many ways, and a good little singer too. We were very close. I shared my dreams with her walking down to school, talking of how I wanted to go aboard the Millennium Falcon, the *Star Wars* ship. Joanne was always ready to listen to me, and had a wonderfully vivid imagination as I have. She used to talk to me about pictures. Joanne and I were alike in many respects; there was an affinity between us.

Claire Louise's character was full of contradictions. She could be very affectionate and loving at times, but on other occasions hard. She was a child of extremes, a very determined little girl whom we could not persuade at any price, then suddenly, inexplicably, she would change her mind. She was frisky, wiry, slim. Claire and Joanne used to fight like cat and dog. Joanne would accuse me of giving in to Claire too easily. Yet if ever Claire was in trouble Joanne would champion her.

They both loved the television and would get engrossed in it as most children do today. Joanne got lost in it, entirely immersed. There could be a third world war with everything in pieces around her, but as long as the TV worked Joanne would not notice. Her mother used to chide her for becoming so engrossed in television; I couldn't say much about it because I was the same. I think I was a bit of a kid myself; I used to enjoy some of the children's programmes such as *The Mister Men*. I still have the sound track of all those adventures even now.

Telling bed-time stories was a real pleasure for me. I made up a lot of my own as well as trotting out the usual standards that have stood the test of time. I made up stories about Andrew and the Pixies to tell Joanne as she lay in bed, and she would stay awake for hours just to listen. I also have all the old well-loved children's songs of our day that I have passed on to Pat's grandchildren. They will always be popular with each generation.

I have some sweet, fond memories of little Joanne and Claire once they both started nursery and school. I composed a religious song about Moses for their school assembly. I think that was the time when I realised I could write songs. I often played the piano for the school.

Because Lin needed a great deal of help my work suffered, partly because I wasn't free much during the day and partly because my nights were so disrupted by the baby that I was permanently tired. There were many difficulties between Lin and myself. Yet I found comfort in my music. In June, in the middle of a heatwave, I plucked up the courage to buy "Trick of the Tale", the latest Genesis disc, although Lin disapproved of my buying, or listening to, music. One evening, at home alone when the children were in bed, I listened to the LP. It blew me away. The words spoke to me:

> *"Sleep won't you allow yourself fall*
> *Nothing can hurt you at all...*
> *With your consent I can experiment*
> *Further still"*

In other words, the music could reach me, take me, guide me, heal me. The words seemed to be saying to me that if I agreed, the Genesis music could do whatever it wanted. I had only to allow it. The music filled me, so haunting, so distant, as if time did not matter.... as if nothing mattered. All my troubles were way down there on earth and I was up in space in another time warp, in a ship far, far away from everything.

I had been introduced to a drug far more powerful than pot or mushrooms. It was the drug of Genesis. Even now I cannot explain their effect on me, their tremendous influence, but just at the right time came the right words, the right sounds, and they transformed my soul like a religious conversion. That drug gnawed at me, ate into my brain, got into my very bones. It slept with me. At night Genesis permeated my dreams; all I wanted to do was to talk about them.

At that time I frequented a record shop called "Scene and Heard". Upstairs was the light stuff; downstairs they stocked the heavy music, including Genesis. The staff came to know me. "Downstairs, sir? Progressive, sir? Genesis downstairs." I needed music as a refuge to survive, to live, to breathe, to be aware. I tried to talk to many people about my feelings, but no one understood how unhappy I was.

Towards the end of 1980 Lin was pregnant again. It was hard work coping with two children. How would we manage with three? I had a sleepless night while Lin was in hospital awaiting the birth. At six o'clock in the morning the telephone rang. I was summoned to the hospital because Lin was in labour. I rang Lin's Mum and Dad, who promised to look after the children and have dinner ready when I returned, and off I went, shattered because I had not slept all night. Later that morning the sister told me it was another girl.

The years of bringing Leanne through babyhood were fraught with so many problems at home that it was difficult to feel I really knew her. I was undergoing so many emotional crises that there was little of myself to spare for this child. My greatest consolation continued to be music and when I couldn't take any more I played a Genesis record. Their songs matched my feelings; their songs were me:

> *"Life is so lonely..*
> *am feeling like I'm locked in a cage...*
> *No way in, no way out."*

But there had to be a way out. At the end of 1982 I heard there might be some work in France. Here was a chance to make a clean break, to have a job, to escape to a new environment. I was willing, even eager to do this, met the French employer in February 1983 and came to an agreement. On March 15th I was due to depart for France, although I knew I would miss my children desperately. This was the heavy price I had to pay. I still have dreams of when they were little even to-day and I know that despite all that went wrong later on that I will always love them. Having to leave them was the greatest wrench of my life.

On the day I left I loaded the suitcase and bags into a car and the wheels turned, taking me away from my old

New Beginnings

life, from wife and home and beloved children. No one will ever know the long years I agonised over what I should do about my future, and how torn in two I was. Despite the pain of it, I would do the same if I were presented with the choice again, for their sake as well as mine. I knew it was the last time I would ever see Lin. It was the end of an episode in my life which was a very big mistake. It took me a long time to realise it, and it was a mess before it was finished. There were mistakes on both sides. We were both culpable, but looking back, I married too young and was flung into a situation which I did not know how to handle.

I stayed with a friend until I was ready to set off for the new job, but by the following Tuesday the deal seemed to have fallen through. Rash promises were not fulfilled; it was obvious I was not going to France. But there was no going back. Lin had always been close to her Mum and Dad. I was confident that she would be happy in our old house with her family and our three lovely children around her. But I was bruised and battered, alone in the world, desperately lonely, longing for someone to care, to show tenderness towards me. Despite all this I knew I had burst out of my cage and would never be imprisoned again.

I met up with Paul and Keith, two old friends, who mentioned a room which was available adjacent to their workshop, which would just suit me. Within a week I moved in. I had my own room in a house shared with two students. But I was nervous, tense in company, became jumpier by the day, and was unable to sleep. My friends noticed it, worried about me, and took the matter into their own hands.

"We know exactly what you need," they said. "We can get you someone, but you'll have to pay. OK?"

As I prepared I was full of trepidation and doubt,

Touch Me Please

with old prejudices nagging at me. Was I doing the right thing to associate with this type of woman? But since I had left home I had been indulging in excesses, overeating, drinking too much, wallowing in music regardless of time, driven on by what I was only partly aware of – a desperate yearning for some peace of mind which, I thought at the time, could only be achieved by a physical release of the tensions inside me.

At last I was ready. It was a stormy day as the four of us set off through a thunder storm, first to The Cobourg for a drink to boost my courage, and then to the Star and Garter where they left me to wait. I was alone, apprehensive, as if I was waiting to see the dentist, like sitting in a queue in the waiting room with muffled conversations of other patients around me. I didn't know what to expect, or what would be expected of me. A few minutes later there was a tap on my shoulder.

"Already?" Like many a patient in the dentist's waiting room, however long the wait, it was too soon when the summons came. An old quotation from a Hancock sketch came to me. When he was called to give blood he asked: "What me? Now? Surely there's someone else before me?"

Brian introduced me to Elaine, the woman who was sitting in the back of the car. Thoughts raced through my mind. What the hell was I doing? What was I getting into? Yet I knew there was no turning back. It was something I needed and wanted at the time.

She was a kind person and treated me well. She made me feel a new man, even if I had to pay for the experience. Elaine did so much for me that I was bursting to express myself in song. I was up all night writing words, the lyrics for a tune which was already shaping itself note by note in my mind. I described the feelings I had earlier that evening as we set out:

New Beginnings

Through lightning, hail and thunder
All the strain that I've been under
My cold emotions shivering in the rain
My life blood pulsing, racing,
Thoughts running, jumping, chasing,
Like a puppy whose young mind is yet untrained.....
Something deep inside
Became impossible to hide
And I knew I'd have to find myself again.

Then I poured out what Elaine had achieved:

You held me oh so tight
Wondrous lady of the night
My whispered thoughts I'd never dared exclaim
Though you'd never know me,
Through your guiding hands you'd show me,
Calm my fears and let my feelings live again.

During the following weeks, buoyed up by the transforming experience with Elaine, I was helped by my friends, Paul and Keith, to sort out my future. I had always had a dream of setting up my own business. The Government Enterprise grant of £40 a week for those embarking on new schemes was heaven sent. With guidance and support from the Department of Industry and a safety net of a regular, if low, weekly income, I could hopefully get myself established and build up enough business to be self-supporting. It had been an unattainable goal to me for many years, but now seemed a distinct possibility. The business was due to be launched in September, and I had some impressive leaflets printed to publicise my work of piano tuning and repairs.

My horizons seemed broader than ever before. For years I had been trapped, suffocated, exploited, unfulfilled, and suddenly everything seemed possible. The hostile world was offering me new life, and the seeds of the Tuneathon germinated in the warm spring of 1983. Someone had been reading the Guinness Book of Records to me. The only piano-tuning record was the quickest ever – only four minutes to tune a piano. I did not think I could beat that. Why not go for quite a different record where I would be the first person to tune pianos over a prolonged period. So the idea was born. Sue Thornton, my business advisor from the Department of Industry, agreed to help me set it up.

In the meantime, I received a sudden surprise invitation from Paul. Would I like to go to Holland for a couple of days to help him take some furniture to Rotterdam? I had ten minutes to pack before we drove to Hull to catch the ferry. When we arrived, Paul went off to sort out his business and I enjoyed a drink in a bar, chatting to people. It was a new, exciting experience to be abroad on my own, and I found the Dutch very amicable. I fell into conversation with a particularly friendly woman who invited me out into the country.

"Do you know what women are like?" she asked me as we strolled in the sunshine. "How do you imagine them?"

"Well," I replied, "I can hear their voices and make judgements from the way they talk to me."

"Yes, but do you feel them?" I was taken aback for no one had ever asked me that before.

"I don't often get the chance," I replied. "You can get arrested in England for that sort of thing."

"Well, here I am."

I was speechless momentarily. Then I was respectful. The penalties for sexual interference in Holland are severe. Besides which, I didn't want her to think I was after one

New Beginnings

thing. So I touched her shoulders, her hands and her arms, and thought to myself, "Very nice."

Then she said, "You haven't touched everything yet." So I touched her dress and her legs, still very respectful.

"There are still things you haven't touched yet," she urged. I was getting worried. I felt I would have to be careful. It was too late. She took my hands and directed them. I was seduced. The rest was wonderful.

I stayed in Holland for three days. I met Rose van Dyke, a Dutch pop star. I sang her my song and she liked it. Then I embarked at Rotterdam to travel home alone, leaving Paul to conclude his business affairs. On the journey I played the piano for members of the crew in the crew bar. When I finished, a tall, slim stewardess wearing a voluptuous scent, asked me if I had a cabin, or whether I needed somewhere to sleep. I was overwhelmed by her consideration and replied that I hadn't booked a berth. She offered to find me one, and soon we were inside the small cabin with two bunks, one up and one down. I was expressing my gratitude when the door was firmly shut and I heard the latch click and the bolt close. My mind flipped. I wondered how far her consideration extended. Was I going to be seduced for a second time? I trembled, wondering what to do, but she had the situation in hand.

"Why don't you get ready now?" she suggested. "We'll only need one bunk, won't we?" she asked, to which I heartily agreed. She was an artist, she was superb, and stayed with me two hours or so. I suppose one of the things that attracted her was my singing and piano-playing.

I went down to breakfast the next morning a new man. The boost to my morale was unbelievable. That someone should want me physically was a new experience. Yet at the back of my mind there was

Touch Me Please

something not quite right, something missing. At that time I didn't know what was wrong, and it seemed to me that a physical relationship was the ultimate.

Meanwhile I got work playing and singing in a couple of pubs and took what tuning jobs I could find. In September the grant for my new business was approved and I was ready to start. The name wasn't difficult to choose. 'Project Genesis' reminded me of that June day in 1976 when I suddenly thought in an entirely different way.

One early June day in 1984 I tuned the piano for a client I had known for a long time. Over the years we had exchanged news. She had heard of my marriage and the birth of my children, and I had followed the birth and development of her family. But she was a reserved person, very proper and unemotional. To my surprise she was much more friendly than usual so I invited her to come and see my new house not far away. She rang me a few days later and we made a date. I was surprised that she had contacted me.

We sat talking and listening to music and found a great sense of companionship. We met again over the next few weeks, trembling on the brink of intimacy. I began to find a new meaning to life. I was beginning to feel the strength of love and the security of kindness around me. What was this new thing? By July I knew I was falling in love. A multitude of questions crowded into my brain. I did not understand how or why this could happen. All my thoughts were turned upside down. All the logic, the signs in the star charts, had pointed to this never happening, yet reason and probability had been totally defied. The rules I had set were completely ignored. My sixth sense, which often warns me of something about to happen, had failed me completely. I was caught unawares. This long-standing customer was of course, Pat, who turned out not to be as cold and reserved as I had thought.

New Beginnings

Meanwhile plans for the tuneathon were going ahead. Suddenly, a week before it was due to take place, I had a call from Jean-Michel Philippe.

"Can you come to France next week, Mike?"

"No, monsieur, I am sorry, I can't. The week after, yes, but I cannot come to France next week. There is something in England I have to do which is very important. I will come to France after that."

PAT: South Pacific

Ever since he was a boy Mick had dreamt of visiting the South Pacific. I used to laugh and say chance would be a fine thing. Supporting a family on a single modest salary had not left much money to spare. Towards the end of the nineties, however, the realisation crept over me like a gentle sunrise that it was, after all, a possibility.

Financially I was much better off, and now that the older children had graduated and fled the nest I was supporting only one son at University. The cost of the air fares were comparable to flights to Australia, and I knew lots of people who went there. We were also computer literate and eager to exploit the comparative ease of communicating by email. Once the tiny thought had embedded itself in my consciousness it began to grow and flourish.

Where should we start? How could we start? I came across The South Pacific Handbook by David Stanley, a wonderfully comprehensive compendium describing all the island groups, how to get there, what to see and where to stay. We enjoyed many months perusing the book and deciding which islands we would visit. Indeed much of the pleasure of the trip was in anticipation. Tahiti sounded wonderful, but much more difficult to reach and more expensive. Eventually we plumped for Samoa, Tonga and Fiji, relatively close to each other but offering enough differences to give us a varied experience.

Our first thought was to travel like our children, without any planning beyond the flight, and to look for accommodation when we got there – geriatric backpackers like the lady we met in Crete. But I freak out at any kind of long-distance travel, and taking a deaf-blind man, who was totally dependent on me, to the other side of the world seemed pretty scary. We compromised by booking some of the hotels in advance and leaving a few gaps so we could be spontaneous for part of the trip. Our one criterion was that we should use locally run accommodation, and not the huge Japanese or American hotel chains which would not give us any idea of how the native people lived. There was also a financial element in this of course, as the local inns and guest houses were cheaper. Our main outlay beyond a doubt was the air fare, followed by the Blue Lagoon cruise in Fiji. The hotels we favoured were fairly inexpensive.

We flew to Samoa in May 1999. On the last legs of the journey the passengers included wonderfully exotically dressed Hawaiians and Tongans, and the Samoan rugby team. The rugby players were celebrating in high spirits and there was no chance of sleeping, but I didn't care, it was so exciting.

As we stepped out of the plane in Upolu and descended the steps we were engulfed by the warm, humid, scent-laden air, heavy with the richness of fruits and lush vegetation. Mick found the smells of the South Pacific delightful throughout the whole of our holiday, and nowhere more so than in Samoa. It was morning and the children were going to school. As we drove into Apia in a taxi I described to Mick the villages we passed with their open fales: raised platforms with palm leaved rooves and wooden pillars instead of walls. Chickens and pot-bellied pigs were running about. I told him of the colourful uniforms the school children were wearing: reds, yellows, blues and brilliant greens. Everywhere I turned the view was bright and luscious. Everyone seemed happy and smiling.

Our first accommodation was at the Harbour Light

Touch Me Please

Hotel on Beach Road, which runs right round the harbour in Apia. We overlooked the water where teams of rowers frequently practised in their long boats – magical in the early morning light or setting sun. This inn was listed in the 'budget accommodation' and I found it did not meet my standards. Mick laughed at me because I was squeamish about the profusion of tiny insects crawling about the floor, and complained on the second day that the one towel provided by the hotel smelt awful because the humidity prevented it ever getting dry. "What do you expect in a tropical climate?" he asked. The hotel staff, however, were warm and friendly and were typical of a pattern of behaviour that Mick came to greatly appreciate. They were eager to touch and to help. They showed a tenderness and concern for disabled people that is totally lacking in the west. On the first morning the waitress was keen to butter his toast for him, so it gave me a break.

Everywhere we went we found kindness. Walking back downhill from Vailima, the house where Robert Louis Stevenson spent the last five years of his life, we found the heat and humidity very enervating. A local resident pulled up to offer a lift. He was driving a Toyota pickup which we noticed was the most popular vehicle in Samoa (they could carry livestock or equipment in the back). We squeezed into the cab gratefully. The driver displayed the friendliness we found everywhere in Polynesia and particularly in Samoa.

Exploring the market we admired the range of fish for sale and the curious vegetables such as tapioca, yams, taro, cassava and breadfruit. Coconuts, papayas and bananas were plentiful, but to Mick's disappointment it was not the mango season. There were various craft goods for sale – carvings, garments and jewellery. Mick bought – and later wore – a lava-lava, or wrap round cloth worn by the Samoan men. He wanted to live like the native people

South Pacific

as far as possible, and found it cooler than his shorts.

We stopped at a stall to sample a local drink, and this was Mick's first taste of kava, made from the root of that plant. It is the South Pacific alternative to alcohol and is popular in social and ceremonial contexts. One official description says "Not only is it a pleasant drink that can be a safe alternative to alcohol, but Kava has been prescribed as an effective folk remedy for anxiety, insomnia and back pain." Taken in large quantities, however, it can lead to temporary paralysis, and we certainly noticed that our tongues became numb. Mick came to like the drink and enjoyed several kava sessions.

On Wednesday evening we went to the Samoan feast at Aggie Grey's Hotel, one of the most famous and iconic hotels in the South Pacific, further along Beach Road a bit nearer the city centre. After the meal we were entertained by some wonderful music and dancing, which Mick unfortunately could not appreciate. We still needed accommodation for a couple of nights, and the temptation of a dry room with air conditioning was too much for me. We booked at Aggie Grey's, in due course enjoying the luxury, and hanging up all our clothes to dry while we went sight-seeing.

On a memorable trip to the Aleipata and Lepa districts on the south east coast of Upolu we admired the beach fales (for rent by backpackers) and swam in the luke warm sea while the guide prepared a barbecue. He was warm and friendly and described for us the agonising practice of tattooing, illustrated by his own densely patterned body which he was happy for Mick to touch. Then we enjoyed a feast of fish and South Sea vegetables. The School children in their brightly coloured uniforms waved as they went past. This paradise was the area sadly devastated ten years later by the earthquake-created tsunami in September 2009. On the way back to Apia we visited an idyllic hotel in the centre of the island where our guide picked a banana for each of us. The South Pacific banana is small and deliciously fruity, unlike the bland variety available in Britain. We could hardly believe it was the same fruit.

Mick was intrigued by the local buses, like large square lorries with no glass in the windows (it is never cold, and would be unbearably hot if enclosed) and a few wooden benches added almost as an afterthought. Doing it the hard way, like the Samoans, we caught one of these buses to Mulifanua to catch the boat to Savai, another Samoan island we wanted to visit. A friendly young Samoan called Oliva helped us onto the boat with our luggage, and assisted us when we disembarked at Salelologa. Oliva was keen to improve his English and invited us to visit his family for a meal during our stay. This was beyond our dreams, to see inside a real Samoan fale.

Savaii was much more traditional and less touched by Western lifestyles than Upolu. Our accommodation at the Safua Hotel was an enclosed fale in the tropical garden. We woke each morning to the sounds of the island: birds cheeping, dogs barking, cockerels crowing and pigs grunting. Mick was able to identify many of these sounds with his implant and found it magical. Warren, a New Zealand geologist appointed as the volcano watcher on Savaii and resident at the Safua, was fascinating to talk to, and a great help during our stay. He organised trips round the island in the hotel minibus. He took us to see the amazing black volcanic lava fields and the blow holes through which the incoming tide spurted into the air. We practised throwing coconut shells onto the spouting water to see how high it would take them.

Warren did what he could to show Mick the beauty of the island. We had a young Samoan boy on the outing,

Samisoni, who was assigned to collect local flowers for Mick to touch and smell. Only the white flowers, like frangipani, have a scent. Anything tactile, like bits of lava, was brought for Mick to feel.

Mick enjoyed and appreciated the attention he received. Everyone wanted to dance with him in the evenings. The hotel barmaid held his hand and stroked it. She laid his hand on the flower in her hair. (Behind one ear it is a sign that a woman is available, behind the other she is spoken for or in a relationship.) Mick loved the affectionate and demonstrative nature of the Samoan people, and they encouraged him to express his own generous and extrovert nature.

The time came for the visit to Oliva's family. A splendid banquet had been prepared by Oliva and his brothers. We were served first, then his parents, and finally, when we had all finished eating, the children themselves ate. This is the tradition in Samoa and we thought it was a great idea! We discovered, to our amazement, that Oliva was the son of the village chief and he would in due course take over that role.

It was enchanting to sit in a traditional fale with this welcoming family, the warm breeze blowing off the sea straight through the building. We could understand why their houses were designed to be open because an enclosed room would be stifling in that climate. As the sun went down and the wind increased Oliva rolled down a kind of tarpaulin on the seaward side. Changes were certainly coming: traditionally it would have been a woven mat rather than a tarpaulin. Moreover, the television was on in the corner and father (the village chief) was watching an Australian soap, although neither he nor his wife spoke English. Mick could not see the surroundings but the food, the smells and the atmosphere were unique. As we left, Oliva's mother gave us a present of a woven sleeping mat which she had made herself, which we managed to bring safely back to England.

We had only three days in Tonga. We left Samoa on Tuesday and after an hour long flight arrived in Tongatapu on Wednesday, crossing the international date line which bent south east round Samoa (this was changed in 2012). We stayed at the Breeze Inn just west of the king's palace in Nuku'alofa, again giving us a view of the harbour. The accommodation was basic, and it was here I had my first (and only) encounter with a cockroach. The landlady was an expatriate Japanese woman who was very self-contained. Mick, with his strong psychic sense, believed she had in the past suffered a great deal, but clearly did not want to talk about it.

We took a taxi trip round the island, visiting the lava blow holes on the south coast, viewing the giant fruit bats hanging from the trees, and then swimming from the Kolovai Beach at the western end of the island. We enjoyed traditional dancing and more feasting. It is traditional in Polynesia to cook food in an underground oven called a lovo or umu. A fire is set in a pit, then coral stones are heated in it. Food wrapped in banana leaves is placed on the hot stones. Fish and meat are set down first, then vegetables on top. Everything is then covered and left to cook slowly for several hours. We enjoyed a number of these delicious feasts in all three islands.

Then Mick succumbed to a South Sea bug. The landlady organised a taxi to get us to her doctor, who was German and very kind. Mick's temperature was 104, so he was prescribed antibiotics and was obliged to stay in bed the next day. I am ashamed to say I left him at the hotel and went sightseeing on my own. I knew I wouldn't be visiting Tonga again.

Amazingly, Mick was well enough to travel to the airport the following morning and we flew to Viti Levu, the main island of Fiji. The Suva Motor Inn was modest, but very comfortable with an open air dining area and a small pool. It was certainly not basic 'budget accommodation'. Suva is the only place in Fiji where the buildings are taller than the palm trees and it offers an architectural mix of traditional and modern buildings. We were intrigued by the large harbour and the solid white stone government buildings which looked so like fifties Britain. The south west peninsula is warm and wet and we enjoyed a walk in the tropical rainforest a short taxi ride away. The damp foliage was almost intoxicating and we heard the calls of numerous birds as we pushed our way through narrow tracks and dense vegetation. We were caught in a downpour and got soaked but didn't feel chilly at all. The rain stopped as we emerged from the rainforest and we steamed dry while we waited for our returning taxi. Luckily the driver came as promised to take us from this remote spot back to the city.

We arranged to take a river cruise from Navua, which proved to be a bit different from our expectations. I imagined joining other tourists on a coach, but our personal guide turned up at the hotel with a taxi and escorted us on the two-hour ride to the river wharf. We felt rather uncomfortable having undivided attention. We boarded a shallow punt with an outboard motor. The hull barely cleared the stony river bed as the motor propelled us over the rapids upriver. We travelled through a deep canyon with tumbling waterfalls on either side. Mick loved the undulations of the boat and the spray as we tossed and bounced on the river. When the water became too shallow for navigation we disembarked and walked up the hill to Namuamua for a tour of the village, a splendid banquet, a dancing display and sale of local crafts. I loved the dancing, until they urged us – or rather compelled us – to show them how WE danced. We then had a huge array of hand-made goods thrust upon us and felt obliged to buy as much as we could afford. It was a fascinating day, but our hosts lacked the genuine warmth, the unassuming nature and spontaneity of the unspoilt Samoan folk. Who can blame them for extracting what they could from (relatively) rich tourists?

We chose to get to Levuka on the small island of Ovalau by local ferry bus up the east coast of Viti Levu (we have never been so crushed and uncomfortable in our lives) and then by the regular Patterson ferry. At tea time, exhausted and hungry we reached Levuka, the former capital of Fiji and once a significant whaling and trading centre. The quaint main street stretching along the water's edge looked like a set from a Western movie, with its saloon type buildings and covered sidewalks. Indeed its history includes lawlessness just as did the American West, resulting in an invitation from the local chiefs to the British in 1874 to take over control of the islands and clean them up.

We rather fancied an organised walking trip to Lovoni, a traditional village in the centre of the island but when we enquired the booking agent said it would be too difficult for Mick. However, they offered to take us there by Land Rover so that we could join the walking party for the traditional feast. On our arrival in Lovoni, the village tour manager ushered us into the Fijian equivalent of the Gentlemen's Club where the chief and menfolk had gathered for a kava ceremony. Mick was invited to join them sitting cross-legged on the floor and for the next two hours or so he enjoyed the kava and the company of these friendly villagers. The cup was offered first to the chief, then refilled and handed to Mick, and then to everyone else in turn. They repeated the process again and again. When the cup bearer offered the cup, the drinker clapped once, took the cup in both hands, said "mbula", drank the

South Pacific

whole contents, handed the cup back and clapped three times. Mick's speciality was a satisfied 'aahh' after drinking. Every time he took the cup the men waited for the 'aahh' then smiled and clapped. Mick could always be relied upon to make friends and fit in with any company.

Meanwhile I declined the offer of a drink, acutely aware that this assembly was for men only, trying to look inconspicuous and doing my best to keep my knee length wrap-round skirt over my knees. It is considered indecent to show any legs in Fiji, thanks to the influence of the missionaries. I would have loved to take a photo of the event, but felt instinctively that this would be inappropriate and a violation of their hospitality and courtesy. We were privileged indeed to be part of it. Eventually the walking party arrived and we joined them for a magnificent feast. Some of the walkers confirmed that it had been a hard trek and Mick would never have made it. (Nor would I probably.)

Was that the highlight of our visit, or was it the journey back to Viti Levu? The guide book suggested travelling with Patterson north bound and Emosi southbound saying "It's a beautiful circle trip not to be missed". The Emosi Express was a very small craft – just a large dinghy really – with two powerful Yamaha engines. While we were staying in Levuka we heard of a boat capsizing and its passengers lost in the turbulent seas arising from the sudden gales that had sprung up. Local people warned us about travelling by the Emosi Express and I did try to book air flights instead but they were full. Either we could delay our journey and travel on the big ferry, or risk the little boat and keep to our planned itinerary. With grave misgivings I gave in to Mick's wishes and we sailed as planned.

I dare say there have been rougher seas, but I believed my end had come. I thought of the children

Touch Me Please

learning of their mother and step father perishing in the South Pacific ocean. Never had my family seemed so dear to me. The skilled sailors turned the flimsy boat into the waves as they towered above us and rushed towards us and then we were lifted high, so high only to drop and hit the water with a force that knocked the breath from our lungs. We were lifted from our simple wooden seats and hurtled down onto them after the boat hit the water. "Don't worry," Mick assured me, "I'm a life saver. If the boat goes down no harm will come to you." That is all very well I thought, but if I don't cling on to Mick he will neither see me nor hear my screams. I worried that if we were indeed capsized Mick's implant would be completely destroyed by the water. His complete lack of fear in a variety of situations has always amazed me.

Gradually, hopping from island to island we moved nearer to Suva. I was tense and tired with gripping the seat hard; Mick was exultant and enjoying every toss and every roll, laughing at the thrill of it. We hadn't much further to go when a particularly large wave tossed us very high and we came crashing down once again onto the seat, only this time Mick's weight and the force of his fall proved too much and the seat broke from the side of the boat, tumbling us onto the floor. This caused great hilarity and even I had to laugh, forgetting my anxiety. We spent the rest of the journey partly huddled on the floor, or clinging to and sliding down a sloping bench. At last we reached dry land. My legs were weak and trembling, but Mick had relished every minute. "I wouldn't have missed that for the world," he said. Later we heard that all the tourists missing from the capsized boat had been found on nearby islands. That's the beauty of Polynesia: lots of little islands to swim to if necessary. But I was so grateful I didn't have to do it.

Moving on to Laukota in the northwest of the island,

we found the climate was hot and dry, a complete contrast to the area around Suva. We were amazed that most of the population here were of Indian origin, transported by the British to tend the sugar cane. We saw the first cane harvests travelling by train to the factories. At present about half the population of Fiji is Indian and half Melanesian. This has led to some tensions between the ethnic Fijians and Indian Fijians and we were saddened to hear of the coup almost exactly one year after our visit when Prime Minister Mahendra Chaudry was removed from office by hard-line Fijian nationalists. The problems continue with further coups in 2006 and 2009.

We had a restful time at Laukota, waiting for our cruise which we hoped would be a splendid culmination to our holiday. We spent a whole day lazing on a beach. When a passing Fijian asked if we would like a fresh coconut we readily agreed. He shinned up the nearby tree, cut a large fruit and descended with it. Holding it in one hand he swung his knife with the other and chopped the top clean off. Never has coconut milk tasted so fresh and so good. A long journey across half the world to the supermarket does nothing for the flavour.

The Blue Lagoon cruises sail to the Yasawa Islands off the north west coast of Viti Levu. Here Jean Simmons filmed *The Blue Lagoon* in 1949; hence the name of the cruise company. The enterprise is run by and for the local community and all profits support schools and other village needs in an economy which struggles to be self-sufficient.

We checked into the terminal and the officials called passengers to board the coach. We seemed to be ignored which surprised me, because disabled passengers are usually called first. Then to our amazement we were ushered to a limousine and driven to the wharf. This was the start of our pampered treatment for three days. The crew could not have been kinder. Mick was invited into the wheel room and shown all the instruments; and someone was always on hand to help him about the deck, or up the stairs, or into a landing craft. They were always willing to answer questions or show him what he was interested in. As with any cruise, the food also contributed to our pleasure.

We sailed about four hours a day, anchoring for swimming or snorkelling, or for trips to local villages and craft sales, for Fijian dancing or barbecues on the beach. There were about thirty passengers altogether and we found other people, particularly the Kiwis, were keen to talk to us and to share experiences and friendship with Mick.

One day we went out in the small boat to feed the fish. As the crew threw crumbs into the water we could see the shoal just below the surface, so densely packed that Mick could put his hand into the water and feel them brushing by. Add to all this the warm sun, the turquoise waters, white sand and gently waving palm trees and you begin to imagine the paradise that we enjoyed.

On our final night, having eaten our barbecue on the golden sands, we all had to perform something from our national heritage at the farewell concert. Mick and I gave a lusty rendition of Ilkley Moor Baht 'At. It had been a perfect cruise. We had received such consideration and love, from both crew and fellow passengers, that I was unable to speak as we disembarked in Lautoka. I knew I was too emotional to trust myself.

It was a long, weary journey homeward without the anticipation and excitement we experienced on the outward flight. I was mainly relieved that we were going home. I had felt a long way from those I loved, very responsible for Mick and rather vulnerable. Most of the time I had been anxious and suffered from tummy upsets.

I had wondered what pleasure Mick would gain from a South Pacific holiday. I realised as we returned that even without sight and with minimal hearing it had been immensely worthwhile. It is a place predominantly of scents and atmosphere, which Mick absorbed with delight; he appreciated the different food and drink; he would always remember the warmth and affection of the people. Nowhere else could his remaining senses be so stimulated and overwhelmed.

MICK: Tuneathon

It was a cool October day in 1984. I was sitting on a chair in the middle of the busy concourse of Seacroft Shopping Centre in Leeds. It seemed that hundreds of shoppers were milling around that Thursday morning. I could hear some of them hurrying past; others stopped to read or comment on the large printed posters placed strategically around my little enclave:

> MICK GERWAT'S TUNEATHON
> Mick Gerwat has been blind from birth.
> He gained honours in his piano-tuning
> qualifications and has since worked for
> Siouxie & the Banshees, Rod Stewart,
> Sid Lawrence, Rick Wakeman, Peter Katin,
> Victor Sylvester, Paul McCartney
> and Elton John – to name but a few.
> MICK WILL KEEP GOING FOR 72 HOURS

Here I was about to embark on three days and nights of piano tuning, and hopefully fulfil the boast on the posters. I wanted to become a record holder, not in a marathon or a vast sporting event with which we usually associate record holders, but the first person in the world, the first person so far, to achieve this goal of tuning pianos for 3 days. On that day in October 1984 I felt that this particular event would be significant to me, a milestone on my journey.

For days I had been nervous, tense, the hours dragging by. I had endured sleepless nights, although I knew I really needed sleep if I was to stand a chance of completing my self-imposed marathon. All sponsorship money and collections in the Seacroft Centre were for the Physically Handicapped and Able Bodied (PHAB), an organisation which seeks to normalise life as far as possible for paraplegics and other wheelchair people, and enable them to get out socially. I was sitting at the table where the time chart and records would be maintained. Each adjudicator would sign and verify what I had been doing, that I had, in fact, kept working during that stint.

Four pianos were awaiting my tools, my hands and my ears. As each was finished it would be 'untuned' by the adjudicator ready for my next circuit. Sue had organised an elaborate and impressive rota of adjudicators, some of them my dear friends. There were strict rules laid down by the Guinness Book of Records. Although I had to keep going without proper rest I was allowed five minutes' break every hour for food and other obvious physical demands.

On a large display board beside the posters were the words

MICK HAS NOW BEEN TUNING FOR ___ HOURS

As the days wore on the appropriate number, 1 – 72, from the pile on the table would be inserted into the space in chronological order.

It was now five minutes to eleven. Sue led me to my first piano. I was gripped by a sudden fear and doubt. Did I really expect to make it? I took the tools out of my bag and prepared to operate. An interviewer from local radio approached me, asking how long I intended to keep going. His questions floated over me, past me, for I was too preoccupied, wondering, even as I assured him of my success, whether it was an idle boast. Only a few seconds now remained. My talking clock, which I treasured a great

Touch Me Please

deal - it was bought for me by the BBC - pipped out three pips with a long one on three. Eleven a.m. on October 4th. Tools up and I was away!

It felt just like an ordinary job, tuning any piano. I had worked in the piano tuning business for fifteen years. It seemed a long time. As I worked I had so many things to think about. I knew that a week from today I would not be in England but in France. What future did I have after that? Thoughts mingled and raced through my mind as I started on the first of my four pianos, which were to become my companions, my soulmates, my blessings, my curses, over the next three days.

The first few hours seemed just like a normal tuning, except that people stopped to ask questions, wanting to know what was happening. Initially we also had some trouble with youngsters of around fourteen or fifteen banging on the pianos: a huge joke to them, but distracting for me. Eventually someone dealt with them, and for the time being, all was quiet. How boring it must have been for the public: ping, ping, ping... on and on through the afternoon; ping, ping, ping, on and on through the evening. Just a normal day's work, I thought. There are no problems here! During my five minute breaks I was even willing to read palms of shoppers and passers-by.

Then we moved into the first night. After nine o'clock in the evening I had to do some urgent repairs on one of the pianos. All was still in the deserted centre. A cold wind was wafting through the empty concourse. It seemed to me one of the coldest nights of the autumn so far. A couple of fan heaters were brought in, but they didn't produce much warmth in the centre of a vast, empty, draughty space in the cold night. I was particularly annoyed with the piano I was repairing. It was proving difficult, but I didn't feel tired, just excited. As time wore on, however, I began to feel more acutely the strangeness

Tuneathon

of working in and walking about the empty shopping centre during the night. All the shops were closed. There was only one person with me. We two were alone in the huge, deserted complex. It was silent, eerie, haunting, strange. At four in the morning we stopped for a cup of tea. The hot liquid warmed and strengthened me. I had now been tuning about sixteen hours.

Suddenly it was half past six. Our radio interviewer wanted to speak to me again. He was waiting on the end of the phone for a live broadcast. "Mr Gerwat, did you enjoy your first night at the Seacroft Centre? Are you feeling tired?" I answered enthusiastically, thinking of the handful of listeners at that early hour, and the warm beds of most sensible people. Then it was back to the pianos and the tuning. I was hungry, although I was being well looked after. During the first day plenty of food had been brought in for me. I could ask for what wanted. I felt like a king. It was like having a string of servants. I could snap my fingers and they would come to my command. Do this, do that! This was a total reversal of anything that had happened to me before, and wakened within me latent tendencies towards megalomania! Why not make the most of it?

Nine o'clock. Just time for a quick wash. Up the stairs at the baker's shop, a squirt with the deodorant and back to the pianos. The first sprinklings of shoppers disturbed the long silence of my vigil. By ten o'clock on Friday morning it was as busy as a shopping precinct should be, with noise on every side. A particularly noisy commotion indicated the approach of something special and I learned to my astonishment that it was Yorkshire Television. The interviewer held his microphone up to my face as I pinged at the piano. Was I enjoying it? How was I managing? Was I finding it tiring? He posed the usual questions, which I was finding increasingly easy to

Touch Me Please

answer. Then he asked about my music, and I admitted that I wrote songs. "Can you sing us one of your songs now?" I willingly agreed, put the finishing touches to the last few strings and played my song Elaine for television. The presence of the TV cameras – surely not my singing – had drawn a large crowd of spectators round our working space. Then the music died, the TV crew melted away into the background. The crowd dispersed. I worked on. I still had all Friday and Saturday and half of Sunday to go.

During my five minutes' tea break I tried to relax completely. I had been working for more than 24 hours. I needed rest, solace, comfort. Some illusions were beginning to attack me, unusual, unnatural thoughts preyed on me. Tiredness plays strange tricks with the mind. But I had set myself this task and I would complete it. Sleep was calling me, if only faintly....

It was midday and my adjudicator changed again. There was a steady flow of interested spectators after the television episode. They bombarded me with questions, asking me if I could play or sing their favourite tunes. Would I read their palms? The exhilaration which I had felt earlier seemed to have seeped out of me, leaving me tired and a little depressed. By three o'clock sleep wasn't calling gently anymore; it was pulling at me, dragging at me like some irresistible force from which there was no escape, a force which I had to grapple with and conquer. It was pulling at my muscles. My arms and back were beginning to ache. My finger ends were sore with constantly touching and tuning. My adjudicators caringly rubbed them with surgical spirit to toughen the skin. Each time I picked up or grasped the lever my hand protested, the muscles crying out with too frequent use. I did not want any food, I just wanted to sleep. I knew I would have to fight sleep all the way from now on. My unyielding adversary, far stronger than I was, kept up his ceaseless

Tuneathon

and merciless attack for the rest of the tuneathon. I knew his victory was inevitable, but could I hold out against his onslaught until eleven o'clock on Sunday morning? Should I give up now and go home? But immediately a little voice inside me revolted against the idea. Far too many people had done so much for me. Both for myself and everyone else around me I must continue.

I felt strange and lonely, although there were hundreds of people pestering me. I felt an upsurge of resentment and longed to escape. I experienced an overwhelming desire to cry and be comforted by my lady adjudicator who was kind, considerate, gentle. Comfort I needed, of any sort, from anyone. Minutes passed, hours passed. Ten o'clock, eleven o'clock. Tears were running from my eyes, not just from crying, but from sheer exhaustion. I had now been working for 36 long hours. It had seemed an eternity and still I had as much again to complete. Why can't I just sleep, I thought. But once again the thought of how hard my friends had worked to make the tuneathon possible drove me on. Naturally it would be a painful struggle. Otherwise anyone could achieve it.

At three o'clock on Saturday morning John Cook arrived, another dear friend, the man who promoted my business right from the start, who piloted it through all the difficult meetings, and took the plan through. Strength flowed into me. With him there to support me, I could go on, but I was beginning to feel weak. Dizziness and nausea swept over me in waves and I had to struggle to keep control and prevent myself from nodding off. I was feeling really odd, as if I would fall on the floor if I touched another piano. I worked on, stumbling, fumbling. Accuracy didn't matter too much, as I kept to the older pianos. I had tuned the other two nicely, and left them in perfect condition. There was a peculiar humming in my ears; I was barely able to absorb the notes I was pinging. I

Touch Me Please

seriously wondered if my hearing would be affected for life. When I finished this would I ever tune another piano again? Would I ever be able to work again? These thoughts grew into great worries. I took a brief walk outside, stepping weakly, gingerly, drinking in the fresh night air. All the while John, who had brought his son with him, amused me with stories of the days when he was a runner in the Olympic team, and about some of the women he had encountered. They talked on, as I tried hard to listen and to comprehend their conversation.

At six o'clock the cleaners began to arrive to wash the floors and tidy up the shopping centre. I listened to their complaints of being tired. At least they had had some sleep. If they were tired, what must I be? How did I feel? Tired? Utterly dejected, absolutely all in, but still determined. I would not admit to anyone how I was feeling, and had to control my emotions lest I became morbid or depressed. John took me out to the car park for a breath of fresh air. The cool breeze fanned my face, soothing and healing. I was further cheered when one of the bakery employees brought me a cup of tea. How thoughtful everyone was!

Physically I was really suffering: I had pain in my eyes and ears, my head ached and things swirled around me. Every minute seemed an hour, every second a minute. I could scarcely move my limbs, and found it difficult to grasp the lever in my weakened hand. Each time I clenched my muscles they screeched with pain. My back nagged uncomfortably and my finger ends were increasingly sore. Worst of all was trying to keep awake. Time passed unbelievably slowly. When I asked the time I could not understand why so few minutes had crept by.

When Sue arrived that morning to monitor progress I didn't know how I could go on. "Come on, you can do it," she urged me. We asked John if he could suggest

Tuneathon

anything to help me. As an athlete he would understand the feelings of a body when it is drained, no longer propelled by its own mind, lacking in character, when every reserve is being sucked from you as a leech sucks blood from your veins. My final reserves were being sucked away. People were a nuisance, their questions irritating. At ten o'clock I was given a cup of coffee with two Pro Plus tablets. Oh heaven, something to give me a little energy, to help me survive.

Then Brian arrived, bringing me some moon boots and a space blanket in case I was cold at night. "These will be more comfortable than the shoes you're wearing," he advised. I thanked him with tears in my eyes. We reached eleven o'clock. In 24 hours I would be finished. It was very busy now at the shopping centre. Lots of shoppers were milling around, coming and going. Some youngsters touched the pianos, banging discordantly on the keys. "Leave the piano alone," I begged, "I can't stand the noise!" My ears whistled. My emotions were letting me down. I cried at the stupidest things, feeling such a fool, such a child. I was offered some food at lunchtime but couldn't eat anything. Paul and Keith were on the rota again. They were enough to cheer anyone up, bouncing around the centre with their collection boxes. "Come on, dig deep. Let's have your money." They were doing a wonderful job shaking the boxes. Paul was my guardian, my protector. "No, he can't read your palm. He's too tired."

"Yes, but you said he could read palms."

"Look, he's been tuning pianos for two days. He's very tired. Leave him alone. He's got to work until tomorrow morning."

At three o'clock I called to Paul, "I'm going to faint, I know I am, and I don't know what will happen when I do."

Touch Me Please

"Come on," he said, "I'm going to take you outside. You can take an extra break and make it up later. I'm taking you out to my car and putting you in the back. Then you can sleep for ten minutes. I put my head back against the seat, my moon boots keeping my feet warm and comfortable. Sheer heaven, sheer bliss.

Suddenly Paul was calling, "Come on Mick." His voice seemed far away. "Time to wake up, time to get back to the pianos." I dragged my weary body, which refused to acknowledge consciousness for some time, slowly to its feet. Now I knew how people must feel on endurance tests, or climbing Everest, or how men felt when they were cut off and lost during the war. I sympathised with their aching bodies and longed just to lie down, give up. We walked back into the centre towards the pianos. I went dizzy. "I know I'm going to faint."

Everything blurred in my mind; my hands dropped to my knees. I knew nothing, I sensed nothing. Miraculously from the unconscious areas of my mind I had a sensation of something I could not describe. My nose picked up a feminine perfume. Suddenly a burst of adrenalin coursed through me. I began to lift my head and found Helen on one side and Hilary on the other. "Come on," they rebuked me, "why are you putting us through this?" implying it was all fun and games for me. Geoff took me over to the piano and put my hands on the keys. "Let's have a song, Mick. Play a song."

My mind sang the first few bars of "I made it through the rain", but my fingers wouldn't play. My mind knew I should play the notes, but my fingers didn't respond. I couldn't make my fingers play. Suddenly I heard a tiny, feeble tinkle – a B flat. Then the A followed. I started to play and my friends clapped. "We've passed the danger point," said Geoff. "He can keep going now." As the song died away, Helen and Hilary applauded and

Tuneathon

pampered me. Next week I would be in France far away from my friends and those I loved. I would be working in a foreign country with strangers for two or three weeks a month, and making the journey across the Channel regularly. Hopefully my financial worries would be at an end. My whole future lay open, full of opportunity, but uncertain, insecure.

At half past five the gates opened to admit dear Isobel who brought me a full dinner. Painfully I lifted the knife and fork and ate. It gave me new energy, new purpose, gave me a second wind. Geoff urged me on. "Mind you," he said, "Helen says I'm too hard on you. She says I'll let you die before I'll let you give up! I would too," he laughed, "and I wouldn't pay for the funeral either!"

I worked on, trembling, jumping at every sound. I felt as if I wanted to die. I'd never felt so bad in my life before. "Why can't I just go to sleep?" I begged. "If I give up now I've still got a record." But my friends said no, that I had vowed to continue until Sunday. My will power was no longer sufficient to propel me towards the goal. For the rest of my endurance I was encouraged, driven, goaded by my supporters. I was incapable of self-determination, and they kept me going out of love, although at the time it seemed heartless. Every note made me jump. I still kept to the old pianos. In the past I had said I would do things which I didn't carry out either because I was too scared or too shy, but now I would show the entire world, even those who had hindered or hurt me in the past, that I could achieve something when I put my mind to it.

By nine o'clock I was beginning to feel sleepy again, and the second wind which had revived me earlier in the evening was dying away. I pinged slowly on the pianos. Oh my hands, my aching hands, wanted to stop. I could hardly carry on. I couldn't stand any more. I felt I had to give up, but still a tiny spark inside me burned, urging me

Touch Me Please

on. My mind groped weakly, wearily, with difficulty separating reality from illusion. Colourful memories of the past engulfed me – grass, trees, summer days – I was drifting gently, so sweetly, into a painless, effortless land of dreams.

"Come on, someone talk to Michael." A voice shattered my reverie. Geoff started to talk to me on all sorts of subjects: women, music, anything that would keep me awake. He recounted some of his old childhood stories. The others talked, joked, and sang with me to keep me awake. Someone called for a song. I tried to play but I didn't want to. "I can't do anything," I said feebly. I rested my head on my arms and started to drift off. Someone shook my chin.

"Come on, wake up. You are not going to give up now after you have come so far. We are not going to let you. We'll keep you awake if we have to shout at you all night. Come on, play us a tune." It was midnight. An old, familiar piano piece from way back came into my mind: Beethoven's Moonlight Sonata. I learnt this when I was about fourteen or fifteen. I began to play hesitantly, but gathering strength.

I heard Geoff's footsteps as the last notes of the sonata faded and he whispered, "There's a surprise for you." Suddenly I felt an arm around me. I couldn't believe who it was – the one person I most wanted to see. I must be dreaming. "I want to go home," I told her. "Why don't you just take me away?" My hands rested on hers. I wanted to snuggle against her and sleep.

She shook me gently. "Keep going Mick. You are nearly there. How about some soup?" Dear Isobel had made me a delicious vegetable soup. "That will keep you warm later on," she had said. Now the hot soup was poured from the flask. I didn't have the strength to eat it. Like a baby that has just woken out of its sleep I allowed myself to be spoon fed. I hardly had the strength to open my mouth to eat. She held the spoon to my lips patiently until I could sip from it. Spoon by spoon the rich energy-giving soup was consumed. Energy! I was going to find it difficult to summon up enough of that. I still had another eleven hours to go. Then she was gone and the cold, empty night stretched before me. Those hours seemed the longest of the tuneathon.

Jim checked my fingers and rubbed them with some more surgical spirit. I struggled on with the piano until suddenly Sue and her daughter Zoe appeared. "What are you doing here at this time?" I asked them. "We were sitting at home worrying about you, so we thought we would come and see how you are." Tears came to my eyes. I was crying about the least little thing, and their concern moved me. They chatted for a while to raise my spirits and then went home.

Mother Hen Jim was looking after me through the night, caring for me like his little chick. "I've decided," he announced solemnly, "that you need an hour's sleep whether the rules say so or not!"

"I don't think I'd better," I said, "I'd better keep to the work."

"You look to me as if you need it. Let me look back at your breaks and see when you took them." He examined the book meticulously. "Oh yes, there are a few extra breaks, I'm going to let you lie down, if only for twenty minutes or half an hour." He put me down on the mattress and I drifted off to sleep. Suddenly I was woken. Mike Kelly, the Chairman of PHAB, roused me from my weariness speaking to me breezily: "I've just been to the Lord Mayor's reception, and there's a lot of money riding on you, old boy." He had obviously had a few pints and was merry and jovial, whereas I was just the opposite. The last thing I wanted to do was exchange pleasantries.

Touch Me Please

Someone being jolly and joyful at two o'clock in the morning when you are struggling through your third night without sleep is not really welcome.

"Come on, Mick. Let's walk around the Seacroft centre," he said. We started off at a cracking pace. I wished I had had a pair of skates so that he could just pull me along without me having to make my legs move. Then it would require no effort on my part. I had reached a point where I was beyond tiredness. My body was like lead, just mechanically carrying out what it had been programmed to do for three days: tuning, working, tuning, working. My brain was somewhere else. I listened to endless waffle from Mike about this and that; all of it passed through my head without me understanding much about it. At last he was off. "See you in the morning for the finish," he promised exuberantly. "Don't let me down, will you?"

Then Jim told me there might be someone special coming to see me later. I couldn't have cared if the Queen had arrived! "Come on," Jim said, "twenty minutes sleep." I lay on the mattress once more, again my rest was brief and Jim awoke me. "Here's the Sergeant-at-arms come to see you." An emissary from the Lord Mayor of Leeds. I managed a feeble "Hello." He had been to the Lord Mayor's reception and was drunk, as Mike had been. His speech was barely intelligible. I was too tired to appreciate dignitary waffle in the small hours of Sunday morning but I tried to tolerate him. I wondered what I was in for when he told me in a slurred voice that the deputy Lord Mayor was coming to see me. I dreaded the mere thought. I was to be presented with a tie! I suppose I must have seemed unreasonable and antisocial as I failed to respond enthusiastically to his affability, but I had been awake for three days and things were beginning to mean nothing to me. I needed all my presence of mind, all my instinctive responses, all my reserves, to keep me awake, just to keep

Tuneathon

my attention fixed on that goal of eleven o'clock later that morning.

At six o'clock Jim went off duty and a young Buddy Holly fan took over. Suddenly there was a piercing screaming noise outside. A security alarm had gone off in the Seacroft centre. It went on and on, penetrating my brain. Couldn't someone come and turn it off? It was beginning to undermine me. That was the last thing I could cope with at this time of the morning exhausted as I was. It cut through my mind like a knife, on and on, ten minutes, quarter of an hour, twenty minutes, half an hour. "Can't they turn it off for pity's sake, can't they turn it off!" I moaned, my head feeling as if it would explode, my nerves in shreds. I felt as if I would go mad. At last... silence.

Seven o'clock. Only four hours remained. My arms and legs had gone beyond the barrier of tiredness. If I fell off a cliff or out of the window or fell off the stool it wouldn't matter. Nothing seemed to matter anymore, not even my future, or the fact that in forty-eight hours I would be setting off across the sea for France on one of the strangest experiences of my life.

At nine o'clock Sue arrived. She drove me hard keeping to the rules firmly as all the adjudicators had done. "Come along," she said, "keep going." I pinged along slowly. I was finding it an effort to press the keys. I never thought a piano key could be so hard to press. I moved my lever up and down the pins. My ear had gone. I couldn't hear what I was doing. I had to stick to the older pianos. I just kept tuning for the record. It was almost ten o'clock when I called out, "I feel sick!"

Sue walked me up and down the car park. "For God's sake," she said, "if you are going to be sick, be sick." Waves of nausea washed over me and died again.

"I'm okay now," I told her.

Touch Me Please

"Well tell me if you are going to be sick and we can take you outside."

Now my friends and supporters were beginning to turn up to see me finish. At twenty minutes to eleven the dignitaries began to arrive. The deputy Lord Mayor of Leeds and his wife came along to help me to celebrate my new record. I was gratified by this attention, but part of me felt resentful. I had been up working for so long, but they expected me to be chatty, responsive, dynamic. Moreover they took the centre of the stage, when my friends who had supported me so loyally had to retire to the background. The deputy Lord Mayor had brought some champagne. I did not think it would suit me, constitutionally weakened as I was, but I knew refusing it would look unsociable and discourteous.

"Its five to eleven," Sue told me. "Have you got your talking clock?" When that clock pipped I knew it would be the end, it would be finished. Strangely I felt a new burst of energy in those last few minutes, then a wave of nausea came over me. "I feel sick," I appealed urgently to Sue.

"Don't be sick now," she commanded. "You can't be sick now. You are nearly finished, and everyone is waiting here." I fought off the sickness. Only two minutes remained. I didn't care where I tuned now. I tuned any note, pressed any key just for the last two minutes. As we entered the last minute everyone started counting down. My clock had the seconds digitally displayed. Thirty, twenty nine, twenty eight, and so on. The sense of achievement of what I had done began to grip me. At the same time a feeling of anti-climax pervaded the Seacroft centre. Nineteen, eighteen, seventeen, ... now that it was all finished how long would people remember my name? Twelve, eleven, ten,.... counting down as if we all were taking off into space. Five, four, three, two, one... The pips of my clock sounded with them. The last long tone

Tuneathon

sounded right on eleven o'clock. I put my lever down. There was clapping all around.

"Mick," someone suggested, "why don't you give us your own song?" Elaine? Elaine now? At this time as if I hadn't had enough? As if they wanted me to go on. Didn't they want me to go home then? I put my hands on the keys. I felt I could play it now. No problem. I seemed to have new strength now that I knew I had finished.

"Do you want to go on for another twelve hours?" some joker asked. I started to play my song. My loyal friends who were with me through the hard times were there as I played. Then it was time for the formal celebrations. I was presented with a tie bearing the coat of arms of the City of Leeds, a congratulatory scroll from the city. The deputy Lord Mayor praised me on reaching the goal I had set myself. Next we drank champagne and photographs were taken of me holding the scroll and the tie victoriously flanked by the deputy Lord Mayor and his wife.

"I would like my palm read," the deputy Lord Mayor asked me authoritatively. I submitted reluctantly, much too tired to concentrate on the task, and longing to go home and rest. At last we were ready to go, I was free to leave my prison after 72 hours. Sue took me to the car. We had one last job before I could sink into my longed-for rest. Radio Leeds was waiting to interview me.

"You sound annoyed about something," I said to Sue.

"I damn well am," she replied. "You have been working for seventy-two hours and that man has the cheek to ask you to read his palm." She too resented the prominence of the officials at the tuneathon at the expense of my friends who had staffed, organised and supported me, fed me, talked, joked, laughed and provoked to keep me awake.

Touch Me Please

Tragically that achievement, which cost so much pain and anguish, was never officially recognised or recorded. Although it did not occur to me at the time, perhaps it was symbolic that we sipped champagne from plastic cups rather than glasses, an indication that the whole venture had a tawdry ending. I was not aware on that October day of the disappointment I was to suffer, that the whole purpose of the tuneathon would be lost, and that I would be left disillusioned, cynical and bitter as a result. Sue, who had worked so hard throughout to organise everything, disappeared to take another job. I tried to contact her on several occasions. When I finally tracked her down, she assured me she had sent all the information to the Guinness Book of Records. I checked this with the Guinness organisation and found they had received nothing. As Sue was the only one who possessed evidence of what I had done, the whole Tuneathon turned out to be for nothing.

What evidence is there that the event ever took place? Even the scroll which was presented to me disappeared. The last I heard of it was that it had gone to be framed at the East Leeds Women's Workshop. Attempts to try and contact this organisation proved impossible, since they will not talk to men. I never received any promised copies of the photographs with the Lord Mayor and other dignitaries. For all my troubles I am left with just three flimsy pieces of evidence: my Leeds City Council tie which in itself makes no reference to the tuneathon at all; a few old copies of the posters put up round the exhibition, which do not indicate that I completed the 72 hours; and tape recordings of my interviews with Radio Aire and Radio Leeds, which provide the only shred of proof that I achieved my goal.

It seems ironic that PHAB, the organisation for which I was raising money, could not be bothered even to collect the money from various shops in which I personally had put posters. So far as I know the money could still be there to this day.

The posters, as well as carrying information about the Tuneathon, and recording the passing of the hours, included a vast panoply of advertising about benefits and grants available from Leeds Industrial Estates. I was quite happy for this to happen since I felt it helped both causes. In the end the only cause it helped was the Industrial Estates. The publicity did not bring in work as expected. Nor did any of the promises from our eminent councillors, who were confident they could find openings for me tuning pianos in nursing homes and council premises. This left me feeling as if I had been used merely as a political pawn.

Thinking of it now, I still feel a sense of bitterness. Once again I had been taken to the top of the hill only to be hurled from its very heights. Could I trust anyone? It amused me to think that Sue was annoyed with the mayor for wanting his palm read when she went the way of the rest of them, along with all their phoney adulation and empty promises.

Parting of the Ways

PAT: Following our South Pacific trip, I was finding our large Edwardian house and garden a burden. I was still working full-time, supporting Mick in my spare time and getting older. The family had all left home and were never there to cut the grass or the hedges. I suddenly felt we needed to move and initially found an ideal house large enough to accommodate the family when they came to visit. Unfortunately a problem arose and it took some months, a temporary lease and lots more house hunting before we were settled in a small new-build three-bedroomed house. All this was stressful for both of us, and the move brought new problems: the house was less robust and less spacious. I don't think I had foreseen how unsettling a move would be for Mick. But we seemed to settle down into a routine and time passed.

I was looking forward to the theatre one March evening in 2002. My friend Jean and I had booked to see *The Wizard of Oz*. The following weekend, which was Easter, Mick and I had arranged to visit Bristol to see Andrew. When I got home from work I found Mick sitting on the sofa with his coat on. "I didn't know you were going out," I said, surprised.

"I'm waiting for my taxi. I'm going to my new flat," he told me. The room spun. I felt as if something had hit me. I could not comprehend what he was saying. What did he mean? He had once mentioned that he would like to go away and live alone, but I had not taken this at all seriously, not believing for a minute that he would be able to cope on his own, or that he would even want to. I realised sadly that we had not been really close for a while but surely he knew that I still loved him?

I asked him "What flat?" He confessed he had been negotiating and waiting for a council flat for about three months. He had been supported and helped by the staff at the Deaf Centre and by Mike, his guide. Now it was ready and furnished and he was leaving me.

I was distraught, pacing the room and appealing to him. "Don't go Mick. You can't go." He seemed unmoved but told me he had written a letter explaining everything, which I could read at my leisure. "Tell me where you will be," I begged. He didn't even want to give an address (he explained later that he was afraid my children would seek retribution for his actions if they knew where he lived), but he eventually agreed to let me have his new phone number. Then the taxi came and he was gone.

I was alone and desolate. I rushed upstairs. His wardrobe and clothes drawers were empty. In the study there was a letter printed out on the desk. Only his leather swivel chair was gone. He had left me his computer, the talking kitchen scales and the talking microwave oven (these last two I later took to his flat). My emotions were in turmoil. I felt angry. How could he do this to me after all we had shared, after all I had done for him? How could he be so deceitful? At the same time, I felt of a twinge of guilt, wondering how I could have let this happen. I had obviously failed him. And I was deeply sad, grieved at the loss of a special love. I knew I would miss his gentleness, his warm support for everything I did and his sense of humour (although it had been markedly absent of late). I was desperately anxious about him. How would he manage without me? Who would read to him, cook for him, wash and iron his clothes, take him on holiday?

I read the letter. He wanted his own space as he felt I did not understand disabled people and did not allow him his independence or his dignity. I found this very hurtful.

Touch Me Please

At the same time he thanked me for all I had done and said I could now have a life of my own. He wrote of hurts of which I had been unaware, which he had never talked about. If only we could have discussed the problems and sorted them out we might have found a way forward.

MICK: As I sat there, all alone with my coat on in the house we had moved to two years previously, I thought of the last fifteen years I had spent with Pat. All my past came back to me. Why was history repeating itself? Nineteen years on from my last leaving, here I was doing it all over again! How could this have happened? This time however, I wouldn't run away without at least explaining, or facing the person I was leaving. How quickly these last three months had passed. Once the process had begun it became like a production line and I was on auto pilot. It's so easy with hindsight to look back over all the preparation, securing a flat, collecting things together and enjoying encouragement from those who would, in the end, gain by my leaving poor Pat. Everything was mixed up in my mind on that day but all was ready and there could be no going back, the die was cast, just as it had been all those years ago with my first marriage.

Pat would be in soon and I would have to face the one I still loved but whom I felt I could no longer stay with. Why had I not been able to talk things over? I suppose I was afraid of actually trying to talk it all out; stupidly I feared reprisals. Since my early childhood I had lived in a world of rows, and had built a protective shield around myself which had kept me from facing up to problems and discussing them with Pat. On the one occasion I had brought up the subject of leaving, Pat, I suppose in panic, had 'gone teacher' on me. "You can never live on your own, don't be silly," she said in lecturing tones. I felt I had been put down again, as so often happened in my past.

From that day on the fire of rebellion was kindled. I am not proud of it, not at all. When Pat came in and saw me with my coat on, she asked innocently, "I didn't know you were going out." When I haltingly explained what I was going to do, it provoked a storm of mixed anger and emotion. How absolutely rotten I felt, how cruel, but once down that dark path there was no turning back. All the arrangements were in place. I knew before ever she entered the house what had to be done. Like an actor reading a script I persisted. Pat was desperately clutching at me and protesting vehemently. "You can't, you can't do this! " But I could and did.

I had agonised over it for quite some time. Is it fair to expect someone who has full sight and hearing to constantly have to worry about a person in my situation? I remember reading way back in the early nineties a biography of a deaf-blind man in the United States. True, it was way before the time of modern computers, but he stated he would never marry because of the difficulties of deaf-blindness and inflicting it on a partner. Pat has told me – and I fully understand – that had I lost both sight and hearing before we married she would have had to think very hard about whether she could make a commitment to me.

In my mind there was also, I have to admit, a rebellious streak. Sighted people are kind and well-meaning. They believe they can see more clearly and know better than we disabled folks. In many ways they are right but sometimes we stubborn people with disabilities don't see it that way and want to prove our independence.

The horn of a taxi beeped, and I left in a confused state, in the end giving in to Pat's pleas for my new phone number. As I drove away, I wasn't me, I felt numb inside, I was just an empty shell. I arrived at the new flat, lit up a cigar and had a glass of beer. Mike, who stood to gain a job caring for me, was there as well. After about forty minutes he left, leaving me to work out my way round the house and to locate everything. The flat had been carpeted, I had my own living space, no one to tell me what to do, what to eat, what not to touch. The part of me that rebels, that cries out for that elusive thing called "freedom" was having its head. I would cope, I'd done so before, I would do it again, but oh, how I felt somehow empty, and feared that a blow would fall on me for undertaking the great escape a second time.

I hardly slept that night. I woke early and listened to *Jurassic Park* on Talking Books. I got lost in it all the following day. I would have to face all the appointments with the benefits people, all the queuing, all the frustrating explanations to poor overworked employees who were overwhelmed with requests for help. I also had to arrange various renovations for the flat, such as a rail in the garden to stop me falling down a drop. Now that I had decided on yet another new life, I knew it would be up hill in many ways but I had picked myself up in the past. Now I had to start all over again.

PAT: *The Wizard of Oz* dropped off our list of priorities the day Mick left. Jean came round to console me, but I could not take in what had happened and tried to understand how this had come about. My life had been dedicated to supporting Mick, not just morally and financially, but with love and kindness and physical closeness. The outside world existed and I was part of it – going out to work, attending Quaker meeting, supporting the family, because these things needed doing – but that world was not the real essence of my existence. For a long time I did not pursue the usual leisure occupations of television, cinema, music or hobbies. My whole being had been centred on Mick and his needs. I did this willingly. It was a privilege because he tackled his situation so bravely.

It was, however, demanding to have so little personal space, time for my own interests or just for chilling out. As he gradually built up new interests and friends, and grew accustomed to a different, restricted life, I mentioned one day that I did not think I could go on giving support at this level of commitment. I did not mean it unkindly, but with hindsight it was a mistake. He said nothing at the time but later threw it back that I had said I didn't want to help him any more. That was definitely not true, but one of the misunderstandings that came between us.

It is sharing activities and mutual experiences that succour any relationship and keep it strong. We could enjoy food, drink, books and, of course, sex. But we had lost music, the real catalyst in the relationship. We had different political outlooks, and now different religious affiliations. Mick became an important figure in the deaf-blind community, from which I was excluded either by accident or by Mick's choice. Whereas he had been welcomed and supported by my Quaker meeting I was hardly ever invited to any Buddhist event (apart from one when the lama gave a talk).

I was also getting older and feeling more tired when I got home from work. It was less effort to sit and watch some TV, and this became a habit – me in one room and Mick in the other with his computer or talking books. Mick too was getting older and more weary, forever sad and missing his music and changed by his isolation from the cut and thrust of the world. We allowed our love for each other to dissipate. Many times afterwards Mick said that our circumstances made our breakup inevitable and whereas I wouldn't entirely agree the situation made it much more likely.

In our new house we had less space and were more on top of each other. Mick hated the more confined accommodation and the flimsier walls that he felt he would demolish if he wasn't careful. I didn't realise what an effect this change of environment was having on him. I think if we hadn't moved house we would have stayed together.

I was also irritated by his increasing weight. I worried about his health as he grew heavier. I realise that it was hard for Mick because one of his few pleasures was eating. I was careful what we ate at home and provided a balanced diet, but clearly Mick had lots of opportunities, now that he went out more, to eat what he most enjoyed – and what was least healthy for him – when he was outside the house. What we did not realise at the time was that Mick was developing an addiction to food exacerbated by his situation.

After a sleepless night I went back to work, barely able to concentrate during the day. That night I rang Mick and asked if he was still coming to Bristol. The answer was no, but after much pleading I persuaded him to give me his address, which turned out to be about as far away from my house as possible without leaving Leeds. He agreed I could call to see him on my way back from Bristol. Until then I had no idea what sort of accommodation he had, what conditions he was living in or whether he had proper food.

I was reassured when I saw his ground floor disability-friendly flat. He had a garden at the back and a little patio at the front where he could sit in the sun. But for weeks I was anxious because I had been so protective since he had gone deaf. I could not believe anyone else could care for him, or that he could be comfortable without me. It was a very long time before I could let go. I had the choice of erasing him from my life completely, or holding onto him as a friend. After we had been so close and shared so much I could not bear to be cut off from him entirely.

I was extremely angry with the Deaf Centre and with his guide, Mike, who had colluded with him behind my back. I wrote to the staff at Centenary House complaining of their underhand behaviour, to which they replied that they acted in the interests of their client alone and were bound to maintain his confidentiality. So irrespective of the years of devoted support I had given Mick, and the very little he had ever received from the professional services who should have helped him in the first place, I was seen as the oppressor from whom he was helped to escape.

Looking back I now understand why it was all done in secret. I would never have agreed to him leaving. I would never have believed he could manage without me. And although it gave him his freedom I really think he also wanted to give me mine.

Still today we ponder on how it all came about. I felt then, and still feel, a strong sense of failure. In spite of the difficulties we had to face, we should have been able to resolve the problems and keep that tenderness and closeness we had once known.

MICK: Sea of Troubles

The failures of the Tuneathon goals were unknown to me as I set off on the long journey across the channel to France. All that Sunday afternoon when I got home from Seacroft, and well into Monday morning, I slept. Then a young lad called Neil travelled with me to the coast. He was uncommunicative and concerned only with his own petty problems. We arrived in London in the early evening and changed buses for Newhaven, where we looked desperately for accommodation for the night. It was nine o'clock as we walked the streets of the small town. Wearily we knocked where we saw a Bed and Breakfast sign. A wonderful, kind, jovial cockney man opened the door. In reply to my query about cost, he asked, "How much can you afford? Would a fiver for two of you be OK?" His wife behind him asked us in. I was surprised how cheap it was, and was cross with Neil who didn't even show his gratitude. I thanked them warmly on behalf of us both.

Soon afterwards the bewitching smells of frying bacon and eggs, and bubble and squeak reached us. Neil started to complain, saying he couldn't eat this or that, and didn't like some things. Was it organically grown? Were the eggs free range? Anger began to well up inside me. "Look," I said, "if you don't want the meal I'll eat yours as well. That's up to you." We were summoned to the dining room where a real Balmoral spread awaited us. I slept peacefully that night on a very full stomach.

Next morning, not only did I have a job persuading the landlord to accept payment, but he also insisted on transporting us down to the quayside in his car. At ten o'clock Jean-Michel Phillipe met me and we boarded the

Sea of Troubles

ferry.

I felt numb as the boat drew away from the English coast, a feeling of utter loneliness engulfing me, and complete disbelief in what was happening. I knew there would be no friends to help me out of any trouble in France. The phrase "standing on your own two feet" took on a stark new meaning. As for my new employer, all he was concerned about were the gambling tables, and ignored me completely. Was this an indication of how he would treat me in the future?

At Dieppe I was introduced to M. Phillipe's partner, Jean-Francois Tar, who journeyed with us to the workshops in Caen, with only a brief stop on the way for a minuscule egg sandwich.

I was immediately set to tune two pianos, without any rest or refreshment, before Jean-Michel dumped me unceremoniously at my hostel and abandoned me. It was Wednesday night and there was no work for me until Monday. The hostel required two weeks advance payment of 500 francs for my accommodation. I had changed 2000 francs on the boat for emergencies only, and had not envisaged having to use my reserves so quickly. I was staying at the Centre International. Lucien, who could only speak two or three words of English, took me upstairs. "Your room," he said curtly, and closed the door on me. I was at zero point, with nothing, starting afresh in a strange country surrounded by people I could not communicate with. In fact, to all intents and purposes I was deaf since I could not understand the language. I walked round my small room, comprising a little washbasin in one corner, a tubular framed bed with a thin mattress, a sheet and bedspread, a plug socket of a continental style I could not use, a small wardrobe and, in another corner, a radiator.

My immediate concern was food. This presented a

Touch Me Please

serious problem as I had no idea how to ask for it. The place itself was a maze of corridors which would have surpassed Hampton Court. As I sat puzzling what to do my hunger increased. I was left with no choice but to try and find the stairs leading down into the main hall. After wandering aimlessly for quarter of an hour or so, I literally stumbled down the flight of stairs. As I reached the hall there was the distant hum of machinery but no sign of anyone about. I circled the vast room looking for a door I could knock at. Footsteps approached me. They sounded like Lucien's so hope rose within me. "Excuse me," I called loudly to attract his attention, "I am very hungry. Where can I find some food please?" There was a pause.

"Pardon, monsieur?"

"Food," I repeated, putting my fingers into my mouth and biting them. Comprehension dawned.

"Ah, restaurant finis," he muttered and left me. Though I knew no French it was obvious I was too late for the restaurant. There was nothing other than water for me that night. Sue had lent me her cassette deck to take to France. I recorded my feelings on a blank tape, using the machine sparingly as I had only one set of batteries. After lying awake for what seemed like hours with hunger gnawing at me like a dog at a bone, I eventually fell asleep. I woke next morning with a determination that I would have what I wanted to eat at any cost. Never in my life had I felt so hungry. My stomach felt like a big bass drum. How I longed for a traditional English breakfast of bacon and egg and toast. Imagine my dismay when I was presented with a Continental breakfast consisting of a small baguette and a demitasse of coffee. The way I felt I could have eaten the Cherbourg Peninsula and still had room for pudding.

There was no alternative but to set out to seek food elsewhere. Tasks which in England seemed small and unimportant now became vast problems, such as finding the hostel gates. It was not as if I could ask anyone the way if I got stuck. It was only my empty stomach which drove me on. I walked round and round the hostel grounds bumping into fences, running into walls, my frustration increasing each moment. Finally I found a gap which I thought was the main gate. Passing through it I was in what seemed to be a narrow country lane. In point of fact I had found the small back gate and was on the main road into Auville St Clair, the village in which the hostel was situated. As there was no pavement on either side of the lane I was forced to walk along the edge of the tarmac. Forgetting I was on the continent I kept to the right hand side of the road, believing I was facing the oncoming traffic. I was startled out of my wits by the very first car that passed by me. Not only did it come from behind me and pass me on my left, but it was going fast enough to be propelled by turbo jet engines. I was puzzled at first by the cars passing so close until I realised the reason, but couldn't cross to the other side of the road because of the volume and speed of the traffic.

I trudged on doggedly in my pursuit of food for what seemed like miles. From out of the passing traffic a car pulled up and stopped beside me. A kindly woman got out and greeted me. A smattering of French from school days entered my mind. "Je suis Anglais," I said desperately. She shook both my hands warmly and chattered away at break-neck speed in French. I felt helpless. At last I had found someone who was kind, but I could not communicate with her. Further footsteps approached as her husband and their small son came to try and help. I went through the action of putting my fingers into my mouth and eating them. This brought a volley of laughter from the little boy who was about five. His father rebuked him. The lady took my arm and led me

Touch Me Please

towards the car. I followed meekly, hoping they had understood my gesticulations. I sat in the back between the two children. They were sweet-natured and were trying to be very friendly. They chattered to me, tapping my shoulder and taking my hand. I turned to each of them, trying to smile as broadly as I could. My rescuers took me to what I assumed from the smells was a large super-market. The father left me in front of the automatic doors saying, "Ici le carrefour."

Once inside I was as helpless as before, wandering from counter to counter, unable to communicate, until I heard a voice speaking English behind me. The sense of relief was so great that I could almost have hugged the man. He helped me to obtain food and a plug which would fit the socket in my room, and took me back to the hostel in his car. That afternoon I relaxed with two large bottles of Normandy cider and three giant baguettes stuffed with liberal supplies of cheese and butter, at which I tore like a rabid tiger.

The work, when I eventually started, was arduous but rewarding. There were some good pianos but others were dilapidated wrecks. The latter I nicknamed in pidgin French "pianos du feu", or pianos I would like to have burnt. This phrase was taken up by the other employees and caused much amusement. After a couple of weeks in the warehouse I was taken out to tune pianos in ordinary French homes which enabled me to make gradual progress with the language.

As regards my employers I had moved out of the frying pan into the fire. I was shocked at having to pay for my accommodation without any assistance from them. There was no limit to the number of hours I worked. In one three day period I had only six hours sleep. Moreover, they always paid me late, and gave me less than they had promised, both as regards my wages and my keep in

France. As I did not receive any wages until I returned to England my debts accumulated and I was always in arrears.

After my first taste of France the vacation to England came like an oasis in the desert. During the three weeks abroad I had deeply missed my friends and my familiar surroundings. It was with a great sense of relief that I turned the key in the front door of my own little home. The very sounds and smells of the country I was born in gave me pleasure. This was, however, short-lived, as I felt an alien in an alien place. It is often the same if you wish to contact friends. They are either out, away or busy. On this occasion they seemed to be all three. The thing I most looked forward to was to hold in my arms the woman I loved so dearly. I was thwarted even in this since she could spare only half an hour throughout the whole week because of her heavy commitments. In the brief meeting we had she was cool and reticent, completely changed from our last encounter. We were both in need of support and affection, but neither of us felt in a position to offer it to the other. I felt isolated and lonely.

I was further aggravated to find several messages on my answering machine offering work, which of course I had missed. Immediately I had to grapple with debts and outstanding bills. Without realising it I had become caught up in a vicious circle. I had been living in poverty since I moved into my house at the beginning of the year, not even being able to afford a bed. Though I had the enterprise grant up to the end of September it barely covered my mortgage and rates, let alone other essential bills. My stubborn resolve to cling to my independence made things worse. I felt reluctant to sign on and slip back to where I had come from, after having fought so hard to hold my head up with dignity and pay my own way in the world. The phrase that my mother had instilled into me

Touch Me Please

continued to haunt me, "Don't depend on anyone for anything. Always pay your own way. That way no one can throw it back in your face." I was paying a high price for my obstinacy. This left me with a difficult choice: sign on and sink deeper into debt, or return to the uncongenial conditions in France to keep my head above water.

With great reluctance I sailed once more across the channel and resumed work in Caen. One day a rusty steel splinter from the iron frame of a piano lodged itself in my finger. I mentioned this at once to Jean-Michel, who looked at it briefly and told me he could see nothing wrong with it. "We will get a doctor tomorrow, or maybe next week, but you will have to pay." As I was short of money I worked on with the finger throbbing throughout the whole of that day.

I had a sleepless night because of the pain, and appealed to Jean-Michel next morning that I needed treatment. With a heavy sigh he reluctantly agreed, "If I am not busy this afternoon I will take you."

By that afternoon I was feeling dizzy, my finger was swelling up like a balloon. First he took me to a doctor who whistled loudly when he looked at the finger. He referred us to an emergency clinic, emphasising that if I did not have treatment immediately I would contract septicaemia and could possibly die, as the metal poisoning was entering my bloodstream. The doctor commented on how considerate Jean-Michel had been to bring me to him, especially when my employer added, "It is all right. I will pay." I thought there was a chink of mercy in this iron man. Not so. As we left the doctor's he told me, "I will have to take it off your wages."

Never have I known such pain, as I lay on the table in the clinic and the doctor slit my finger with a sharp needle. In order to carry out this operation the anaesthetic needle had to puncture the centre of the wound three times. I almost passed out with the pain. The wound was bled and cleaned. Once again the cost of this was to be taken off my wages. The final bill amounted to 1000 francs, money which I desperately needed to meet commitments in England.

I was taken back to work immediately next day although the doctor recommended three days' rest. My employers had no idea what the word consideration meant. On one occasion they went away for three days leaving me without a penny for food. Despite my pleading with some Americans who had moved into the hostel, and others, I starved for three days.

All this was only made bearable because in November I met some English students who were studying in France. They were staying in the same hostel as I was. Vividly I remember the Sunday I first met Jan at the hostel bar. I was standing alone with a beer in my hand. This French beverage tasted disgusting, not far removed from sheep dip, but I had to drink something. Soft drinks were half as expensive again as the toilet water I was drinking. A fresh bright voice beside me said, "Hello, I'm Jan." My face lit up. An English person at last – and a woman! In her typical casual way she asked, "What are you doing over here then?" I began to pour out my tale of woe, to which she replied, "My friends are coming along soon. Perhaps we can all go for a meal." So I met Gail and Tim.

I struck up a close friendship with all three, and we visited the D-Day beaches the following weekend, something I had been longing to do since I landed in France. It was a remarkably warm day for the time of year. I recorded myself on the radio cassette, walking into the sea. A local French fisherman was able to tell us which troops had landed on that particular beach. All of us spent that day having lots of fun. Soon afterwards, Janet, Gail and Tim moved into a flat together. I can never praise these three people highly enough; it was entirely due to them that I managed to stay in France.

As regards my work, things did not improve. One thing however did make things a little lighter. The young lads in the workshop were, as far as possible, friendly. They knew very little English, but still managed to be kind to me.

My home vacation for Christmas came round and with it a most terrifying incident. Coming home on the ferry I particularly wanted to bring Pat a nice present from France and some tobacco for myself. Jean-Mi, as we used to call him, had fallen asleep as he had been driving for some time. It was, after all, four in the morning. He always seemed to choose the most outlandish times to travel. I wandered around the somewhat ancient and creaking French boat.

At last I came upon a guy who seemed to be one of the French crew because he offered to take me to the duty free shop to choose some goods. He on the other hand had other ideas. Rattling the keys in his hand he walked briskly towards the door and opened it. As we entered I heard a husky sigh of pleasure and found myself being led to the gents' toilet. Pushing me through the door the man pressed close to me, attempting to take my trousers down and anything else that he could. He was stronger than me and of course he could see. I felt the icy chill of terror grip me. Turning round I pushed my way past and tried to run. I forgot of course that I was in the small confined space of the shop. This fact seemed only to please him. Obviously he was into chasing around as part of his perverted pleasure.

Running around the shop I shouted and started knocking some of the items off the shelves. As he could not speak English, I thought that the noise would frighten him. In the end it did and he unlocked the door. I ran anywhere until I came upon a young English student. I gasped out my story to him urgently, hoping that he would get someone, anyone. All I got was a sleepy uncaring "Oh yea". I rushed on and quite by chance came upon Jean-Mi still fast asleep. He was very annoyed at being woken up. I told him what had happened. "I suppose this means that you want to tell the police. More hold ups! This is a nuisance." It was all right for him, I thought. After that he went to see the captain and I saw the immigration officer. "I will certainly see about it when we reach port," he said, in a very concerned manner.

On reaching port all the crew were interviewed but nothing could be done. All of them to a man closed ranks and as they were all French citizens there was nothing that the English police could do. Finally we proceeded on our way to Leeds. I was still feeling weak with the shock of the whole thing.

Arriving at home I poured out the story to Pat who was most understanding. On this occasion I spent well over a month in England. The last thing I felt like doing was going back to France. However problems of the heart overshadowed even this. My relationship with Pat wasn't going smoothly. She was unable to commit herself, I could not stand the uncertainty. We agreed not to see each other.

The world seemed to have crashed about my ears. I returned to France in a daze. I didn't care what work I did. I just stumbled on blindly. When I returned home Pat wanted to see me. Again, we were drawn together like two magnets but the basic problem had not been solved.

I decided that the next trip to France would be my last. I was so short of money and getting so far behind with my mortgage I was in danger of losing my house. Jean-Mi was opening a little shop in the town centre and I was going to sleep in a flat above it. That was a laugh.

Touch Me Please

When I arrived, there were no facilities for sleeping and I had to get some new clothes for work. Of course the cost of these was, as usual, taken from my wages.

On my last night in France I had a farewell party for all the friends I had met. Richard, the only decent French chap I had met, came along as well. He had helped me to learn French. I departed from the country forever the next day and never returned. Jean-Mi rang me and asked why I was not coming back. I told him I could no longer afford to work under his conditions and left it at that.

So it was back to signing on again, right back to where I had been before – on the dole. Pat had persuaded me that it was the only way to carry on. I reluctantly agreed. That summer I wrote another song. Pat had wanted to write some lyrics while I wrote the tune but she didn't have the time. I set to writing yet another romantic song about the way I was feeling. Everyone seemed to like it; it spelt out my thoughts. All through the summer and autumn of that year I struggled to get little bits and pieces of work.

At the beginning of December I decided that there could be no future in continuing to see Pat. We shared a last meal. I drank plenty of cider to dull my senses against the coming shock. This time I said I had to be left alone because I wanted total commitment to the relationship and nothing less.

After we parted that night I cracked. This was the end. I was alone in the world and I thought nobody would miss me. My money troubles were at an all-time high. I could see no way forward so why not finish it and quit the world? A little earlier I had caught one or two mice in the kitchen. Jim's wife had purchased some mouse poison for me. I had quite a lot left. I went to bed that night and prepared to die. Debts were weighing me down; financial pressures were increasing. There was no point in going on.

I had lost the only source of true love I had ever known. The world was desolate, empty, meaningless. Better end it all and escape from the twisted and tangled ruin of my life.

I felt I could not depart from this world without telling someone about it. The only person I could think of talking to at this late hour was Vanessa. It had become a habit to phone Vanessa, a friend I had met the year before. Regularly we would converse very late at night. I intended to make a brief farewell call, but I stayed chatting to her about the way I felt and about subjects in general. Suddenly I remembered I had promised to play the uke for a local youth club the next day. This recollection, combined with the cider and Vanessa's sympathy and support, saved my life.

One of the great comforts at this dark time was my talking book that I had been given the previous summer. I spent a lot of my time listening to it. In March I appeared on a small radio programme called Calypso on a regular basis, telling people's fortunes using their date of birth. Members of the public could write in and consult me. I enjoyed this work a lot, although it was voluntary and consequently brought in no money.

Sleep was difficult, my life had no pattern and I did not care. I ate vast amounts of fatty foods to comfort myself. Many a time I was sorely tempted to ring Pat but I was determined not to give in, not to go back on what I had said. My money problems continued. The gas board had lost my forms and claimed I owed them over £500. Despite my arguments they went to the social security and the money was taken off me for the payment of all those arrears. Because I couldn't prove the bill was not mine I was forced to pay it. (It is an irony that I did not, in fact, owe any of this money. Eventually the matter was cleared up and they sent a cheque returning my payments. I

Touch Me Please

wanted to frame the cheque.)

The peak of all my troubles came when my mother died. The previous October I had gone down to see her for the first time for years. We had got on very well. In March my brother Ron curtly told me over the phone that she had gone into hospital. He had a lot of money, three cars and yet he didn't even tell me which hospital she was in or where it was. I only found out when the hospital rang me to tell me that she was very ill and wanted to see me. I scraped up the money somehow and went down to see her. What a state she was in, no life in her at all, resigned to quit the world a mere shadow of her former self. A shabby end I thought to her blighted life.

At the end of August I received a double blow all in the space of ten minutes. First there was a loud knocking at the door. It was someone from the building society. "As you are so far behind with the mortgage we have no alternative but to take your house from you. I shall also report you to the social security as well for failing to pay. I mean it, we have been patient with you." This was rubbish as they hadn't even contacted me, or as far as I knew written to me. As I was blind I thought they could have at least phoned me to talk about it. As he had finished speaking the phone rang. I answered it and found it was my brother. "I know you don't care but your mother has died and I am not prepared to take you to the funeral." This was the last straw.

There was only one thread to hang onto once again. A few days earlier the phone had rung and I heard that voice I had secretly been longing to hear for so long. "I would like to take you on a surprise outing for your birthday if you are free." The old magnetic attraction that had been between us worked its magic charm again and I agreed. So Pat picked me up and we set out the day after the abusive phone call from Ron and the visit of the building society representative.

We went to see *Chess*, the very musical that I had bought for Pat and myself on cassette at the beginning of the year. Our story seemed to be encompassed within it; there still seemed no hope to me of the commitment I so badly wanted. I tried to take the weekend for what it was and nothing else. I had no expectations. The Sunday of that weekend was actually my birthday. That night I was playing at the pub. I felt so deflated, so sad I got drunk and didn't care. I had no idea what Pat was thinking. How had she taken the weekend, I wondered.

On the Monday evening of September 1st I was making a recording when the phone rang. A soft voice said "Mick I would like to come down and see you now". I agreed and by the end of the evening we were in each other's arms. We both decided to give things another try.

But what about the mortgage arrears? Pat and my bank between them helped me to solve the immediate crisis with short-term loans. I was lucky to take part in a clairvoyants' convention, where I read a lot of palms. Following this I was invited to several palm parties and whilst the tuning work was slack I earned enough through playing the piano and palm reading to repay my debts in a remarkably short time.

PAT: Some New Gains

During the months following our separation we struggled through a maze of emotions to find a new way of life which suited us both and allowed us to keep in touch. I found it hard to accept the new situation without feeling angry or bitter. I couldn't let go of that sense of responsibility since I still felt he needed me. I was often upset and more than once we agreed not to see each other again, but each time I rang Mick and we made up. Eventually we established a pattern of meeting at weekends, going swimming, perhaps taking a walk, occasionally going for a meal or a drink. We had a delightful trip to Norfolk on our own, and the following year with the family.

Now when we met at weekends we were more tender with each other than for a long time, and I felt sure he would come home soon and we could resolve all our minor difficulties. I don't think he ever felt the same way. After two or three years I gave up the idea. By then I had come to enjoy my freedom, the ability to do whatever I wanted whenever I liked. He said in his parting letter that I would one day come to thank him, and indeed I came to appreciate living alone, although it hurt me so much at the time. I also had a grandchild and could visit my daughter and her new family without worrying about Mick.

I think he also enjoyed his freedom, to wear what he liked and eat what he liked. The downside was that he kept putting on weight! Mick had claimed in his letter that he could manage by himself. The irony was that he could not. He had funding for a carer because he couldn't shop and cook and wash and iron or go out alone. Only years later I discovered that he didn't actually have the freedom and stress-free life he had sought. His paid carer became more and more insensitive, unkind and manipulative. So it was definitely a case of out of the frying pan into the fire.

Some months after Mick moved to his own flat, towards the end of 2002, he was invited by the Cochlear Implant team in Manchester to undergo some hearing tests. They were very impressed with his performance and concluded that the part of his brain normally dedicated to sight was now being used to assist his hearing. He was thrilled when they offered him a second implant on the strength of this. There was some mention of further experimentation into how well he could make use of this as a blind person, but almost at the same time I read a report of research into this very issue which had come to the same conclusion. It didn't appear to be a new discovery. The cause or reason was immaterial and Mick was only too glad to accept. He had always said he would benefit from two implants. How could he not? And he had waited ten years for the chance to prove his point.

The operation was fixed for December and Mick invited me to accompany him since I had helped him through his worst days and his first implant. This he saw as a kind of reward that was due to me and I was very pleased he had asked me. When it came to the event, however, I felt it was, after all, a dubious privilege. This time I was not offered accommodation in the hospital (we didn't ask) but I found a nearby hotel which meant travelling between my room and the hospital. There was a lot of sitting around with little to do and as the festive season was fast approaching I spent some of the waiting time writing Christmas cards. The day of the operation I was relieved when it was all over and looked forward to a celebratory glass of wine with my dinner, only to discover that I had unwittingly booked into a Muslim hotel.

Touch Me Please

Although the room and the service were fine it was a dry hotel. Despite these drawbacks I wouldn't have missed being with Mick for the world.

He was discharged fairly soon after the operation and I was glad to be driving back one Saturday evening over the M62 for perhaps the last time. However, we had no sooner got home than he was in severe pain and when I rang the hospital they asked me to take him back. We arrived once more on the following Sunday morning and, having been diagnosed with a severe infection in the newly-operated ear, Mick lay around on a trolley in A & E for most of the day until they eventually admitted him. In all the rush and panic I had not packed his pyjamas and dressing gown (never thinking he would be re-admitted), so I drove home and after work on Monday made yet another journey to take over all the things he needed.

A few weeks later and Mick was 'switched on' again. He expected a big improvement in the second implant following ten years of research and development. Again he was disappointed. It had a narrower range than the first, although speech was slightly easier to hear. As for music it offered no more opportunities. Over the following weeks the audiologist laboured to balance the two implants to give Mick maximum benefit. Now that he had two implants Mick worked very hard at recognising stereophonic sound and tried music again. Classical music was impossible, but popular music which he had known and appreciated during his hearing days began to offer some satisfaction. Despite the fact that he could not recognise pitch and tone, the rhythm and sometimes the words became accessible. Once he recognised a tune by the rhythm his memory filled in the gaps and I suppose you could say he enjoyed listening to it. This only applied to music he already knew; anything which came after the onset of his deafness was totally inaccessible.

Some New Gains

Now, for the first time in eleven or twelve years, we were able to listen to music together: the lively tunes of the sixties, the romantic recordings of the seventies. The irony was not lost on us: in less than a year from the date we split up we were enjoying music together, which was a thrill and a novelty. It is possible that if Mick had been offered the second implant earlier, sharing music might have given us just the impetus we needed to revive our relationship.

Now that a door had opened Mick began to acquire music greedily. For the first time in his life he could download what he wanted and store it on his computer. It was there for the taking, and he built up as large a music library as was possible within the parameters which confined him: it excluded classical music and had to be pre-1990. His extensive knowledge of the pop world, song writers and artistes was very valuable in building up his collection and recognising tracks.

The next stage was to share it with other people. He thought he'd like to be a disc jockey, so he bought some expensive equipment. At first he provided entertainment for residents at the Deaf Centre in Leeds. This was particularly useful at Christmas or special occasions. Then he was invited to do a few discos for private individuals and organisations. He did one for Adel Quakers when they were fund-raising for a new extension. He became quite well-known locally and for some time was invited to present a regular slot with Leeds11 FM, a local internet community radio programme.

In 2007 his fame had spread to Radio Caroline and Johnny Lewis invited him to present an hour of music on his (Johnny's) show. The challenge was enormous. Mick had to juggle with earphones over his implants and co-ordinate his commentary with the tracks. But he achieved it and I was very proud of him. I was a bit disappointed that he didn't ask me to take him to London. (He never asked me to take him anywhere else after the implant operation.) Instead I tried to record the programme via the internet, with very limited success. Mick was overjoyed to have this opportunity. To use a hackneyed phrase, this was perhaps his finest hour.

While he was enjoying the DJ work he was making a valuable contribution to coHearant Vision (the charity name of The Leeds Society for Deaf and Blind People). He had been teaching deaf-blind people to use the computer for several years and his IT knowledge was very impressive. He had always teased me for being political and a 'committee person' but he became more and more involved in the various blind and deaf-blind organisations and sat on several committees. He accepted the position of secretary to more than one. He had become a trustee, and then vice chairman of the Society. Later he became the treasurer as well. He was a good spokesman for deaf and blind people, and contributed to Deaf Awareness courses and the Guide Communicator training scheme. For a time he was also active in Federation of the Blind and became secretary of the Yorkshire Region. It was immensely important for him to have the satisfaction of doing something useful.

With these various strands, including his Buddhist meeting, life had some purpose. But nothing is simple or straightforward. I would say that in every area of his life Mick was limited by how other people treated him, and he was often undervalued or ignored because of his disability.

He had once told me I didn't understand disabled people, but sometimes my heart ached at the insensitivity of some of his contacts. The deafness was the problem. He had mixed on equal terms in the sighted world when he was blind. But people shy away where communication is difficult. Either they are embarrassed, cannot be bothered to make the effort, or attribute a degree of stupidity to anyone who cannot respond readily. So however much effort Mick put into an activity, however willing he was, there was always a point where he was rebuffed or overlooked. This is often the plight of a disabled person.

Although he listened to and 'enjoyed' lots of music, he hadn't really got it back; it was like seeing a distant star twinkling instead of being in full sun. He simply recalled it in his memory, like Wordsworth remembering the daffodils. His one delight was eating. He loved food and without anyone to restrict it he began to expand. After the joy of the second implant and sharing music again he became so overweight that it was difficult to take him anywhere. On a visit to Harrogate with my daughter we passed several restaurants before she chose one which had sufficiently robust chairs (in her opinion) to support her step-father. I grew concerned about the wear and tear on my furniture when he came to my house. To me his size was a greater obstacle than his dual sensory impairment, and a serious barrier to our relationship. It changed him more as a person. Eventually I suggested he should no longer visit me until he lost some weight. Banning him meant we lost our lovely weekends together. I filled the gap with other things. So did he (where possible). We grew more distant and although I tried to visit him every week it wasn't the same and I really missed our shared time together.

MICK: Family Life and Communication

It was during the autumn of 1986 that I began to visit Pat and see her family on a regular basis. Living with sighted people and interacting with them inevitably causes humorous incidents. Pat and I have had our share of them. Right from our early days, when I first met her as a customer, she always made me a cup of tea, served in a plastic cup. This, she insists now, was quite normal as they were melamine insulated mugs – she gave them to all her visitors. At the time I thought it was because she was afraid that I'd break a china cup.

One day, Pat called me to help her because Chris wasn't well and had to stay off school. I leapt up to her house full of enthusiasm, ready to look after him. One of the first things I had to learn was that older fully sighted children think differently from myself as a blind person. Chris liked the television and we watched this together.

I remember Pat at this time had a Silver Reed electric typewriter. Chris asked if I could type. Proudly I stated that indeed I could. How the Mighty fall. I started typing away. Chris found it extremely funny that I made lots of mistakes. He thought it was great fun to read out to all the family my puny efforts. They were all good spellers and laughed at my inept literary attempts. I felt rather belittled; I had learned braille in which there are a lot of contractions, so we didn't write words out as a whole. They were often represented by only one letter or a couple of letters and therefore I had no idea how they should be spelt. Once I became a regular computer user my English improved.

One thing I did to impress Pat, was to help with the

Family Life and Communication

cooking and make tea for everyone when Pat came home. I really enjoyed doing this, though I was always accused of making far too much or being very liberal with certain ingredients. My curries for instance were very hot and I loved using large amounts of cheese in some dishes. Pat would often ask the family to help me make the tea. This was rather a joke because they usually just stood about, watching me work! I didn't mind at all really.

If Pat and I were working together in the kitchen, nothing I did ever seemed to be right. Flour, ground nuts and so on, seemed to take on a life of their own and fly about the kitchen, much to Pat's annoyance and I'd get a verbal rollicking. The trouble was, if that happened, I usually went on to make far more mess or do more things wrong. Pat would then lose her patience and I'd get the stamping of the foot treatment. Whenever Pat was really cross, she stamped her foot at me. It's funny to relate now, but at the time I found it terrifying!

Luckily she didn't know some of the things that happened, such as the day I dropped a pan of cooked rice on the kitchen floor. Andrew, our elder boy, found this really amusing as was my verbal reaction to what happened, which can't be printed here. No matter, we just scooped up the rice and put it back in the pan. No one knew about it except the two of us. The little terrors used to threaten to tell Mum what I had said unless I gave in to their requests. Of course I found this really amusing and we had many a laugh about it.

Since I couldn't see Pat and I devised a practical arrangement based on our political differences so I would always know which cup, towel, and so on was mine. I always knew that of the two towels hanging on the rail, mine was on the right and Pat's on the left. If there were two cups of tea waiting to be drunk, mine would be on the right and Pat's on the left.

Touch Me Please

Once when Pat was away I had been called on to keep an eye on the family, though really I didn't need to do so. They were very capable of looking after themselves, as long as I did all the washing up. I used to go out to work during the day and sometimes go out at night for a few beers and a little snack.

I well remember one day, I'd had a particularly good night singing and having a few beers. I had brought home a lovely take-away. I crept into the house, and thought I was going into the living room. I prepared to sit down and enjoy my well-earned supper. Unfortunately, I'd gone past the door and ended up in the sitting room. I lowered myself onto what I thought was the chair. I soon discovered how wrong I was when all the notes of the piano jangled loudly in chorus as I sat on them. Luckily, nothing got broken – at least I'd have been on hand to repair it – but it woke Chris who came down to see what was going on. Oh how he enjoyed my embarrassment and chagrin when he saw me, with this lovely supper. "Mick, now I've caught you. I'm sure Mum would love to know what you've got there." Little terror. I don't know if Pat ever heard the story from him, though I've told her since.

Sometimes the boot was on the other foot. Years later, I came downstairs one morning and made my way to the sofa to switch on some music. I felt a body, lolling like a dead weight. I lifted an arm and it just flopped back. It turned out to be Chris and for a moment I thought he was dead, but eventually ascertained he was still breathing. Apparently he had been too far over the limit (or maybe just too tired?) to get upstairs to bed the night before.

Silly flair-ups also caused the stamp of the imperial foot. Like when I had just washed up and was putting all the dishes away. I placed a cheap casserole dish on the very high shelves in a tower of Babel. Unfortunately I'd

Family Life and Communication

put it on the shelf the wrong way up. It stayed where it was and seemed all right to me. I moved into the dining room flushed with success after my washing up stint. Suddenly there was a loud crash from the kitchen. Lying on the floor were the remains of the casserole dish. Oh boy, I knew I was in for it now.

"Do you realise one of my family bought that for me?" she complained. "Time you went home I think." Not just the stamp of the foot this time, but banishment back to my little house. I felt really deflated, like a naughty boy at school.

The pipes incident was another example of the wrath of "she who must be obeyed" as the old saying goes. It was winter and there had been a particularly hard frost and the waste pipe from the bath was frozen. Like a Knight gallant, I offered to try and rectify the problem. I took off the panelling at the front of the large enamel bath to get at the offending pipe. With much gusto and aching arms, I bent to the task, turning on the hairdryer to try and thaw the pipe. When Pat came upstairs and saw that I had removed the panel she was very cross. She thought it would be impossible to put it back on.

There were lovely things to counter-balance all of this though, many good times we had in those days before my deafness. I well remember the concerts we used to attend at the Town Hall, all that beautiful classical music we heard together, the joyful day we went to see *The Mission* at the old ABC picture house.

Long walks along the coasts, through woods, hill and dale, over bridges and rivers and round reservoirs – we did it all in those days. Life was so different back then. We were learning to enjoy each other's company, appreciate our strengths and tolerate our weaknesses. Another lovely thing was the first Easter present Pat bought me. I had been wanting an album by Chicago.

Touch Me Please

Things were tight money-wise back then. I wasn't earning much and Pat's wages were low and she had a family to keep and a house to run. So I felt really honoured when she bought me the LP. I treasured it for many years afterwards. Sadly, all those LPs have long since bitten the dust. I got rid of them all after I went deaf.

There were outings with the family as well. Whilst Pat was working hard, I took the family swimming in town. It was their job to guide me. On one occasion they were all chatting together and obviously let their concentration slip. I ran slap bang into a bollard placed at a dangerous level for my manhood. I clearly remember my eyes watering as I stood still in extreme pain. Everyone wondered why I had stopped so suddenly. When they found out the reason they all burst out in an uproar of laughter! I'm glad they thought it so funny. I can tell you it was no joke for me.

In those days I was more outgoing on our holidays than I am now. I used to enjoy a few nights out. I remember when we took the boys and their friends to Northumberland for a week. One evening Pat and I went out to the pub for a drink and I joined in the singing in the bar. There was a bloke there with an accordion and another had a ukulele. I asked if I could have a go on his uke. This I did with great success and thanks to that and my lusty singing I didn't pay for a single drink that night. Well, when folks were kind enough to buy me a few beers it seemed churlish to refuse them.

Pat went back to supervise the boys and I returned to the cottage later. I think she heard me singing down the street before I came into view. Full of the joys of the occasion I forgot about the little trip step on the landing, fell flat on my back and rolled about on the floor. Oh dear, I'd get another telling off I thought but I didn't mind or really care; I felt good and nothing was going to put me

Family Life and Communication

from my good mood. As it happens, I got away with it on that occasion since Pat found it very amusing.

One problem I had was being unaware of the time during the night. I often used to come down and put on my cans, or earphones, to listen to music. Forgetting it was the middle of the night, I would lustily join in with one of the songs. My voice was quite – how shall we say – stentorian at the best of times. The sudden pulling of the hair and irate admonishment of "Do you realise what time it is!" stopped me in my tracks.

The centre we had at the time was a rather fine Technics. It had lovely speakers, powerful and very high quality. Before you used the earphones however, you had to press a button to cut out the speakers. This was rather unusual, since normally when you plug in earphones this is done for you. I remember once forgetting to do this and donning the cans. I set the gain nice and high and put on the record. Unbeknown to me the loud music boomed out making everyone else in the room leap with shock. Luckily, it was day-time but the folly of this action was vociferously pointed out to me very forcibly. That was me, always putting my foot in it.

There was a funny incident on New Year's Day 1987. I had been out for a few drinks. I arrived at Pat's house in a taxi. I really was in the mood for singing. I entered the house in loud fashion. I didn't know that Pat had a Quaker visitor who was very particular about behaviour and strictly tee-total. Pat, in panic, rushed into the hall to meet me, thrust two Amplex tablets into my mouth, clapped her hands over my mouth in an obvious 'shut up' sign. It took a couple of seconds to dawn on me that my present exuberant mood was not to be tolerated.

Pat's dad only visited us once from the north-east. In my effort to impress I offered to take Joe to the local pub. We enjoyed a few beers and talked about this and that.

Touch Me Please

Then came closing time and we arrived back home. Pat and the family were all upstairs in bed. Joe was stumbling around in the dark. Being blind, I never thought about turning on lights for the poor chap. His competence was also impaired by the evening's drinks. "Where's the light for Christ's sake?" Joe asked me. I groped about for the switch and eventually found it. "Joe, do you want some eggs on toast?" I asked him. "Why aye, why not" he replied. (This was the next best thing to a lovely takeaway.)

Clattering happily in the kitchen I prepared our supper. Stainless steel sinks always make a noise at the best of times when one washes up. Being as I was a little merry and not quite so careful about keeping quiet, we were creating quite a racket, though I didn't realise it at the time. Happily washing up, chatting away not too quietly and going over the night's events we were suddenly interrupted. A cold hand came down on my shoulder. "Oh, hello love, I was just making a little supper for Joe."

"Everyone is in bed and you're making enough noise to wake the dead!"

Joe's gentle voice intervened, "Why aye Pat, leave him alone he's just making us supper." Bless him, I was grateful for his intervention. It did soften the blow and I got away with only a slight admonishment.

Pat could get cross with me sometimes, but she was responsible for one of my happiest moments, when in 1988 she suggested we should get married. I rushed out and washed the car I remember. I was in a haze of euphoria and felt lighter than air. A fully sighted woman wanted me with her for the rest of her life. How could she know just how much it meant to me? My blindness didn't seem to be a barrier as we could share so much together, especially music, and I could get about independently.

Family Life and Communication

How different things were after the loss of my hearing. I could no longer enjoy easy conversation with people, whether friends or strangers. There was sometimes a funny side to it though. During the pre-implant days when we relied on the hand language, I often put my foot in it but didn't realise because I was deaf. Many a time I would make a statement while other people were talking. My hand would be seized and fingers would bang down on my hand almost leaving dents in it. "Quiet, someone else is talking!" would be branded on my hand.

It was at this difficult time that my passion for all technical gadgets and obsession with machines came to my aid. My crazes had continued. In the early eighties I had played around with CB radio transmitters and found them great fun. So I had no trouble coming to terms with computers. Having mastered the Amstrad with the Dolphin Speech System I was ready for the next challenge: the Libra with the braille display and accompanying technology.

The Libra had a row of eighty cells in front of the keyboard. Each cell had eight holes, two across and four down. The top six holes were for the braille characters and metal pins popped up as appropriate; the bottom two holes indicated special characters or upper case letters. I could soon find my away around the screen and operate programs quickly with this limited display. I joined groups that talked about *Star Wars* and *Dr Who*. People were so kind and giving. When I couldn't hear at all, they sent me scripts for these favourite programmes which I could scan and read with my braille display. I came to depend on the computer for my communication with the outside world now that I was denied social contact through work and leisure.

We also had a small braille machine which people

Touch Me Please

could type into. This was really handy for folks who didn't know the hand language. Its real problem was that, if a group of people were involved, by the time someone had typed in what they wanted to say (or what was being said in the group), the conversation had moved on. I didn't know this so I would launch into a statement blithely continuing while everyone else was by this time talking about something completely different. The Alva was best as a communication device between two people.

I remember Peter C, a Quaker friend of Pat's, used to take me out for a few beers. As the evening progressed his typing grew more and more inaccurate the more beers he consumed. The next morning I had an amusing time reading back all he had said. It also reminded me of the subjects we'd covered the night before as for some unknown reason, I had forgotten about much of the evening!

There were extremely embarrassing incidents as well. On one occasion we were staying at a friend's house. The bathroom was at the other end of the landing from our bedroom. I needed to use the bathroom during the night and on the way back I miscounted the rooms and strayed into one of the other bedrooms. Thinking I was in our room I blithely started to climb into the bed. Luckily Pat had come looking for me. She yanked me out in the nick of time and explained what had happened. God, I can never forget that occasion, because it was the room of one of our host's children. I was near apoplectic when I realised what had happened. I simply wanted to sink through the earth! After that if we stayed in unfamiliar surroundings Pat tied a scarf or a ribbon on our door handle to make sure nothing like that ever occurred again.

I did a bit more of this earth sinking one day when in 1991, on a really hot summer's day, I was sitting at the computer in my study. Pat and the family were walking

Family Life and Communication

the Cumbrian Way and I was totally on my own in the house. It was so hot that I decided to remove all my clothes and work in my birthday suit. I knew there would be no danger of anyone seeing me since everyone was away. Never trust to luck like that! I was to learn that the unexpected can happen!

I was working away, using my braille display. Suddenly without warning I felt a hand on my shoulder. I nearly leapt through the ceiling! Was it a burglar come to rob the place? Who was this? How the hell did they get into the house, since it was all locked up? Every nerve in my body was at snapping point. I couldn't even speak I was so terrified.

Then my left hand was taken and the words "It's Linda" were spelt out on my hand! Oh my God, I thought. I'm sitting here starkers and poor Linda is standing there. Thoughts of what might happen went through my head. I was really going to be in trouble now! I stammered out something, I can't remember what. I tore into the bedroom and frantically got dressed, apologising profusely all the time. It turned out that Linda had so many blisters she came home early, but of course no one could let me know since I could not use the phone, and I couldn't hear if anyone came in. So that explains how I was caught totally unprepared. It took me a long time to get over that little episode I can tell you.

Being deaf I often felt so shut in, so frustrated that quite often when I was in the shower, I would forget and sing at the top of my voice and sometimes be reprimanded for doing so.

Once I had the implant fitted, things became a little easier. I could at least communicate with people although I was a different person and there were still many frustrations to cope with. It was a whole new ball game working with the implant. After all the initial problems I

Touch Me Please

had to settle down and accept what communication was available. It's not hearing as you would know it. I once described it as a radio station off-tune on FM. No pitch, so I couldn't always tell women from men. This was to cause many embarrassing moments over the years. I usually tried to use other senses to detect gender. It normally worked but there were exceptions if blokes wore strong aftershave or women didn't wear any scent. In this case, I had to rely on the gist of the conversation or the person's name, which is usually a good guide but not always.

Even with the implant it was impossible to go out on my own. I occasionally travelled alone by train if Pat put me on at one end and there was someone to meet me at the other. In these situations we always arranged for assistance to help me board and leave the train. However this system broke down on one occasion when the British Rail conductor forgot to put me off at Stevenage and my friend failed to turn up at the station on time. Before I knew it I was travelling on to Kings Cross. On our arrival the passengers ignored my pleas for help so I had to find my own way to the end of the carriage and locate the exit. Luckily the train had electric doors so I couldn't fall out of the wrong side (as happened to me once). Then I stood and shouted loudly in the hope that someone would hear me. Eventually I was rescued and put on a very slow stopping train back to Stevenage.

The phone was one of the hardest things to use. If only people spoke clearly life would be so much easier for those of us with implants. It's something that people have totally lost sight of. Trying to chain conversations, getting the pattern of what people are trying to say, that's what I had to do. Again, this led to many misunderstandings. As time went on, the implant was slowly upgraded and this improved things just a little. There were times though, like swimming, where I couldn't wear the implants. This

Family Life and Communication

meant reverting to the hand language again. Making other people aware of the situation was hard for Pat at times.

The easiest voice to understand was, of all things, my computer. This was a godsend because it meant that I could work much faster with it. I ditched the Libra and moved through a few machines to a Compaq. We were visiting Linda in Derby at the time when we bought it. This machine was really advanced for its time. Pat thought I could do well enough with the cheaper model but I put my foot down and insisted on buying it. Well do I remember being firm, standing at the counter insisting that I had the extra memory that my particular model included. Then we had to get it into the car – we couldn't believe the boxes were so large – because otherwise delivery would have cost a fortune. I marvelled at Pat's patience that day. Very soon after, she was going away on a walking tour. I remember setting up this machine while she was away, installing all the necessary software.

By now, I was on the internet. It was early days, dial-up connections were the order of the day. How did we manage back then? I mainly relied on emails because the web at that time wouldn't work for me. I can never be grateful enough for all the users who came to my rescue time and again. I joined groups that shared my interests: off-shore radio, sci-fi and so on. Once I had my implant, long before DVDs were available, people sent me tapes from all over the world of old *Dr Who* episodes. I can never forget how kind people were. It meant so much to me at the time. I also found wonderful contacts from the old off-shore radio days and revelled in the past. The world was at my fingertips now, I had emails from around the globe. I made some good friends back in those far off days of the mid-nineties. I came to spend more and more time upstairs with my computer. It was my world while the family were busy setting up their own futures.

Life was hard for Pat, in a full-time job and trying to juggle with youngsters working or at university. Only Chris was still at home. Sometimes I used to visit Andrew at his digs in Liverpool. We usually went out and I supported him by paying for some drinks and meals. The family would take me out sometimes, but I had to keep my pockets full of money of course. I didn't mind because I was relating to them and they seemed to like me. I wonder why? Was it perhaps the free treats?

I remember one incident very clearly. Having returned from her year in the USA Linda was going away to university. She wanted a stereo and I took her into town to buy her one. We went for a meal at Whitelocks afterwards. Oh how we both enjoyed it. Linda and I get on very well now and often laugh together over the old days.

Chris too enjoyed going out with me. We had many an evening out. After he left home to study in Edinburgh, I visited him and met Emily for the first time. It was hot and I had been on the train and was worn out with travelling. Off to the pub we went. I was feeling thirsty and we had quite an evening! I told Chris that Emily would be the one he married. I turned out to be right on that one.

Communication was difficult outside the home as well. I was to meet members of Genesis on two other occasions. Pat, bless her, helped me to arrange a chat with Phil Collins when he was on tour in 1990. She took me all the way to Birmingham and I met Phil again. By that time, I was almost deaf and knew I had very little time left to communicate. I wanted to tell him all my music had gone. Stupidly I thought he should know. He reacted with "What can I say?" taking my head in his arms and rocking it. To me, it meant so much! Silly really, now I look back on it all. What funny creatures we are. It is crazes once again I guess.

My final meeting with Genesis was a couple of years

Family Life and Communication

later in 1992. Pat once again had contacted the agency and I had a letter from Phil himself. He invited us to Roundhay Park and I remember the day the letter came. The family at first didn't believe it. I soon proved it to them though. By this time I had a scanner and scanned the letter so I could actually read it in braille. When the day came, it was quite warm. There were crowds outside and we were led through interminable barriers to a lawn. Here, the band came out to say hello to me. Pat said they looked fed up. I guess it must be hard doing rock tours and I was just another nuisance.

Blind to all this, all I knew was that I was there with them for the last time. I actually met all the band: Mike, Tony and Phil. Of course they had to type into the Alva braille display to communicate with me. Mike typed that they would always remember me. I'm sure they forgot me as soon as I left, but I didn't believe that back then.

All idols have feet of clay, they are simply humans who have become famous. Genesis are long gone now, retired and old like me. Well, getting on shall we say. It's ironic that I now have all the possible recordings, live and otherwise, that Genesis ever made but I can't hear them though I try so hard to do so. I just rely on my memory for their music.

But my love affair with technology continued and my computer knowledge grew. Eventually the web became accessible to me and it meant that I could find out literally anything I wanted. With the introduction of broadband in 2004 many new possibilities opened up. I was very interested in text adventure games, completely losing myself in them. I could now access sites that kept them and I downloaded hundreds – all types of games, simple text or games with sound effects that made them feel real.

With my scanner I could access any printed book –

'sighted books' we used to call them. You simply put the open book face down on the scanner, pressed a key and hey presto! up came the text of the page. This opened up new horizons to me.

Then the CD was born. I could now write CDs just like making audio tapes except it was much quicker. It was not without its failures. I acquired a large collection of 'beer mats' in those early days but things got better.

As my implants improved, and especially after the fitting of my second one, I dreamed of being a DJ and bought a unit for this purpose in 2007. This had two CD players and lots of controls for fading music in and out and for using a microphone. Though I could not actually hear the tunes of the music, I could use my memory of how the tunes sounded as a basis for identifying them. I began to acquire music avidly. Then I found a site where I could buy jingles. Using a computer program, I could tailor these to suit my needs. By careful editing I could put in jingles along with the music tracks. Now I could really be professional in my DJ sessions. Sadly, it's who you know not what your skills are that matters in that kind of business, so I was not destined to achieve much. My appearance on Radio Caroline was my crowning moment I guess.

Eventually, to supersede the terrible line I had at home, I moved on to mobile broadband. This has proved a real boon since I can now access the internet on several devices. My current favourite is my small braille computer which is totally portable and goes most places with me. I also have an Apple Mac. For many years I longed to try one and only last year, I found out that they can be used by blind people. I have an independent 'Wireless for the Blind' internet radio. This is wonderful because you can get literally hundreds of radio stations. If I add to these my talking i-pod and my Kindle I have the best of all technical worlds. This equipment is essential for my communication with both friends and the outside world. My gadgets give me books, newspapers, games, music, current affairs, tennis at Wimbledon and the Ashes progress.

It's not quite the end. Thanks to the generosity of Pat and family, I now have a braille printer. This means I can print hard copies of any documents I want to have 'hands on'. We often talk of how life would have been without computers and I am immensely thankful that my deafness has coincided with their development. They have enabled me to be part of the world in a limited way.

PAT: The Final Obstacle

Eventually Mick's weight was approaching thirty stones. I worried he would have a heart attack. I think he worried about diabetes and strokes, but we never discussed it. I felt he didn't care or he would do something about it. He was now so large that we didn't go anywhere, just sat in his boring room. He wasn't the same person. I had lost my Mick.

Then one day he told me he had asked the GP to refer him to hospital for a gastric bypass. He felt this was the only way to tackle the weight problem. Then I understood that he really did care about his weight but was powerless to deny himself food. I suppose he got to the stage where he was addicted and the task was too enormous to tackle. I encouraged him to go for it, even offering to help pay for the operation if he couldn't get it on the NHS. But once I had looked up the details I tried to dissuade him. It looked so drastic. Mick was not to be moved; he was adamant he had no choice. It took a while, but nearly two years later he was admitted to Bradford Royal Infirmary. I was not invited to accompany him this time; in fact I had arranged several visits to friends over that period and didn't even see him until two weeks after the operation. We communicated through text messages.

He found it a painful experience. When I saw him one of the three incisions had not closed up and was infected. It had to be treated by inserting 'seaweed tape' into the gaping hole from the outside and patiently waiting for the open wound to grow together. As I am a squeamish person it was quite a challenge for me when he asked me to dress it one day! It took around four weeks to

The Final Obstacle

heal. As for food, he was barely able to eat anything at first. By that I mean both quantity and variety. I think he lived on soups for around two months. At one point I joked that if he couldn't start to eat more he would be back in hospital being fed intravenously. On the positive side, he lost a lot of weight very quickly and was around ten stone lighter within eight months. At some point during this process he was light enough to be invited once more to cross the holy portals of my abode.

The rapid weight loss caused bruising on his face and arms. He had difficulty maintaining his balance (it is hard enough if you can't see) and one day fell backwards going upstairs in my house, straight over through 135 degrees. You can imagine the thud which shook the house, and my fright when I discovered what had happened. Miraculously he survived with only bruising – to add to what he already had. His processor, flung off during the fall, was retrieved unscathed, but getting him out of that position was not easy. With no room to roll onto his front, he had to continue sliding backwards head first, aided by me, until he reached the ground floor. He had several falls because of his balance and said it was because he was used to pulling backwards to carry the heavy weight in front.

It was difficult to provide food which he could digest. When I first cooked salmon he was sick. He happily ate and retained a boiled egg at my house, but was ill when he tried one at home. Things improved gradually; the weight loss bruising mostly faded, the variety of foods he could tolerate increased, and his balance stabilised as he got used to his new size and proportions.

Within nine or ten months he was able to eat most things, even if the portions were quite small. Having worn successively a whole wardrobe of old clothes of varying sizes that he had previously outgrown, the day came when he had to buy some new trousers and sweaters. He weighed several stones less than he had when he went to live on his own ten years earlier. He could now rejoice that he had made the right decision to go ahead with the operation. He could bend over to put on his socks and fasten his shoes. He could walk without getting breathless. He could take a bath again without getting stuck. He was looking like my Mick again. On a very bright frosty day early in 2012 we walked round the lake in Roundhay Park for the first time in years. Lots of people were training with army instructors, doing press-ups on the frozen ground, running up and down steep hills, but none of them achieved more than Mick that day.

While Mick was relishing his new fitness and relative slimness, most of the activities he had enjoyed so much were winding down. Leeds City Council decided to withdraw their annual funding from CoHearant Vision and outsourced provision for the deaf-blind to Sense. They had already moved all service users out of Centenary House, which was a large old building near the centre of Leeds and very costly to heat and maintain. Now they closed down the Centre for the Blind in Headingley and Sense acquired some inadequate premises in the centre of the city. The new staff – in Mick's opinion – had very little idea of what the service users wanted and provided even less. Mick no longer had his little I.T. domain and eventually he was so bored and disenchanted that he stopped going altogether.

The decision of the City Council also meant that Mick's committees and offices came to an end. He was no longer a trustee of CoHearant Vision. This stimulating part of his life was now closed. Since much of his DJ work had been at Centenary House, that too dried up.

Mick had already given up his sessions at Leeds 11 FM, the community radio station, because he felt exploited. They were unwilling to provide a taxi to get

The Final Obstacle

him there and back and he was buying vast quantities of CDs out of his own money. He also felt that they didn't take the trouble to communicate with him. Any discussions or decisions were taken without any reference to him. After all he was disabled.

So, apart from the pleasure of becoming thinner, there is very little left in Mick's life. He is still a Buddhist and sometimes attends the meeting on Tuesday evenings. There are also pujas occasionally at weekends and visits to the lama. He enjoys swimming and the gym up to three times a week. He fills the rest of his time with the computer and books, and sometimes his beloved toneless, imperfect music.

It is June 2012. We are sitting in the Mitre Hotel, at a table in the window overlooking the Thames. It has been a busy but satisfying day when we fulfilled a long-standing promise to visit Hampton Court. This has been on hold because Mick simply couldn't walk far enough. Today we were walking or standing almost continuously – apart from a short lunch break – from 9.50 when we left the hotel until 5.30 when we got back again. Mick is looking smart in a new shirt which he had to buy because everything else was too big. He has finished his tomato juice and is tucking into a very large Greek salad. A few months ago I wondered how he would cope with food away from home, but the timing was good. Now, about thirteen months from his operation, he is eating most things and can manage a small to middling plateful, but he won't touch alcohol or chips, although he enjoyed sharing a packet of Minstrels earlier.

The pelican crossing is a few yards from the hotel entrance. Once over the road, a further few yards takes us to the gates of Hampton Court Palace grounds. It is an ideal arrangement, allowing us maximum time at the

Touch Me Please

palace. Even so we have by no means seen everything today, but what we did cover was amazing. Using the audio guides for visually impaired visitors in the morning, we explored the Georgian rooms and those of William III. There was little to touch, but Mick felt some flock wallpaper, some wood panelling, the door locks with crowns on them, a marble fireplace. The audio guide effectively recreated for him the progression through the various rooms to the throne room itself. He smelt incense in Queen Caroline's bathroom, which prompted a long conversation with the warden responsible for ghost watching at Hampton Court. Apparently various smells come and go at this location. We peeped inside the Royal Chapel with its amazing ceiling (which I could appreciate even if Mick could not) and he was able to feel the heraldic beasts holding their standards with coats of arms in the delightful Royal Chapel Tudor garden.

Mick was able to enjoy historical re-enactments. In the Fountain Court we bumped into Lady Anne Boleyn and her companion, who very obligingly let Mick feel their beautiful headwear and long sleeves, and posed for a photo with him. In the distance we saw Henry VIII storming about with Lady Anne's brother George, Earl of Rochford. The king was trying to appease and win the favour of Lady Anne.

After a brief rest and a Tudor sausage in the Tudor kitchen, we meet Dana and Winifred, our room describers for the afternoon. Mick has brought his transmitter and receiver (the 'conch') so that he can hear the ladies despite the noisy atmosphere. By now the palace is full and we are visiting the Tudor sections which are always most popular.

Our guides take us first to the only surviving Tudor kitchens in Europe. There are three rooms with baskets of food, copper pans, pewter serving plates and great

The Final Obstacle

fireplaces with spits. There is plenty for Mick to feel. He explores the great serving hatches, then we go upstairs to the haunted gallery, where the young Catherine Howard ran screaming for mercy from the king, but was dragged away to imprisonment and then execution. There are many ghost stories associated with this place. Dana and Winifred tell us of their experiences and Mick feels the atmosphere instantly. I don't; I never do!

We continue along the processional route, only to find ourselves in a melée surrounding Henry who is sweeping his entourage into the Council Chamber to discuss the problem of an heir and possible marriage to Anne Boleyn. Lord Rochford sees that Mick is disabled and invites us to take him in, although no other women are admitted. The Privy Council is strictly for men only! But Dana and I slip in with Mick and enjoy a ten-minute enactment which consists mainly of Henry putting forward his requirements. Then Lord Rochford reads out the proposals. Naturally no one dares to object.

After this delightful interlude, which Mick manages to hear because the room is small and there are no other distracting noises, we make our way to the Great Watching Chamber. Here our friend Lord Rochford catches up with us and Mick has a fascinating conversation about Tudor history with him and the guides. He (Mick) claims to have read fifty books on Tudor England and he certainly impressed us all with his knowledge. Even allowing for a little exaggeration, he has read a lot! I am so pleased because he has a chance to share it and to blossom. Then we enter the Great Hall itself, with its magnificent tapestries and hammer beam ceiling. Our ladies describe it to Mick and bring it to life. Everyone has been immensely kind and helpful to make the day memorable.

And now we are reliving the experience at our river-

Touch Me Please

side table. This is the first time Mick and I have been away together for years. It is as if he has come back to me, restored and renewed. I so enjoyed his company today. I think back over his life, his unhappy childhood, the loss of music, the sadness of marriage breakups, the exploitation he has endured as a disabled person.

I know him so well, with his (sometimes) irrational distrust of anything left-wing, his impetuous dismissal of anyone who doesn't share his opinion, his bursts of anger, his stubbornness, his inability to face up to and talk about problems within a relationship.

But I also know and appreciate his warmth and romanticism, his passion for history, his longing for escape to another world, his overwhelming generosity, his love of technology, his determination to overcome the many obstacles he has faced, his remarkable patience and acceptance of his lot without complaining. I feel privileged to have shared some of his life with him, and hopefully I can go on sharing at least part of his future.

MICK: Epilogue

So here we are, both of us a little older now and wiser perhaps, having come through so much. In an ideal world I'd like to be able to say that I am a world-famous piano tuner, have been happily married to Pat for twenty-four years and enjoy music from dawn till dusk. But despite our lives taking a very different direction, there is still much to be grateful for.

Pat, always "perfect", as far as she is concerned never doing anything wrong, is just about the most honest person I have ever known, strong in character and beliefs, proud, unwilling at times to show her true feelings, kind-hearted but firm, maddeningly frustrating at times, wanting to be in the driving seat, but just occasionally she likes to be told what to do. She loves everything about the earth, gardens, trees and so on, a person of nature with a deep concern for the world and its people, wanting everyone to get on with each other.

Although I decided to leave and find an independent life of my own I still have a great love for her. Even though she has never achieved the career she longed for, she has lovely grandchildren, all her hobbies and interests and, most valuable of all, her freedom, at last being able to do exactly what she wants, to follow her own desires after so many years of having to bring up a family and then look after me. I don't think we could ever live together again, not in the foreseeable future certainly, but we can still have a loving relationship based on respect and concern for each other.

I too have my freedom. I can no longer wander here and there as I used to do in the days before I lost my

Touch Me Please

hearing, but I have all my modern equipment to keep me in touch with the outside world. I am surrounded by computers which enable me to access the internet, talking books and audio-described films. Even for my hearing, with implants embedded in my cochleae, I depend on computers. I have just had one of the implants upgraded though it still cannot bring me back the gift of music for which I yearn.

To try and describe what music was to me when I had it would take a book in itself. It represented the whole gamut of my being from happy to sad, from boisterous to moody and everything in between. It was the breath of life, it was the monitor by which I could judge how I felt. It was my doctor, curing me many a time of my sadness, my anger and my depression. I recall how affected I was at the Genesis rock concert I attended in the eighties. I could hardly breathe, I couldn't believe that pleasure could last so long or be so poignant. My whole being shouted out, literally, and I recorded my feelings on a small memory machine.

Of the modern artistes I know nothing. My music stopped back in 1989. I live in a kind of time warp, taking advantage of all the internet stations which play old music. My time with the rock bands, though, is something I will always remember with affection and pride.

Despite the long twenty four years of deafness, I still ardently wish I had music, indeed dream that I have it. I can actually hear it in my dreams as if I still had full hearing. Then I awake and there is nothing there. For a very long time this feeling of nothingness paralysed my every waking morning. Over the years this has gradually eased, though at the back of my mind, like a nagging tooth, I still grieve. I long to hear the dawn chorus or a lovely piece of classical music, to be able to find beauty again. It is lacking in my life since sounds used to provide

Epilogue

that beauty for me in so many ways. Hankering after what one cannot have, however, gets you nowhere and after a short time, I have to don my implants, switch on the day and carry on with my life.

What then of the future? This is very much an open field at the moment. There is a lot of space in my life with most of my activities having come to an end. Despite my limited options, I am thankful to be alive and in many ways, very lucky. Although I have tried to kill myself in the past I am really glad that I didn't succeed. There can be no escaping from the endless skein of existence as we Buddhists believe. We know that precious human birth is so rare that it is not to be thrown away lightly or put aside just for our own convenience. That is why I would never consider attempting suicide again. I have a happier outlook now and am ready for anything that comes my way. Besides, one never knows what is around the corner. I am sure that I still have a lot to give to the community, though I don't yet know how. I still want to write that elusive adventure game. I have the tools on my main computer so I guess I should get down to it.

I am thankful that I can live without being breathless, walk without getting exhausted, no longer so large that no one will bother with me. Drinking and over-eating no longer interest me; I don't touch alcohol now and eat healthy food. The agonising decision I took which enabled me to lose weight reminds me of the valuable lesson Mr John taught me when he said "Help yourself and others will help you". I really believe this to be the case and despite all I have suffered, I still have plenty to give. If only the outside world will treat me as a human being, then I can continue through life with a smile on my face as I try to do now.

When I eventually take re-birth, will I return with sight as well as my hearing? Have I really learned in this

Touch Me Please

life to fully appreciate what I have lost? All these things I can never know. All I can say is that I have a strong spark of determination in me and I'll continue to try new ideas and new technology.

Pat and I will grow old gracefully I guess, keep in close contact and help each other where we can. We both have regrets but that's all in the past now. Forward is the only way, now is the only important moment.

Printed in Great Britain
by Amazon.co.uk, Ltd.,
Marston Gate.